"Lanier is a fine writer with a refreshingly realistic story to tell. Few lives are saved and no achievement gaps are wiped out during her two years at a very bad Baltimore high school, but you get a vivid sense of what is wrong with the culture and organization of such places, and how much it will take to make them better. This book is, among other things, a great gift for a new teacher."—Jay Mathews, *Washington Post* columnist and author of *Work Hard. Be Nice: How Two Inspired Teachers Created the Most Promising Schools in America*

"What shall happen to us with our hope? *Teaching in the Terrordome* tackles the hardest possible questions, not only for educators, but for anyone who treads the line between optimism and the gritty reality of our age. Heather Kirn Lanier's memoir is both compelling and wise."—Stephen Kuusisto, author of *Planet of the Blind*

"I loved *Teaching in the Terrordome*. It's a heart-wrenching, sometimes humorous, and much needed account of what it's like to be a new teacher—one with smarts, courage, compassion and still—totally unprepared! Who could be prepared? I couldn't put it down."—Deborah Meier, senior scholar at the Steinhardt School of Education at New York University and co-author of *Playing for Keeps*

"Heather Kirn Lanier's insightful analysis of her experience as a new teacher provides readers with a unique vantage point for understanding what is wrong with American education. Her example shows us that it will take more than a few dedicated, young Teach For America corp members to save America's schools. In fact, this myth is perpetuating the mistaken notion that all we need to do is fire the "bad teachers" and shut down the "bad schools" to solve the education dilemma. Lanier shows us that the problems are far more complex, and she makes it clear that hard work and good intentions can never make up for failed policies and weak leadership at the state and federal level. Clear, well-written, candid and occasionally funny, this book is a must read for those who want to understand many of the problems facing urban schools and are willing to honestly consider what we must do to address them."— Pedro A. Noguera, Peter L. Agnew Professor of Education, New York University and author of *The Trouble With Black Boys and Other Reflections on Race, Equity and the Future of Public Education*

TEACHING
IN THE
TERRORDOME

TEACHING

IN THE

TERRORDOME

TWO YEARS IN WEST BALTIMORE
WITH TEACH FOR AMERICA

HEATHER KIRN LANIER

UNIVERSITY OF MISSOURI PRESS

COLUMBIA AND LONDON

Cataloging-in-Publication data available from the Library of Congress
ISBN 978-0-8262-1986-2

Jacket design: Susan Ferber
Text design: Stephanie Foley
Typesetting: FoleyDesign
Printing and binding: Thomson-Shore, Inc.
Typefaces: Palatino and Reprise

FOR THE STUDENTS,
AND FOR THEIR TEACHERS.

CONTENTS

I

FIRST YEAR

II

SECOND YEAR

ACKNOWLEDGMENTS

I'd like to pile mounds of gratitude upon the following folks:

Clair Willcox, John Brenner, and the staff at the University of Missouri Press, for providing this book a home.

The good people at the Rona Jaffe Foundation, who graciously sent me to the Bread Loaf Writers' Conference, and the writers I met there, including Vicki Forman, for some really nourishing words of wisdom; Ara Tucker and Janette Timm, who deserve all the applause of a Cosby episode; and Ted Conover, who encouraged me to let the book out of hiding and—unbeknownst to him—kicked my butt into gear.

My former teachers, particularly Jeanne Murray Walker, who's warm and wonderful and urged me to keep a journal, "Make it like a soap opera"; Steve Kuusisto, for more than his stellar Nixon impression, who said to throw words down like Jackson Pollock threw paint, and who faithfully reminds me that writing should be fun; Nancy King, who offered the best advice any graduating senior can hear: "Go make mistakes."

And Lee Martin, who said nearly everything else, who taught me almost all I know about how to shape true material, and even more about how to navigate the writer's world with kindness and compassion.

My fellow Buckeye nonfictioneers for your steady, smart feedback, especially the relentlessly positive Joe Oestreich; the super-smart super-momma, Christine Kaiser-Bonasso; the animated enthusiast, Amy Monticello; and the devoted Dave-Chapellian Jon Dibbs Chopan. I cheer you guys onward.

Kit Ward, for giving it a shot, and Joy de Menil, for wisely re-envisioning the beginning.

The editors of *Prairie Schooner* and *Meridian: The Semi-Annual from the University of Virginia,* for publishing excerpts from this book.

My fellow TFA-ers, Noelani, Brooke, Amy, and Ellen. Without your camaraderie and good humor, walking through those side doors would have been far less enticing. I miss you women. Please move to where I am.

My students, all of them, for the privilege of being your teacher.

Justin, for pretty much everything, including all that sage counsel, and for handling my bleary-eyed, post-writing moods with love.

Above all, public school teachers, for all that you do. You who spend extra hours perfecting your lesson plans, extra evenings calling or visiting students' families, extra dollars at the office supply store because your students deserve more than the district allotted, extra energy trying to reach another and another kid. . . . Thank you. The nation does not pay you nearly enough.

AUTHOR'S NOTE

This is a work of nonfiction: the people, places, and events are real. Some lines of dialogue have been re-created, though only if I felt certain that a) the speaker said something similar to the quote and b) the way I quoted the speaker reflected his or her speech, personality, and perspective. To protect identities, the names of all the students and most of the adults have been changed.

TEACHING
IN THE
TERRORDOME

I

FIRST
YEAR

CHAPTER 1

THE SCHOOL BESIDE THE CEMETERY

"Never drive west of MLK," a friend advised before I learned I'd teach every day in a school two miles west of Martin Luther King Boulevard. "I drove west of MLK last night," said another friend, a future teacher, "and a cop stopped me at a light, told me to turn around. Go back, he told us. He said a white person's car got set on fire west of MLK. He said they were just sitting there, at a light—the white people—and someone set their car on fire." I imagined cars west of MLK spontaneously bursting into flames.

But so far, I've never seen any. I'm heading west again today, as I did yesterday and as, should I survive another seven hours of teaching, I'll do tomorrow. After passing through Charles Village, the neighborhood of Johns Hopkins and brightly painted, Victorian row homes, and after passing through Mount Vernon, Baltimore's upscale, urban-hipster scene of posh bars, galleries, bead stores, and transvestite prostitutes, I turn right onto West Franklin. White flower boxes sit perched on the sills of tall, arch-shaped windows. Park benches and potted plants line one building. I am not yet west of MLK.

But West Franklin becomes a freeway, and it's here, on a slab of concrete hovering twenty feet or so over MLK Boulevard, that I do what those voices warn me never to do. The elevation of the freeway lowers until it dips below street level. I now speed below the short Baltimore blocks that my students freely, almost cheerfully call "ghetto." I pass under the names of streets they live on, the ones that make the news for the latest shooting or drug arrest: Calhoun, Gilmor, Monroe. If I were to head south on the last, I'd hit West Fayette. North Monroe and West Fayette: a drug intersection made famous by an HBO series.

I merge from West Franklin onto Route 40, and with each passing meter the road rises to street-level, the walls diminish, and it's like emerging from a concrete tunnel, like being birthed from a concrete mother into a depressed world of more concrete that's now just trash-riddled and broken. In a mile, the city has transformed. Trees and shrubs aren't sculpted around banks and homes. Instead, dead vines and branches wrap around phone lines and chain-link fencing. Row homes line the streets. The homes are no wider than a window and a door. They look conjoined and sad, their varying brick façades stuck together like dulled Lego bricks. Several are boarded up, the doors and windows covered by plywood. Homes should have entries, openings, ways in and ways out. The boarded-up homes look like faces with sealed eyes and mouths. Occasionally, when I spot a real home—a home with glass, a working door—it's almost inviting. Except its rarity seems foreboding.

At a traffic light at North Warwick, an old black man crosses in front of me. With his back bent forward, he makes shaky, pained steps across the road. I smile when I read his stretched out, threadbare T-shirt. *Walk to Win*, it says. In another year, Mayor O'Malley will plaster Baltimore's billboards with his simple marketing scheme: *Baltimore Believe*. The white capital letters will stand starkly against a black background, and no image or border will clutter the signs. Right now, the billboards advertise mattresses and McDonalds and the importance of keeping one's virginity. Right now, the city's slogan is "Baltimore: The City that Reads." City workers stenciled the phrase long ago onto bus stop benches. Baltimore's reading test scores are a national embarrassment, so locals like to mock the motto. Even the kids know it's a lie. A friend of mine asked his students to re-create the city's ad campaign. "Baltimore," they said. "The City that Bleeds." They haven't been the first to say it.

I turn left and pass a gas station, which I've stopped patronizing. While my car idled at this intersection on the way home one day, I watched a man fill his tank, turn away, head to pay. Another man hopped into the driver's seat and sped off. The tires screeched as the car veered right onto Route 40. "My car!" the owner shouted and ran after. No, I don't use that gas station. I use the ones downtown.

North Warwick is a small backstreet squeezing between parking lots of trucks, a towing service, used tire places, more row homes, and a ton of ambiguous brick buildings. The exteriors of the commercial spaces rarely reveal what's inside: they look like brick cubes planted on overgrown grass, and if they have signs, some of the letters have peeled away. "INTER STA E UE" reads one. Its windows are barred. Overgrown trees and shrubs fill the right side of one block. The greenery might be refreshing if it weren't so unruly. "Sit under a tree this weekend and write your poem," I once told a class for homework.

"Under a tree?" a girl scowled.

"Yeah," I said, and nodded, "A tree."

"What, Ms. Kirn," said another, the brightest in the class. "Right next to the hypodermic needle?"

I tilted my head to the side and reconsidered.

After passing four black teenagers, some smoking, all cutting me eyes with dark almond suspicion—what am I, the white, short-haired, glasses-wearing woman, doing around their way?—and after passing a skinny white woman wearing a stained T-shirt for a dress, wavering down the sidewalk in a zig-zag, her knees and elbows jutting out from her shirt like ashy knobs, I reach Font Hill, the driveway of Southwestern High School. It's a long, steady hill that Ms. Patterson says is the reason we never meet anyone at Parent-Teacher night. "It's too hard for them [the parents] to walk up that hill," she says. "After a long day, who wants to walk up that hill in the dark?"

Noelani and I first navigated west Baltimore for our interviews, that tale of the flaming car firmly in the backs of our minds. Once we got here to Font Hill we saw, between the brambles and dead vines raveling around still more fencing, a few tombstones. When we reached the top of Font Hill, two jaw-dropping forces competed for our attention: the high school—a tan, five-story mega-complex—and the seemingly endless acres of graves that spanned south and west. Perched on top of dead grass, Southwestern High School stood like a mammoth, intimidating god of the dead.

"Woah," Noelani said. "My high school was *small*."

I was more preoccupied with the graves. Mount Olivet Cemetery covered a square half-mile of ground. Our eyes were gazing across 34,000 tombstones. *Don't go west of MLK*, they'd said, and here we were, south and west, and even south and west of Southwestern were none other than a lot of dead people, like the further south and west in Charm City you went, the bleaker the outlook.

Like a prison, the *Baltimore Sun* often says of the school, and the newspaper isn't speaking of (or only of) the emotional atmosphere inside. *Prisonesque* is always the first observation anyone makes of the exterior. The school is a drab beige color, and when you approach it from its only accessible road, Font Hill, there's no clear entryway. There's no grand sign, no front door. Very little landscaping, including a charred tree that might have been picturesque before lightning evidently split it. Two rows of tiny windows span the length of the biggest building. A few tiny rectangular windows puncture the side. As I round it, I'm sandwiched between gravesites and a fortress.

"We got you an interview at Southwestern High School," Jeremy Beard, the Program Director of Teach For America-Baltimore, told a handful of us only two weeks before the city's first school day. We'd promised two years of our lives to Teach For America's mission (*One day, all children in this nation will have the opportunity to attain an excellent education*), and though the organization was responsible for procuring us positions in the district, sometimes jobs came through at the last minute.

Someone asked Jeremy what the school was like. To this, Jeremy clapped one fist into his palm and gave a diplomatic Teach For America response. "It's definitely a school in need." Another fist-to-palm clap. "It's definitely got challenges." *Challenges*, I'd learned, was the preferred TFA parlance for obstacles, difficulties, things that would make the job grueling. But *challenges* implied surmountable possibilities. And a *school in need* meant Southwestern needed us.

What were the challenges? I asked.

Again, Jeremy paused. "Every Baltimore high school has issues. There's almost like a checklist . . ." He held both hands together and then stretched them apart like he was unfurling an imaginary scroll. ". . . Like a laundry list of problems common to the high schools. Low attendance. Low test scores." He started tapping his fingers on one hand with each count. "High incidents of violence. Poor special ed services. . . . " He stopped, dropped his hand. He could go on, but I got the point. "Southwestern has," he paused, nodded, "a good many of the problems on that list."

Southwestern has every problem on that list, I took him to mean, which was accurate. I must have looked hesitant.

"Just go in there and talk yourself up," he said. "Know you can handle it."

Know I can handle it, I thought. I, an introverted white woman from the suburbs, a student of Virginia Woolf's prose and Gwendolyn Brook's spontaneous metric verse—I can handle teaching in an inner-city school without ever having taught. Ever. But this is the very premise of Teach For America: that overachieving recent college graduates can in fact become change-agents in the most economically depressed of American corners. If the others he gathered that day harbored doubts, they didn't show it. Noelani, tall and half Hawaiian with silky straight black hair, exuded a calm presence. Amy and Brooke, both blond, were fast-talking and intense. Ellen, brown-haired and the shortest of us at 5'2", seemed to hang back a bit but still voiced no concern about heading west of MLK (as Jeremy had instructed) or handling the "laundry list" of challenges.

As the five of us were making plans to carpool, Noelani's roommate piped in. "South*western* . . . That sounds familiar." She racked her brain but failed to recall how she'd heard the name.

The next day, when I got into Noelani's car for the interview, she relayed the news. Her roommate had paged through *The Corner: A Year in the Life of an Inner-City Neighborhood*, by David Simon and Edward Burns, the same guys who would later go on to make HBO's hit show, *The Wire*. The nonfiction account follows a family entangled in the drug culture of west Baltimore—a son dealing, a mom and pop addicted. Noelani's roommate swore she'd seen Southwestern's name somewhere in there. And in one line of the nearly 600-page book, Southwestern High School is referred to as *The Terrordome*.

"We're about to interview," I said, "at the Terrordome?"

I've driven here every workday since. I park in the back. It's 7:45 A.M., and from the looks of the cars, about a dozen administrators and teachers are here. Among them are the four other Teach For America teachers—Amy, Ellen, Noelani, and Brooke—along with Ms. Davis, the science department head. She arrives faithfully each morning at seven, puts in twelve hours of work. But school won't start until 8:45, and about half of the faculty will roll up that hill in a sudden line of traffic. They'll crowd the parking lot only a few minutes before the first bell, fight for the closest spaces, and rush to the front office so they can sign their names and prove they're on time. Some of these teachers will be the first to bolt from their classrooms when the final bell rings at 3:25.

A year from now, Amy will confess to me that for the first few months of school she feels as I do now: like she's going to puke. I'll be surprised to hear this, in part because, by default, I tend to believe everyone besides me has their shit together. Yet Amy is also amazing at feigning confidence, as are the other early risers, Ellen and Brooke. Other than Noelani, who from day one has echoed my concerns, I think I'm the only one who worries about walking through the single unchained side door of "The Terrordome" and doing what Teach For America has charged me with: bridging the achievement gap. Playing a role in providing my students with educations on par with their middle-class counterparts.

Just as TFA has armed us with alarming statistics on low-income students ("only one in ten will graduate college"; "by the time they reach fourth grade, low-income kids are two to three grades behind their high-income peers"), the organization has also armed us with optimistic evidence of our successes, or at least of the successes of those who've gone before us. Ninety percent of all principals who've hired TFA teachers in their schools say that they'd hire another if given the chance. And the anecdotal evidence of our effectiveness is inspiring. According to TFA, former teachers have raised their classrooms of elementary school kids two and three grade-levels in nine months; they've transformed resistant kids into engaged students by linking subject matter to fun things like football; they've founded movements of nationally recognized charter schools. We've heard the stories. We know we're meant to achieve similar results.

The stories once led me to believe that the faculty here would receive us with open arms, but we were quickly warned otherwise. "Don't. Trust. Anyone," said the first TFA teacher to be placed in Southwestern, a woman from the very first TFA corps back in 1990. Noelani and I had met up with her prior to the school year. "You might think you're making friends," the veteran said, "but they'll stab you right in the back when you're not look-ing." She lasted two years at The Terrordome and then escaped to Mervo, a technical high school with admissions standards, strict attendance poli-cies, and a smoother-functioning administration.

At first, I thought of chalking her advice up to paranoia, but when the five of us first met Ms. Davis, the science department head, she delivered a similar message.

"Come give Ms. Davis a hug," she said when she found us in a hall-way. A pear-shaped woman with wide, plastic-framed glasses stretched her arms out. "You are all my babies!" She hobbled in between embraces. We smiled and returned her hearty bear-hugs. "I adopt all you Teach For America people. Mm-hmm, I do. Just ask some of my former teachers. They'll tell you. Mm-hmm, yes, I still keep in contact with Teach For Amer-ica teachers. Teachers from 1990." She looked at Noelani and nodded, "That's right." Then she grew quiet. "Now, I want to tell you something. This information is between you and me."

She beckoned us closer, and the five of us huddled around her. I pre-pared to learn a secret.

"I don't go around telling people how I feel about Teach For America. You know how people are," she said. I realized then that Ms. Davis's secret was her support of us. Her opened arms were a gift we should keep pri-vate. "And if I were you, I wouldn't tell anyone you're a part of Teach For America. No. Uh-uh. They don't need to know that. You can just keep that information to yourselves."

It was impossible, though, to keep it a secret. To the faculty, we were obvious outsiders—dubious, energetic white people straight out of col-lege. None of us knew Baltimore, none of us spoke with a B-more accent. Before the school year started, I didn't have enough desks, and my own department head, Ms. Wallace, said she had no extras, so I had to scavenge some vandalized ones from Ms. Davis. "FUCK YOU" one read in Sharpie marker. On another, an erect, life-size penis, also in Sharpie pen, was about to enter a girl's open mouth. Other desks had the names of housing proj-ects tagged all across the tops. Noelani was helping me carry these—the last desks to be had in Southwestern—downstairs to my classroom, but we were stopped by a tall woman in clacking red kitten heels. "Can I help you?" she called from down the hall. I knew she was a science teacher.

"No, we're fine," I said, thinking she meant, literally, *Can I help you?*

"What're you all doing up here?" She wore tight red Capri pants to match her heels.

"My room doesn't have enough desks," I shouted back, and side-nodded toward the one I'd heaved into my arms. Half a hallway still separated us. I sensed that I'd crossed an unwritten "No Trespass" sign, the ones that hang on the wire fences of ramshackle homes nobody actually wants to enter. "I teach downstairs," I said, certain this would put her at ease. *I know I don't look like I teach her, but for real, I teach right down there.*

Her neck slumped forward and she put her hand on her hip. She wore a semi-disgusted, semi-bored sneer. She turned to a stout teacher behind her. "What do all these teachers think they're doing, coming up on *our* floor?" I went to respond, but they both turned away, mumbling to each other. "These are *our* desks," the tall woman shouted over the clack of her kitten heels. "People shouldn't be taking things that aren't *theirs.*" I heard the other teacher huff and *mhmm* as they rounded the corner and walked out of sight.

Noelani and I were baffled. *You can make a difference,* we'd been told by TFA. *You can level the playing field. America's schools need you. Ninety percent of all principals request more of you.* Why wouldn't our colleagues appreciate our presence? Back then, I thought TFA teachers were seen as some kind of youthful, revolutionizing commodity. Now, just a couple of months later, I look back at my assumptions and cringe. How could a person so naïve survive even a few weeks in this place? "People have bets on whether or not you'll make it," a teacher had told us before the first day of school.

So far, though, we've survived. And now I see us from our colleagues' perspectives: they're experienced teachers of a tough inner-city school system where they've worked for five, ten, twenty years on lower pay than their county colleagues. In some cases they've lived among their students all their lives. And suddenly a bunch of eager, mostly white, twenty-something kids storm in under the banner of a white-founded organization and believe, or have been taught to believe, that they can make the experienced teachers' same students perform two and three times better? And without having ever taught? Yep, our presence can appear insulting. The teachers think we believe we can do their jobs better than they can.

Which is, depending on how you look at it, what Teach For America has taught us to believe. This again might sound insulting, but not if you take a hard look at our faculty. There are some solid, hard-working veterans here, but there's also Mr. Johnson, the math teacher, who openly derides his female students and makes derogatory, sexual remarks. There's Ms. Jones, the reading teacher, who only shows up the first few weeks of any semester and then calls out sick, using her racked-up sick-days and leaving her kids with a permanent substitute who shows movies. And there's Mr. Sypher, a thirtysomething, white history teacher who, when we first met him, told us how we should best handle our future kids. "You just have to fuck with them," he said, and when Brooke scoffed and my brow furrowed, he rephrased. "Never let them know what to expect."

We were eating lunch at a neighborhood fast food joint. I glanced at Noelani, whose round, dark, half-Hawaiian eyes had gotten wider than usual. Noelani wore floral skirts and proved easy to make giggle; she didn't look like the type to "fuck" with people.

"One time, a kid picked up a chair to throw at me. That's right," Sypher said. "A chair." He paused to look around. We were sitting in a Burger King three blocks from Southwestern. Bulletproof glass separated the cashiers from the patrons. The black girls at the registers were chewing on their gum and taking orders, and the black customers were standing in line or eating sandwiches at the tables, and the white teachers were we, sitting in the center of the restaurant. "I leaned right into his face . . ." Sypher leaned toward Noelani. ". . . raised my finger, and said, 'I'll fucking kill you. If you throw that chair, I will fucking. Kill you.'" Another pause, another look around. "You have to fuck with them like that. That's just what it takes."When Brooke asked if the kid threw the chair, Sypher conceded. "Yeah. But they suspended his ass!" he said smugly.

If you compare us TFA teachers to ones like Mr. Johnson, Ms. Jones, and Mr. Sypher, Teach For America is right: we do better. We show up daily and speak to our kids respectfully.

But we've been taught to expect even more from ourselves. We've been taught to believe we can change the results of the nation's underperforming schools, which are failing our students at abysmal rates but which don't have to fail them, not if we work hard enough. Not if we get up early enough, and stay at school late enough, and call enough students' homes, and plan enough engaging lessons. Not if we attend enough night-courses and create enough systems for classroom management. Not, in other words, if we teach well enough. Six months ago, I was a college student writing poems for a degree. Now, I'm attempting what I think might be the toughest job in all of America. When I come to work in the morning, I wear, like a rock-filled backpack, the responsibility of what TFA calls *the nation's greatest injustice*, and I park my car in the school lot, and I grab my large caffeinated tea and my black work-bag, heavy with papers I thought I might have the residual energy to grade the night before, and I trudge into school with it: the weight of this task, the heavy burden of attempting to manifest what was once a breezy idealism: excellent education for all.

Already, a few students linger on the outside of the school, their faces vacant and lethargic. It's early. They're waiting to get in. They're waiting to enter a prison-like complex that chains every one of its side-doors, other than the single one on the end. The doors are chained for their protection, so no one from the outside can get in, and the doors are chained for their control, so that, once in, they can't easily escape. They're big kids: grown guys a half-foot taller than I am, hefty girls who hold their bodies like walls and smack on their gum. The girls' hair runs down their shoulders in braided extensions, or swirls around their scalps in elaborately braided up-do's. If they know that they belong to sad statistics, they don't really show it. As students of this school, less than half of them are expected to graduate; those who do will perform four or five grade-levels below the national expectation. I recently heard on NPR that Baltimore has the second lowest graduation rate of any city in the nation. The school beyond that one open door is, for the most part, failing them, and still they wait here, early in the morning, not yet able to enter.

I grab the metal handle of the heavy, opaque door and lean away, hurling it open. Once I'm in, it closes behind me with a thud, and I begin the several flights up the dusty, windowless stairwell. When I first came to this building, I expected tough questions. An administrator told the five of us to arrive for our interviews in scattered intervals, but each of our designated times came and went and no one's name was ever called. The five of us waited in the main office. Why hadn't any of us been called in yet? Together, we waited fifteen, twenty more minutes. Did any of us know what we might be teaching? We all shook our heads. No one knew. Amy set down her briefcase. Brooke let out a large sigh. Looking back, our reactions are funny to me now. Teach For America chose us for our impressive track-record of achievements and our eagerness to get things done—we weren't necessarily used to institutions blocking our way. We hadn't yet learned just how much of a barrier a school system could be to its own purpose.

A woman finally appeared, a frail but curvy middle-aged African American woman with rouge-red cheeks and aqua-blue eyelids. She introduced herself as Ms. Brown and called us—all of us—into a back conference room.

"You want us *all* to come in?" Amy asked.

Ms. Brown beckoned with her hand. "Yes. Everyone. Please do come in."

The five of us sat as upright as possible in a cinderblock room so small it was filled primarily by the table between us. We each wore the newest of work blazers and readied ourselves for the tough questions, the ones we'd practiced answering (*Why do you want to be a teacher?*) or the ones we'd avoided considering (*What will you do when a kid tells you to fuck off?*) or the ones we'd never even thought of (*What is your teaching philosophy?*). I clasped my hands tightly together and waited for the interrogation.

Instead, Ms. Brown asked, "How are you enjoying Baltimore City?"

A softball question, I noted. We said we liked it. The harbor was pretty.

Ms. Brown nodded. "You know," she said, "Baltimore has an excellent transportation system. You needn't always rely, on the car as a vehicle." The syllables of Ms. Brown's words were meticulously modulated and well-pronounced, and she paused mid-sentence as though she were dictating. "Have any of you, taken the bus? From time to time, a person might make use, of the Baltimore Bus System, which runs reliably, between all areas of the city." She seemed to take great pains to avoid the *ums* and *ahs* of everyday speech. There was something unnaturally perfect about it. She smiled steadily, as steadily as she spoke, and I decided just to smile back and enjoy her cordial demeanor. To pretend nothing about her seemed off. To start picking my thumb's cuticle and tell myself that if a woman like her—a pleasant, formal person—could survive in a supposed "Terrordome," maybe the school didn't deserve its nickname. Also, how nice was she, warming us up in this friendly way before the intensive inquiries: *How will you handle discipline problems? What kind of unit plan ideas do you have?*

But after a list of factual questions about places of birth and colleges attended, and after we answered briefly because the group interview suggested that we were a single entity—one large, multi-limbed, five-headed body that needed to answer unanimously—Ms. Brown said, "Well, we are all certainly, very happy, that you have decided to begin, your teaching careers, here, at Southwestern High School." And just like that, the group had the job.

"You will find that teaching here, is often a challenge, but we all, do our best, to," and here Ms. Brown had the first long, unsettling pause in her cadence. Her mouth stayed open as she wrestled to find the right words. But before an *umm* slipped from her mouth, she said, "*weather* the storm." Once again, she smiled, looking satisfied with her finely wrought speech.

That's when I saw it, a glimpse into the reality of this frail woman's life. Her dark eyes were shrouded in gray half moons. Her voice sometimes quavered, cracking her painfully faultless speech. She seemed weary. And after having figured out her polite metaphor for the unspeakable—*weather the storm*—she looked at me with a sad, knowing glare. *You know this job is tough*, I felt she was saying. *So tough that I can't even tell you how tough it is. If you want it, then here: it's yours now.* Ms. Brown knew little more than our ages and our alma maters. Our willingness alone deemed us fit, or fit enough, to teach Southwestern's youth.

What I didn't know at the moment was this: the administration had no choice but to hire us. According to Teach For America's records, the Baltimore City Public School System needs about 650 new hires every year, and the closer the summer creeps toward those first September days, the more desperate principals and administrators become. Whoever had shown up on that hot August day would have filled the opening slots. The school needed us because the school needed teachers, and the standard for that word, *teacher*, was now akin to *warm body* in a city where few wanted to teach.

Despite that the school can, in fact, be a place of terror, despite the prisonesque aesthetics, the manic, raucous hallways, the lack of resources, my colleagues' mistrust of me, and despite my own inexperience, I'm here. I'm here to teach kids five grade levels behind, kids diagnosed with emotional disturbances, kids not fed breakfast or dinner in the past twenty-four hours, kids who walk past more violence in one day than I probably see in a year. Right now, they're riding the city buses and heading up Font Hill and waiting beside the closed doors of this school building with, as Jeremy Beard said, *challenges*, and in my classroom those challenges become mine. And against reason, against most people's opinions, against what are on some days my own ardent doubts, I stand in my empty classroom, face my vacant desks, and do this morning what those billboards will soon tell all of Baltimore: Believe. Believe I can teach in The Terrordome. Believe what Teach For America believes. "Southwestern Is a Better Place Because You Are Here," says a motivational poster on my wall, and I will myself to believe that, somehow, on the end of this long day, I'll drive down Font Hill, past the cemetery, past the boarded-up row homes and abandoned lots, onto the freeway and back into downtown Baltimore with, not a war-story of letdown, not a minor tale of tragedy, but a triumph, however small, a victory that makes The Terrordome even a centimeter better for its students than it was before the day began.

CHAPTER 2

TEACHER BOOT CAMP

Should you decide to become a Teach For America teacher—should you decide, that is, to throw yourself without any teaching experience into one of the nation's toughest rural or urban schools and vow to work relentlessly for its improvement—you'll hear plenty of dissenting voices. You'll read them in newspaper commentaries and from education critics, and maybe you'll hear them from friends.

"Just don't park your car in the same spot twice," one friend said to me, thinking he was offering advice.

I told my mother about the latent racism in the comment—*He assumes inner-city kids key cars*—but she only bit her bottom lip and said softly, "Heath, that's not such a bad idea."

After I bought a small collection of new pants, skirts, and blouses for my new job, another friend asked, "Why would you buy new clothes?" He added, as though my tan skirt would get soiled beyond repair in the classroom, "Baltimore's a dirty, *dirty* city." He didn't mean that soot filled the Charm City air, that a person couldn't walk from A to B without attracting unbearable stains. He meant my future students wouldn't appreciate—maybe didn't deserve—a teacher who wore an Ann Taylor silk-blend V-neck blouse.

When I told a thirtysomething teacher friend of mine that TFA was supposed to cover, in five weeks, all the training I needed to succeed in the city classroom, he burst into a hearty, alienating laugh. Then he asked, "Do you even know how to write a lesson plan?" to which I just shook my head.

"But it can't be *that* hard," I said.

He laughed again and added a sardonic "Good luck."

And as I finally headed to Houston, Texas, for my five weeks of summer training, the man beside me on the plane nudged my elbow with his, asked what I did for a living. I told him that soon I'd teach in Baltimore.

"Baltimore *County*?" he asked hopefully, his eyebrows raised, his thick fingers dipping into a salty aluminum bag of nuts.

"City," I told him, and he grimaced. "Would have been better if it'd been Baltimore *County*, huh?" He chuckled, and his belly jiggled against his opened tray table, and I thought he was about to nudge me again.

When I landed in Houston, the airport was filled with a disproportionate number of youthful, neatly dressed college-age people (mostly female, mostly white). They walked quickly and with purpose to luggage conveyor belts, grabbed their bags, and followed the signs that read *Teach For America*. They walked, I thought, like they were used to charting successful paths through the world.

I grabbed my luggage and rolled it toward the signs. I didn't know what we were in for. I only knew that my insides weren't nearly as self-assured as the others' outsides. But the months of dissenting voices were a strange, ironic form of encouragement. *Nobody can teach those kids*, I'd heard again and again, all from suburban white folks who had no idea.

We were told this five-week "Institute" would be akin to military training, minus the physical excursion. We were told to expect grueling, eighteen-hour days, mental, physical, and emotional exhaustion, and no time for rest or relaxation. But mostly, we were just told it would be "really really hard." Like "teacher boot camp." The organization's thousand new teachers had flown from around the country to train, without pay, at the University of Houston. On the first evening, we gathered in the auditorium for the Institute's "Opening Ceremonies." A huge TEACH FOR AMERICA banner hung above an empty stage. We settled, row by row, into the auditorium's seats. I scanned the room and saw that, while a disproportionate number of us were indeed white and female, we were still a fairly diverse group: male and female, Latino, African American, Asian American. Some of us were dressed in button-up shirts and ties, or blouses and business skirts. Others looked like they'd walked right off a college campus in their T-shirts and shorts and flip-flops.

The chatter of the auditorium died down when a white woman in a tan pants-suit walked across the stage. She had straight, mid-length, sandy brown hair. As she approached the podium, I checked her shoes. Soft, sensible flats. This seemed meaningful. I'd brought nothing but heels I'd never worn before.

Once she introduced herself as Wendy Kopp, the audience went wild. They hooted, they whistled, they cheered, all the while pounding their hands together with a force that sounded storm-like. So this was the founder of TFA. And though I joined in the cheering, I had to ask myself why. Why were we all so ballistic? Maybe we were celebrating our collective company, the knowledge that the one-thousand voices surrounding us would finally offer optimistic words rather than nay-saying ones. Maybe we were relieved to begin the road that even the most courageous of us still undoubtedly worried about. Maybe if you collect a thousand earnest, high-achieving twentysomethings into a room, and you tell them they can improve the nation's greatest injustice, despite the fact that they've been raised on heavy doses of irony and sarcasm, they'll make a lot of noise.

"This is truly my favorite part of the job," Kopp said in a soothing, even-paced voice. "Opening Ceremonies. This is when you're still *thank*ing me instead of *blam*ing me."

The audience laughed—aware of both our present naïveté and our impending difficulties. We thousand or so had a sense of humor. But her comment was also a warning: in only a few weeks, we wouldn't respond so jubilantly to her presence.

After Kopp's remarks—about the national crisis, about our importance, about the fact that we should never, ever quit—eight or so TFA alumni lined the stage. Stoically, they stood, their faces cast down, their hands clasped behind their backs. They looked like an un-singing chorus-line of serious young teachers. The audience hushed and waited. A guy named Brian, a tall white guy with a Ken-doll poof of hair, stepped forward into the stage's lone spotlight. In a slight southern drawl, he began a story of what seemed like total failure.

Every day, Davon and Marcus mess around. They talk in class. They don't do their work. Every day, Brian assigns Davon and Marcus detention, but they don't care. They still act out. How can Brian get through to them?

Brian stepped back in line, and the next teacher stepped forward. Right down the line, each teacher delivered the beginnings of a story that seemed unsolvable. Another problem kid. A group of resistant readers. The spotlight returned to Brian.

Detention time, and once again he sits with Davon and Marcus. Marcus flicks his pencil across the room. Davon snickers. Brian levels with them. They're two of the smartest kids in class. They could choose to do better. Why don't they choose to *do better*? Marcus turns to Davon and says, "Yeah man, we should quit messing." But would their behavior improve the next day? Brian didn't know.

Brian stepped back in line again, his plot sufficiently thickened, and another teacher stepped forward to bring us to her climax. On and on went the storytellers until the audience was left at the peaks of eight or so suspenseful teacher-tales. How would they all end? Would these teachers succeed?

Brian continued. The next day, Davon and Marcus sit at their desks, bring out their pencils, get to work. They even have their homework. They raise their hands, they give right answers. By the end of the year, Davon gets a B+. And Marcus, good ol' Marcus, he earns the highest grade in the class.

"And *that*," Brian said, "that is why I Teach for America!"

His final sentence became the end-line for each teacher's victorious vignette. *That's Why I Teach For America*. Every story had a problem, every story a solution. All offered redemption, and each gave us a reason to join the cause. *Why are you doing this?* relatives had asked. *Why not Baltimore County?* my fellow plane-rider had wondered. Now, sitting in the auditorium, I had a yearning: I wanted a redemptive story, too. I ached for sheer, unabashed success in the classroom. The classroom in which I'd never taught.

• • •

Like all TFA corps members, I'd been carefully vetted for certain characteristics. Among four thousand applicants that year, one thousand were chosen, and each year, as the applications break the preceding year's record, the program becomes more and more selective. In 2011, 48,000 people competed for roughly 5,200 slots. Today's fresh, soon-to-be-graduates need to show proof of the same criteria I was held to years earlier: demonstrated past achievements, perseverance in the face of challenges, strong critical thinking, the ability to motivate and influence people, and respect for students and families of low-income communities.

"Why don't they just take everyone that applies?" I'd asked my TFA interviewer back in Philadelphia. "If the schools really need teachers, why not just accept everyone?"

The interviewer shook her head. "Because not everyone can do it," she said, an indication that my prospective future contained much more than the smiling teacher-faces of the TFA marketing brochures.

Founder, Wendy Kopp, also had in mind an element of elitism to "the corps" (as TFA-ers call it), which explains why substantial chunks of Yale's, Harvard's, and Princeton's graduating classes also apply each year. Make it as tough to get into as law or med school and maybe, just maybe, a national corps of teachers can attract the ass-busting high-achievers, the presidents of student governments, the relentless advocates for social causes, the impressive A-type college kids who already founded their own nonprofits at age twenty-one.

Perhaps this is how TFA earned its stereotype: according to the caricature, the typical TFA teacher is a white, upper-middle-class, "privileged" (a.k.a., spoiled), recent Ivy League grad with hopes of becoming a lawyer or doctor like daddy but isn't quite ready to head to grad school just yet. Instead, he or she would rather use privileged hands to make this messy, needy world a better place, and so plunges into lower-class America to save all the poor black kids. Or poor Hispanic kids. In just two years. After that, it's a straight path for Yale, the Bar exam, a bar for the celebratory toast. The stereotype appeared on the TV show *Boston Public* when a pretty TFA teacher, Kimberly Woods, tells her class that what she *really* wants to be is a lawyer, but she's here with them to "make a difference." In other words, *they* are her *difference* to be *made*. The stereotype also reared its head in one of my favorite memoirs, Dave Eggers' bestseller, *A Heartbreaking Work of Staggering Genius*. I quote Eggers, who's channeling the voice of his cynical past self: "We fault the nonprofit [TFA] for attempting to solve inner-city problems, largely black problems, with white upper-middle-class college-educated solutions." TFA, he says, is "enlightened self-interest." "Paternalistic condescension." For support, Eggers quotes an unnamed professor: "A study of Teach for America tells us more about the ideological, even psychological needs of today's middle-class white and minority youth than it does about the underclass to whom the project is targeted."

Like many, I didn't fit the stereotype: I didn't want to be a doctor or a lawyer and I didn't attend an Ivy League school. Though I grew up in an over-sized, air-conditioned suburban Philly home, it was my mother's lone win in a drawn-out divorce, a home she struggled to maintain on her secretary's salary so that I'd have some "stability." Until she remarried, we pinched pennies to maintain what was probably a façade of middle-class respectability. And TFA was not a step on my career ladder. I didn't have a career ladder. I had an English Literature degree with a Religious Studies minor. I'd spent my undergraduate years on Shakespeare, Buddhist Philosophy, Contemporary Drama, Death and Dying, Modern Poetry, Taoism, the Logics of God. I knew a fair bit about the Taoist concept of *wei-wu-wei* and the Buddhist notion of no-self, the blank verse in Shakespeare's plays and the narrative consciousness in Virginia Woolf's *Mrs. Dalloway*. But I rarely studied subjects that were tangibly relevant to a world of employers, and I had no idea what to do with my education. I thought maybe I'd find a home in teaching. If I loved learning, maybe I could continue on the other side of the classroom.

Without an education degree, though, where could I teach? I looked into a few private school positions. The more I learned, however, about the academic performance of high-income students as compared to their low-income peers, the less I wanted to serve those American kids who were performing just fine without me. I learned that a child born into a low-income neighborhood was far less likely to finish high school. I learned that I, blessed by a well-funded public school with its swimming pool and planetarium and brightly-lit, weeded football field—I had it easy when it came to education. Out of the 400 students who entered my ninth-grade class, 390 of us graduated. For the kids in my honors and Advanced Placement classes, we expected college like we expected water to pour from a tap. In grade school, when I slapped my right hand over my chest and faced the American flag and absent-mindedly recited my allegiance to it, I'd sensed in those red and white stripes some kind of American birthright that I could *Achieve the Impossible* or *Be All That I Can Be*. But I later learned that my urban peers were likely seeing something altogether different in those stars and stripes—something empty, something flimsy in the fabric even—as they pledged their allegiance to a country that offered, as a primary stepping stone to their American dreams, schools that were failing them.

Somewhere along the way, I became troubled by the disparities between the haves and the have-nots. Somehow I'd formed enough altruistic opinions that my beloved Republican stepfather disparagingly referred to me as "A Liberal."

But I didn't necessarily believe I could "save the poor children." I was raised on the postmodern stance that the victors of wars became the writers of histories, that whoever has the audacity to think they can bring redemption to a people is akin to colonial Chris Columbus and Co. I was an irony-loving child of the eighties, prone to sarcasm, suspicious of Hallmark, and I believed that we were, all of us, a little broken. How could I "save" anyone?

And yet. And *yet*, the world was still broken. And thousands of idealistic college graduates—yes, many of whom were white—were willing to help, or at least try. I had landed in my generation's postmodernist predicament: even if, as Eggers's expert points out, our ways of trying to fix things might say more about our own brokenness than the targets of our salvation, couldn't and shouldn't we still do *some*thing?

Educational inequity is our nation's greatest injustice. You can change this.

So read Teach For America's website, and the second sentence was the key. It invited you. *You* could change this. Not *him* or *her* or some hero in a teacher movie. *You* could make a difference. It tugged at the heartstrings of just the person TFA was seeking—a hard-working believer in something better.

My college roommate, Mark, and I filled out applications, hoping our achievements were enough to prove to TFA our worth. I was: an honors student at the University of Delaware, president of the on-campus student government, founder of a student writing club, and recently named one of the university's "Women of Promise." Mark was: also an honors student, also president of a major student organization, a volunteer clown in a children's hospital, and a full-time worker while putting himself through school. To boot, he was the kind of guy everyone loves—energetic, optimistic, and outgoing. After writing essays that detailed our "greatest life challenges" and how we overcame them, and after ranking where we'd like to devote our two years should we get chosen (we both picked California's Bay Area), we were each offered interviews.

With eleven other strangers my age, most white, a few Asian, I sat in an office room in Philadelphia and began the full-day interview. We'd been told to prepare a five-minute lesson. I stood at the center of a semi-circle of young adults, all of whom acted as my hypothetical high school English students, and I attempted to teach iambic pentameter. The few minutes flew by in a blur of *When forty winters shall besiege thy brow*, and I sat down, having no idea whether I'd just sunk to the bottom of some Olympic-sized teaching pool or swam victoriously across. Others taught fractions, gravitational pull. Some looked sweaty and nervous. One man limped awkwardly to the front of the room but then taught enthusiastically about addition.

Those "privileged" false stereotypes aside, there *was* still something *about* TFA people, I realized as I waited with the other candidates for my one-on-one interview. Something intense and relentless. While we waited, the limping candidate, Jake, who'd quickly become a pseudo-leader among us, told us our odds: out of the twelve, he said, only four would "make it." Only four would be chosen. This led us to look around and wonder, who were the four? Or rather, I wondered, *Who were the other three*, because Jake seemed like a shoe-in to me.

"I want this. Bad," Jake said.

"I do, too," the only other male candidate chimed in eagerly, as though a video camera were capturing the conversation and he had to assert his devotion. We were used to being watched all afternoon, and I understood his difficulty in remembering that there was no longer anyone to impress.

"I definitely want this," Jake said, ignoring the other guy. Both men wore suits. The two talked about which cities they listed as their top choices. With the certainty of world travelers, they hailed the virtues of Baltimore, New Orleans, and every other possible TFA destination.

"What did you write for your 'biggest challenge' essay?" Jake asked the other guy. The gauntlet had been thrown. The rest of us had just become witnesses to a showdown.

The guy rambled about a story I quickly forgot and then asked Jake in return.

Jake lifted one pant leg to his knee and knocked on his shin, which was not a shin but a metal pole. The pole gave a hollow, tinny sound. "Lost a leg as a kid," he said, and dropped his pant.

"Wow," said the other guy.

The rest of us were silent. I'd written about losing my stepfather to cancer and presiding over a student government in the same year, but I was glad I hadn't been asked. The one-upmanship was apparently male-specific—two alphas sniffing one another out. Here's the thing: the guy didn't say "wow" to Jake as in, *How amazing that you've lived your life with an artificial leg.* Rather, he said "wow" as in *That's a good one. That beats mine. That will surely get you "in."*

Jake nodded and then looked toward the closed door of the interviewer's room. He knew he'd just won the showdown. And I knew I'd just witnessed a telling snapshot of at least one kind of Teach For America candidate: fervent; relentlessly competitive; ready to turn tragedy into redemption; aware, in fact, that such stories were commodities. It was daunting to see. Prone to self-doubt—as well as a neurotic compulsion to share my faults—I wasn't sure I could meet TFA's expectations. But Jake's behavior was also fascinating. I kept hearing his earlier remark—*I want this. Bad*—and it itched at me. *How could he know?* I thought. None of us quite knew what *this*—a two-year stint with TFA—would bring, and if we couldn't know for sure, then what exactly was *this* that Jake so desperately wanted? Entrance into an elite group? Another notch on a personal totem pole of triumph?

A part of me wants these things, too, I realized as I waited in the spring for the *yay or nay* letter from TFA. Yes, I loved learning and so I wanted to try my hand at teaching, and yes, I wanted to join the cause—the fight for educational equity—and this accounted for a good ninety-five percent of my motivations. But as I awaited a response from TFA, I noticed another, quieter, less altruistic motive: I wanted to be chosen. I wanted TFA's mark of approval on my undergraduate self. Little did I know that the organization, by design, intended this reaction, that Wendy Kopp wanted us to see teaching as a selective, privileged field.

When the acceptance letters came—one for Mark and one for me—I felt an elated rush, but I also raised a suspicious eyebrow on myself. A need for external validation was no reason to assume a post in front of classrooms of students. In fact, I was fairly certain that a classroom would do the opposite of stroking my ego. On the porch of our college house, where I'd studied for tests that I'd aced and researched papers I'd also aced and written poems that had won their meager prizes, I signed my name to Teach For America's forms, knowing that the swoop in my signature was a final farewell to a diet of steady college accolades. They call this *the real world*, I thought.

Though I never again saw the unofficial loser of the alpha male show-down, I wasn't surprised when I saw Jake in Houston for training.

• • •

It was 7 A.M., and those of us lucky to have the "late" schedules were grabbing our pre-made vinyl lunch bags off the tower of stacked steel trays before catching the yellow school buses.

"Teach For America!" said a stout corps member, Frank, who projected his normally scratchy, nasal voice so that it mocked the voice-over of an advertisement. "Serving, for ten years, the school's *you've* abandoned!" The word, *you've,* hit a peppy up-note and then slid down scale, just like in some outdated commercial.

A bunch of us cracked up.

"Plastic mattresses," his buddy, Ben, said. "Moldy showers. That's why *I* teach for America."

"Four hours of sleep," added another. "Feelings of guilt over decades of white supremacy. That's why *I* Teach for America!"

More laughter from the group.

Listing the difficulties of "Institute" (as it was known) in the satirical style of the Opening Ceremonies became a pressure valve to release our stress. Just a few days into our training, I'd learned that this "teacher boot camp" was indeed as grueling as TFA had said. The five weeks became, intentionally or not, a kind of hazing period to see who was truly devoted to the cause. We woke no later than six A.M. (and some of us woke much earlier), got dressed in our "professional attire," took buses sometimes an hour to our schools, and attended a full seven hours' worth of diversity discussions, lesson planning workshops, curriculum training, literacy training, teaching observations, and one-on-one coaching. In the second week, we would also start teaching classes. When we returned to campus, we squeezed dinner in before heading off to even more workshops on topics like "creating successful management systems" and "making content meaningful." The especially ambitious among us—and in TFA, there were a lot—somehow fit a workout or distance run into the day. By nine or ten at night, we met with our team of three other new teachers, called "corps members," where we completed assignments and, once we began teaching, co-planned our lessons for the next day. In the remaining late-night hours, we read articles for tomorrow's classes and grabbed the midnight shuttle to Kinko's for copy-making. It was an eighteen-hour day. By the afternoon, imaginary demonic thumbs pressed into my skull: a stress headache. I wasn't accustomed to them.

At night we passed out in overly air-conditioned, ice-cold dorm rooms. Our beds were on thin, crunchy plastic mattresses that rolled in and out of the walls like drawers, and the windows in the residential towers wouldn't open. We joked that this was suicide prevention. My particular floor also housed the garbage chute and reeked of rotting fruit. In the few minutes before my roommate, Jada, and I went to sleep, we each read passages from our palm-sized "365 days of inspiration" books. Mine: *365 Tao: Daily Meditations by Deng Ming-dao.* Hers: *365 Meditations for African American Women.*

"In the beginning," I read to her, half mocking and half sincere, "all things are hopeful."

"Each day is new," she read, also equal parts ironic and true. "Praise God that each minute is new."

In the next minute, we passed out.

As a roommate, Jada was the ideal foil to my self-doubting, introverted, and hyper-planned self. She was whimsical, outgoing, and brash. Though I'd read my TFA articles days before Institute, Jada hadn't even looked at hers on the plane. While I'd arrived punctually for training, somehow Jada had strolled in near midnight and missed Opening Ceremonies all together. It wasn't her fault her plane had been late, but I was fascinated by how she'd handled it: she couldn't have cared less. She hadn't prepared, she'd missed the first event, and all she could do was shrug. It took a lot to faze her.

Which was why she shocked me one afternoon when she charged into the room, crying. "TFA's nothing but a fucked up white-person's organization!" she shouted and flopped onto her mattress with a plastic crunch.

Relieved that, for once, it was Jada and not me who showed signs of breaking, I readied to leap into the role of supportive roommate. But then she murmured "Sorry," as though the color of my skin put me in cahoots with the organization, and that one word *sorry* covered up, like a manhole, an opening into the darker emotions Jada had for TFA. When I asked what happened, she just shook her head and said something vague about her CMA team.

The CMAs—Corps Member Advisories—consisted of usually twelve corps members, advised by a single TFA alum, and those groups broke down into three smaller groups of co-teaching and co-planning teams. These teams of four broke down once again into pairs for still more in-depth co-teaching and co-planning. In the larger groups of twelve, the advisors led us through discussions on all kinds of topics, but for the first week, we focused on diversity. While TFA had given us only five weeks to learn everything we possibly could about teaching (planning a lesson, designing a unit, managing classrooms of kids, handling difficult students, accommodating special needs kids, and so on and so on), the organization spent a substantial amount of time unearthing assumptions about race, class, power, and privilege. Issues of race and class, latent in most American conversations, were now the primary focus.

"Stand if you identify as white," our advisor, Tamika, announced to our group early in the first week. We'd arranged ourselves in a circle, and seven of the twelve stood up. "Stand if you identify as African American." Four stood, including Tamika. "As Asian." Two stood. "As Latino." None stood. But then came the more private matters. "Stand if you identify as straight."

"As gay." "Stand if you identify as Muslim." "Christian." "Lower-class." On and on went the categories, and we stood up or remained seated accordingly. My threshold for divulging personal details has always been higher than the average person's, but the activity still made me uncomfortable— TFA had just required all its members to "out" themselves—on religion, on sexuality, on class categories. What if one of our group members hadn't wanted to share with people he or she only met four days ago?

Despite its potential damages, the activity had an eventual point. TFA's first principle for excellent teaching can be summed up in two words: high expectations. Hold the bar high and all your students will rise to meet it, we were told. It didn't matter how swank your management systems were for collecting homework, or how entertaining your lessons were for multiplication. You could erase the benefits of any teacher-magic if you stepped into your classroom believing your inner-city or rural kids weren't really capable of the same work their middle-class peers produced. You could negate all of your training if, regardless of your own background, you let a certain thought pop into your head: *These kids can't do it.* On the road to our students' potential triumphs, we were told, we could be the first to sabotage them. Consequently, our advisors asked us to take inventory of our identities, to reflect on the degree of power that our various categories provided, and to investigate the subconscious beliefs we held about those in positions of less power.

The message we got from TFA was this: nothing could stand in the way of our kids' success, nothing, so long as we teachers believed in it. So long as we set expectations audaciously high for our students, our students would rise to meet them. This was an energizing belief that most, including me, quickly bought. When a corps member voiced dissent by suggesting that other factors played significant roles in a child's success— parental involvement, nutrition, a student's motivation—our advisors steered them back to the message. Students did poorly in school primarily because society expected them to perform poorly. To suggest otherwise was to engage in the same kind of low expectations and racist and/or classist assumptions that dug students into the academic holes they were in. We had to imagine great things for our students. Huge teaching successes. Reading levels raised three grades in one year. Seriously engaged students with hands raised and national test scores raised and everything: raised. These kinds of expectations, at least in my mind, were accompanied by inspirational background music that might accent a movie montage. Children working at desks, writing, erasing. Teacher moving around desks, calling on children, high-fiving students, jumping for joy. Yes! Learning! Hip-hop's closest kin to "Eye of the Tiger" coursed through my mental imagery.

Perhaps eager to hear that we were all that mattered in "solving the nation's greatest injustice," we rarely refuted these theories. I'd heard that when the rare corps members wouldn't come around to this keystone of TFA philosophy, he or she was flagged and put on an improvement plan. This seemed to be the case for Chin, although he exhibited issues beyond just an inability to embrace Institute theory.

After meeting his Houstonian students on the first day, Chin, a teacher in my twelve-person group, announced, "My kids are really sweet. They're nothing like I thought they'd be."

We were reflecting on our first lessons in yet another share-circle. As soon as the two unassuming sentences slipped from his mouth, I cringed. The concept was an obvious "no-no" in TFA. Kendra, an African American woman with shoulder-length braids, pounced first. "Why'd you think they'd be *mean*, Chin?" I'd seen her lighthearted, I'd seen her worried, I'd seen her transform into witty confidence before her students, but in this moment, she'd become a stern pseudo-therapist.

Chin straightened his back against the plastic chair and shifted his eyes. "I don't knooow," he said, lengthening the last word like a kid does when he resists an adult's question.

Much about Chin seemed kid-like. He was a pudgy Korean-American guy with a disproportionately large head. Supposedly a Harvard science genius, he was among the many Ivy-League grads who pursued TFA, but he struggled with everything about Institute—the expectations, the philosophy, the very act of teaching. Though we were encouraged to cultivate our commando-teacher voice, Chin's words were quiet and mumbled, and he sometimes stuttered. On his first day of teaching, Chin plowed through his lesson plan in ten minutes and, instead of asking the kids questions or tossing out a riddle for them to solve or doing anything, anything to fill the time, he simply looked at his watch, shrugged, and *left the room.*

"You can't do that, Chin!" Tamika yelled.

To the rest of us, she talked in a warm, encouraging voice and smiled brightly, but with Chin, she scolded. Often when he said something, she looked at him with a furrowed brow, mouth hung open, head cocked to one side. Then she lifted her eyes to the ceiling, took a deep breath, and plunged into an explanation of what I think she'd assumed was common sense. "When you're a teacher, Chin, you become entrusted with your kids. You have to *stay with* them." That was her first response. "And Chin, these kids are in *sum*mer school. They didn't pass the eighth *grade*! Do you really think you taught them everything they need to learn in ten minutes?"

Chin went verbally limp in the face of these questions. He shrugged, he mumbled, he shuffled away. But, as cruel as it seems, Chin's natural incompetence presented itself with an upside: it showed the rest of us our comparable competence. We knew, for instance, to stay in our class-rooms. And even if we feared that our kids might unleash violent potty mouths upon hearing our introductory sentences, as the kids in Holly-wood's "ghetto-teacher-movies" did, we knew not to say, "My kids are really sweet—they're nothing like I thought they'd be."

Once the question popped from Kendra's mouth, "Why'd you think they'd be mean?" Chin looked like he'd been caught taking some piece of candy that he'd assumed was free. *Who, me? What did I do?* It was familiar territory for him. Kendra wouldn't let his "I don't know" become the final word. She pressed him.

Chin shrugged, said he didn't know why, and then said, "Because kids in the ghetto can be violent?"

I cringed and watched our three black corps members respond. Kendra scooted to the edge of her chair. Mia folded her arms against her chest. Robert, who had the unfortunate luck of being partnered with Chin, kept his lips sealed. He was cataloging the sentence for a clever punch-line that I knew would later make me spit my soda.

Kendra began the justified lecture on how Chin had no prior experience with "kids in the ghetto," so he couldn't possibly assume they'd be one way or another. The rest of us sat back and watched the inevitable vortex of racial tension.

Tamika did the hard thing; she turned the topic back on all of us.

"You have to be really honest with yourself," she said. "You have to be completely honest about what society teaches you, about the kinds of assumptions you're going into your classroom with. What are they? What has society told you?"

Someone offered the responses we'd been learning in the TFA literature. "A lot of people might assume that under-resourced minority groups can't achieve to the same standards as 'the culture of power'. But of course it's exactly because 'the culture of power' has this perception that minority groups face the challenges they do today." This was the diplomatic answer. This was the right answer. We, as relatively high-achievers on things like standardized tests, were adept at offering right answers.

But Tamika wasn't interested in our paraphrase of Lisa Delpit's *Other People's Children*. Someone else talked about how members of "the cul-ture of power" dominate mainstream media; images on the news and television often reflect the inherent prejudices of the culture of power and are then passed on. We all had to be aware, this person said, of these images and not let them obstruct the high expectations we had for our students.

We nodded. I looked at Tamika, who I thought would be pleased. Her brow furrowed. She pressed her pointer fingers against one another and they wiggled back and forth like a charmed snake. "Why is it that when a group of black guys head our way on the street, we tense up?"

No one answered. I knew what Tamika wanted; she wanted us to get personal. I saw a classic scene from my teenage years—a Ben Franklin statue rising above Philadelphia, the rush of cabs and cars on wet Market Street, my mother and stepfather behind me. My sister and I always walked faster than they did; we were eager to roam the city on our own. We weaved through the crowds, laughing at our own jokes. An old lady or two passed. Three black guys passed. I felt my stepfather's hand on my elbow.

Once we returned to our two-story home, surrounded by mowed grass and other two-story homes, he told me, "You might be wise, but you're not streetwise." I didn't know the "dangers of the city," he said. Back in the suburbs, I realized what my stepfather meant by "dangers of the city."

Still, I didn't respond to Tamika. It was hard enough to acknowledge the flaws, the ignorance, the—let's face it—racism of the people who had loved me best and whom I still mourned the loss of; even worse to confess it to near-strangers.

Nobody answered Tamika's question. She finally said, "I even get tense, and *I'm black*." Her long, unpainted fingernails pointed at her temples. Her shaved head accentuated her high-cheekbones. "I sometimes walk to the other side of the street. Now why is that? What have people told us about the kinds of kids we're teaching? What have your friends and family said to you about your commitment to TFA?"

Heads sunk down again, or looked away and out the window. Outside, the concrete ground looked wavy in the hundred-degree heat. I was eons away from my upbringing, thousands of miles from my home. My mother and sister had said they were proud of me. My mother had also said she could never do what I was doing. My mother had also agreed that I shouldn't park my car in the same spot once I'd settled in Baltimore. I looked down at my hands. I saw I'd been picking my thumbnail cuticle. It was raw and pink. If he were alive, I thought, my stepfather would be clutching my elbow. I smoothed my torn cuticle over with my other thumb.

In that moment, Matthew, stocky Matthew with the South Carolinian accent and the striped, preppy neckties—a twenty-two-year-old white kid who might greet you with a hearty "Morning" at a Baptist church—Matthew made a little whimper, bowed his head, and put his hand to his forehead like a visor on a cap. His body shook as he cried. He inhaled again and then let out a sob.

The rest of us were shocked. It was the unlikeliest of breakdowns. The stoic, exceedingly polite, rarely emoting Matthew: now driven to hyperventilation. Someone thought to hand him a tissue.

Eventually, he gained enough composure to speak. "My friends. Back at home. They say to me," he paused to take a breath, and his diaphragm shuttered on the inhale like a child who'd been crying too hard. "They say, Matthew. Why're you going. To teach," another staggered, kiddish inhale, "a bunch a nigs." He blurted the last word in a wet, sudden sob. With that, his shoulders collapsed again.

Tamika asked him what he said to his friends.

"I said, 'Don't call 'em that.'" He wiped his face again with the tissue and looked at us like we were those bar buddies. "'Don't call them that. Call them . . . call them *under-resourced*!'" He shouted the last two words. They were high-pitched and wet, and the slippery echoes of the *S*'s in the word, *under-resourced*, sat in the Houston room with us, where the air-conditioner droned and the windows sealed us from the heat that warbled the lines of the one-story, patched-roof shacks across the street. The table at the front of the classroom stood like a pulpit from where nobody was preaching, nobody was teaching, and nobody said a thing. *Under-resourced*. It felt like the lamest replacement for what Matthew's Carolina buddies really meant.

• • •

If mastering cultural sensitivity had been the only requirement for success in the classroom, perhaps Institute wouldn't have been so grueling. Indeed, it took far more than "high expectations," despite TFA's maxim, and the planners of Institute must have known this, hence the hours upon hours of training on literacy, curriculum designing, cognitive development, higher-order thinking, classroom management, diversified instruction, special needs students, and on and on. The topics seemed as endless as the many ways that a teacher could screw up.

Unbeknownst to me, I'd impressed Tamika with my first lesson. I'd chosen the story "Salvador, Late or Early" for my nine summer school kids to read. As soon as I announced the title, Malika, a vocal girl, complained. "I already *read* this story!" she shouted.

"Oh," I said and improvised. "That's great." I kept counting copies, separating them between my fingers, sending them in small stacks down the rows. "I love reading things more than once. You can always get more out of a story the second time."

This was the comment that led Tamika to believe I was "a natural," an opinion I didn't learn about until another, later lesson had gone so poorly that I burst into tears afterward. But on the first day, before students read the one-page tale about a forty-pound, impoverished, neglected kid named Salvador, I pulled out colored pencils and asked them to draw images of their homes. It was supposed to be an "engagement activity," a "hook," as TFA called it, a way to get students interested in the lesson to come. I knew that they'd be able to relate to at least some aspects of Salvador, who "lives behind a raw wood doorway," as Sandra Cisneros writes, "where homes are the color of bad weather." The description could have fit the shacks around the school.

On a blank white page, one kid set to work on a two-story house with classic four-paned windows, a pointed triangular roof, a chimney, a green yard, and a balanced tree off to the side. I glanced at the desk of the student beside him. He drew a virtually identical rendition of the classic American home. In fact, student after student had drawn, not his or her own place of residence, which I knew more closely resembled the peeling one-story shacks nearby, the ones with broken windows and yards of abandoned debris that we corps members had seen a week ago when we'd toured the communities. Instead, each kid drew cartoon versions of the typical middle-class suburban life.

It troubled me. Why didn't they draw the truth? It was possible that they were too ashamed. But they churned out the clichés so fast that it seemed like they didn't know they were even *allowed* to represent the truth. Or maybe, after years of seeing on television sitcoms what American life should look like, they thought I was asking them to mirror it back to me.

I later told Tamika about the drawings. I thought she'd offer some solution, some way to empower my students to bear witness to real experiences. But she just shrugged and offered a nod. *Yep*, I felt she was saying. *That's the 'culture of power' in action.* "What do you expect, you know?" Tamika said. "When they're surrounded by versions of the world that don't look anything like their lives?" Tamika didn't have an answer for how to empower my students to express the truth. *That's your work in the classroom*, I felt she was telling me. *That's your job to figure out.* It was a motivating challenge, and I left feeling empowered to make headway.

But the track on which a person learns to teach is unpredictable, rickety and ever-undulating, and my empowerment got quickly replaced by feelings of ineptitude. In my third lesson, I'd based half the lesson on the homework I'd assigned the day before. When I asked students to take out their homework, only one student had it. The rest had nothing to show. Flustered and surprised by their apathy, I moved onto part two of the lesson. "Get into your groups from yesterday," I said, a sentence that might as well have been, "Commence doing whatever it is that you desire."

Some kids threw their heads on their desks. Others stood up and talked. Malika wandered around, laughing, cracking jokes to other kids. Nine students. That's all I had. Why couldn't I get them under control?

"Get into your groups," I commanded, but Malika spun toward me, hand on her hip, and shouted, "We don't *know* our groups. We don't re*member* them!"

Later, Tamika told me that this was a lie—students remembered their groups, but they liked to pretend that they forgot them. The charade bought them a few minutes of chaos. But *I* didn't remember the groups. I'd created them the day before, and I hadn't written them down. How stupid, I thought. I couldn't keep track of the simplest things. I threw the kids into new groups and gave them their assignment, which they didn't do, and which, I realized mid-lesson, was just busy work. I didn't know how to salvage the moment, so all I could think to do was let the clock run out. From the back of the room, four corps members and a faculty advisor made disapproving faces and jotted notes down on forms. I was the failure at the front of the class. When I left the room that day, I realized I hadn't even remembered to take attendance.

These were minor struggles compared to what I'd face in Charm City, and I sensed this. How could I handle a full-day of teaching in Baltimore if I couldn't even manage nine students for forty-five minutes in Houston? When I found Tamika, I was on the brink of crying, and we sat outside on a step in the heat where I told her I thought I might not be cut out for this.

She looked stunned. "*Noo*, Heather, you've got a knack for this." She described what she saw on that first day. "I was like, Wow, she's a natural!"

Tamika glowed with her usual optimism, but this time it wasn't rubbing off. I countered with a list of my many mistakes. Tamika proceeded to use each as a mini-lesson for the future. Don't ever base a lesson on homework, she said. She drew a diagram to illustrate why this was so. And if I had trouble remembering attendance, I should make a list each day of all the things I needed to do in a lesson. I should put "attendance" at the top of the list. "Why do you think I carry a clipboard everywhere?" she asked. It was true; the clipboard extended from Tamika's arm like an extra appendage.

When I went back into the air-conditioned school, I felt a bit stronger in resolve but no more competent, and with good reason: I *was* incompetent. To varying degrees, we all were. Herein rests one of the greatest tensions of TFA: it hand-selects, for its mission, those who are typically adept at succeeding, those who in some cases (mine included) are even addicted to success. Though we were diverse in many ways, we'd been chosen because we were over-achieving, talented do-gooders with leadership, charisma, and skill. We'd graduated at the tops of our classes, earned high scores on standardized tests, served as presidents of this organization or that. In classic résumé language, we'd touted our achievements on paper: we'd "facilitated and managed" X and "increased profit margins" of Y and "successfully engineered" Z. We were accustomed to chasing—and catching—the carrot. We thousand were not accustomed to failure.

But teaching is a complex craft, and novices are destined, in some way or another, to fail. Adding another dozen hurdles to the obstacles, our future students would be some of the least prepared in the nation, our schools the lowest funded, our administrations the most unstable. We were assuming the toughest teaching posts in America, posts that many teachers spent their lives avoiding. TFA designed Institute with the intensity of a boot camp because the organization attempted to cover everything a newbie needed, but it could only accomplish so much in five weeks. At Institute, the chasm between the successes we corps members typically achieved and the dire conditions the educational crisis posed created little walking time bombs inside each of us. We had, in most cases, never failed so miserably. (After all, we'd written those "greatest challenges" essays, which we knew were meant to end in victory.)

Among everyone I talked to, this tension—a tension between our proclivities for success and the inevitabilities of our failures—didn't go unnoticed. Many of us saw that TFA recruited a certain "type," the exceedingly hard-working, die-hard type, the type who would sacrifice his or her well-being for the good of a cause. We were often told not to expect to have lives outside of teaching. Bridging the achievement gap would take everything we had—every hour of every waking day. Don't expect to go to the movies.

The combination of this type and the TFA mission created incredible pressure. Some of us unraveled early. Melinda was my teaching partner, which meant we collaborated on every lesson and delivered it identically to different sets of students. A white, extroverted woman, Melinda had a manic, scattered disposition. She worked herself so hard one evening that she crashed only an hour before wake-time, slept through her alarm, and missed the bus to the high school where we trained and taught. This led her with no means of transportation, but in her desperate attempt to arrive on time, she chose what to me was beyond the realm of options: she stuck out her thumb on an unknown street of Houston and pleaded for a ride. Only a few minutes late, she raced into the school unharmed and un-showered. As soon as she had a chance to sit, she burst into tears. She could have been hurt, she said. She could have been raped. But failure—or, in this case, missing a day of Institute—was not an option.

Although almost all of us wore the stress of wanting to succeed, we didn't all wear it the same. Robert used sarcasm, though the increasingly darker bags beneath his eyes belied his good humor. He and I worked on the same schedule at Institute, teaching in the morning and immediately meeting up with others in the faculty lounge for, ostensibly, reading and planning. More typically, we used the time to crash on the old couches and stare at the ceiling like zombies. Whenever I arrived in the room, Robert was sitting in his usual position: torso sunk into a ratty brown couch, head thrown over the top, butt hanging off the old cushion. I plopped down next to him.

"How'd it go?" I always asked, hoping that, for the both of us, he had greater success in his class.

"Oh," he laughed one day and lifted his head. "I'm just the James Brown of teaching. I'm like the Godfather of Education. I'm like, 'Get up, get on up!'" James Brownian enthusiasm leaped into Robert's voice, and then just as quickly leaped out. A low, exhausted tone returned. "And they're like, 'Umm, who the fuck this?'"

The air-conditioner droned.

"It's like," and then Robert simulated his neck hanging from a rope. "Somebody. Help me!"

I wrote the headline: "Teacher Hangs Himself in Middle of Terrible Lesson."

"No, I mean that's what the *students* were doing. *I* wasn't even making complete sentences. Subjects? Verbs? What? Where am I?"

I laughed. Disaster was less tragic when narrated by Robert. We made light of our ineptitude. We asked each other when Teach For America would deliver, along with the daily turkey sandwiches and oatmeal cookies in our packed lunches, the precious microchip, the one we could insert into our brains somewhere next to my theories on the aesthetics of blank verse and his reverence for Henry Louis Gates, Jr. The chip would make us capable of doing what seemed a perfectly feasible profession. The chip would make it so that, by the end of our lessons, our students actually learned; they had internalized some new knowledge and could demonstrate it, and didn't look at us with pained expressions.

On the wall of that teacher's lounge read a motivational sign I stared at each afternoon like a Zen koan: "Sometimes you have to build your wings on the way down."

What happens, I always thought, if you jump out of the plane with your wing-materials in hand but can't build them fast enough before your face hits the ground? In Robert's voice, this would have been funny. But in my own, the question haunted me with dull seriousness.

One day I taught what, to me, felt like a bona fide, competent lesson—it had a clear goal, the activity fit the goal, the students completed the activity, and I handed the group off to Kendra with satisfaction, who taught them social studies. Success! Or at least I had deemed it as much. My school advisor, a veteran Houston teacher employed by TFA, stopped me on the way out. She'd observed the entire lesson, and I readied for her praise.

Her fuchsia lips curled into a smirk but she shook her head. "You didn't *close*," she nearly sang in a melody that might accompany a finger-wagging.

She meant I hadn't reflected back on what the lesson had accomplished; I hadn't reminded students of our goal together and how we'd achieved it. It was a minor aspect of a lesson plan, but one we'd been taught to remember. I sighed and left her behind. She was right. My lesson hadn't been perfect.

I could have beaten myself up for imperfection. A part of me did. Another part of me knew that if I didn't pat myself on the back for small victories, I'd never survive as a teacher. And I'd achieved something that day—instead of pretending to be a teacher, I'd actually taught something. Most of the nuts and bolts of the job had come together that day, and with practice, they would again.

I arrived in the lounge, where Robert sat on the ratty brown couch. This time, though, rather than flopping into it, I sat up and faced him. "I've figured out our problem!"

He lifted his head, eyebrows raised, sensing I was ready to share more than our usual sarcasm.

"I don't know how to teach," I declared.

Robert blurted a single, mono-syllabic "hah" and threw his head over the top of the couch again.

"No, I mean really. I don't know how to teach now, but eventually I will."

It was honestly the first time I realized that teaching was a skill to cultivate, a craft to learn, not a micro-chip to receive or, as I had at one time suspected, a genetic coding to possess upon one's embryonic conception. But that was the trouble with many of us TFA types: we were accustomed to performing well. We weren't used to the humility of failure. As much as I liked hearing Tamika's proclamation that I was "A Natural," I'd figured out that, at least in this profession, no such thing existed. Nobody stood in front of a class for the first time and excelled. I didn't have much of an idea on how to teach, but I believed one day I would. Not necessarily in Houston, as none of us could learn how to proficiently perform our future jobs in just five weeks. But eventually I believed I'd learn. Until then, I'd practice and, if need be, I would pretend.

• • •

On one of the final days at Institute, after all the students had left, several of us gathered in a vacant classroom to pass the time. It had been a long day, a long summer, and we were finally nearing the end. For an anomalous one hour, we had nothing we had to do. Someone picked up a piece of chalk, practiced swooping the cursive letters of her name across the blackboard. The rest of us joined in. *Mr. Hamden, Ms. Arnold, Ms. Kirn.* We created different renditions of our names, shaped the letters this way and that, then stood back and sized up our work.

"You have the best teacher-handwriting," one woman said to me.

"Your name looks most like a teacher," I said to someone else.

We were like kids playing make-believe. *Let's make believe I'm the teacher, and this is how I write.* Though we'd learned plenty of theories and strategies and tools and philosophies at Institute, we were still only pretending to do a job that we'd soon have to do for real.

It's poignant, I think, that I remember this moment better than I remember the Closing Ceremonies of Institute. Compared to our energy at the Opening Ceremonies, the new Teach For America corps was a less boisterous crowd, but we sat in the auditorium and heard a few more triumphant teacher-tales, this time told by the likes of us. My college roommate, Mark, stood on stage along with seven others and offered his "This is Why I Teach For America" moment, a moment he'd accrued during his five weeks at Institute. I remember being impressed with his stage presence, but I don't remember his story. I don't remember any of the stories. I remember, instead, a few newbie teachers, heavy with exhaustion and writing their names on a board in chalk, knowing that in a matter of weeks, they'd be responsible for rosters of kids.

After the Closing Ceremonies had newly minted us ready to teach America's low-income kids, we thousand new TFA teachers popped open plenty of bottles. Without a single additional workshop to attend the next day, without another new logistical system or teaching philosophy or learning modality to master for the immediate tomorrow, we newbie teachers meandered around the grounds of the University of Houston, shouting for joy and cracking jokes in our new Teacher-Speak and rejoicing that, after tonight, we didn't have to sleep on those crunchy plastic mattresses again. I watched even the most professional-seeming of teachers—the ones who'd easily assumed at least a mask of "competence"—wobble drunkenly around the lawns like they were once again college kids, free to wear flip-flops and master the art of leisure. Free to live in a world where the burdens of a social injustice didn't rest on their youthful, athletic shoulders.

After that evening, I never saw Matthew or Kendra or Melinda or Tamika, or Chin, for that matter, again. The next day, we all flew to different cities and rural towns across the country. We left to find apartments to rent, and roommates to live with, and cars to drive, and we left to learn about these new towns and cities that, in many cases, we barely knew. But mostly, we left to do what TFA had charged us with: construct our own teacher stories, stories that began with the challenging but surmountable conflict, that rose to the inevitable climax, that descended into the satisfying, conclusive victory. Stories, in other words, that could prove we had good reason, we had every right, we were destined to teach for America.

CHAPTER 3

FIRST DAY

Don't let them see you vulnerable. Be firm. If you look weak, they will walk on you forever. Engage them. If you don't engage them, they won't care about learning, and you'll lose their interest forever. Smile—it sets the tone for the rest of the semester. Don't smile. Never smile. Don't smile until Christmas. Get contact information from them. You need their contact information. They will give you the wrong contact information. It won't matter whether you get contact information or not because you will have different students in your classes by the second week, thus forcing you to get all new contact information. Assign books. Don't assign books. They will lose the books. Or you will have different students in your class by the next week, and your books will be assigned to kids who no longer show up. Have a system for everything. Give them name tags. Make seating charts. Don't make seating charts. Instead, give them numbers when they walk into the door, which should match numbers that you assign to the desks, and as you do this, write each number down on a clipboard beside the corresponding student's name, and the desk that corresponds to the number the student holds will be that student's seat for the semester. This is how you make a "Classroom Designed for Success." Also, make sure to tape the numbers to the desks—students will try to peel off the numbers.

The voices from a summer of training comprised a schizophrenic chorus. I sat cross-legged on a new double mattress, which had just been delivered a few days earlier to a row house, which I'd just rented with three other women I'd just met, and I stared at a mess: dozens of handouts designed by other teachers; books from my former life as a literature student; scrap paper with my scribbles; an idle pen. The summer's crash-course in teaching had paralyzed me. In the center of my new comforter I faced my first week of teaching and thought about how a "real" teacher would not plan her lessons from a crouched position on her first larger-than-twin-size bed.

Just the other night, I'd gotten a new tip. "On my first day, I played that game," a third-year TFA teacher had told a group of us at a bar. "You know, the game where you go down the line and ask each kid a question and they each get to ask you one question?"

I nodded. I knew the game. It seemed like a good getting-to-know-you kind-of game.

"I just sort of figured they'd ask me about my hobbies or something. But one kid goes, 'Are you gay?' And I just blew it. I froze. So another kid shouts, 'He gay! Look at his tie, he gay,' and that was it. I lost all credibility with that class." The teacher took a gulp from his beer. This was the same guy who, during TFA presentations, had seemed so competent, so cool.

Someone asked how he got his class back.

"I didn't. The first year was *hell!*"

I vowed to steer clear of that game, and on my mattress I finally scrapped together a first-day lesson. A review of class rules. A jeopardy game testing students' understanding of class rules. And from my stacks, I chose a book I'd loved so much that I'd stolen it from my high school in tenth grade: *The Autobiography of Malcolm X*. I flipped through the yellowed, musky pages, searching for the scene where, while in prison, Malcolm turns his whole life around. Word by word, he copies the entire dictionary, pulls himself from nearly illiterate dealer to historic intellectual. *Aardvark* begins his journey from everyday criminal to American revolutionary. *Aardvark* makes a man iconic.

I decided to use the book despite the fact that I thought a white teacher who taught a class of mostly black kids about a black revolutionary seemed fairly condescending. But it was nearing evening, and I couldn't afford to philosophize. And I loved that book. "Students will be able to read a passage of Malcolm X's autobiography and identify the main idea and subordinate ideas." This was one of my first written objectives.

But my real objective wasn't measurable, and I wouldn't write it on paper. *Students will be able to revel in how books open like doors into worlds and ways hereto unforeseen.* Because books *were* like doors, I thought, the way they swung open from their bindings like wood from hinges. With that, I put down my pen. Across the street, in another Victorian row home nearly identical to ours, black and white men of all ages—gray-haired men with bent backs, twenty- and thirty-something men with popping calves, balding men, middle-aged jiggly-middled men—all kinds of black and white men gathered in the yard. They held mugs and sipped from them. They stood in loose circles or sat together in white plastic chairs. They smoked cigarettes. It seemed like a bizarre Baltimore-Benetton commercial for men. I hadn't yet figured out that it was a halfway house for AA. Instead, I just smiled at what I thought was a multicultural, multigenerational, feel-good intentional community. *See,* I thought, *people from the most divergent of backgrounds* could *come together.*

• • •

I unlocked my classroom door, and the morning light shone through the row of windows, which offered a view of Font Hill and Mount Olivet Cemetery. Some of the windows were tinted a urine-yellow hue, and torn shades of beige vinyl covered each of my windows' top halves, but the sad color of the shades contrasted with the yellow streamers that, thanks to Ms. Patterson's advice, I'd stapled to the bottom edges. While some of the Southwestern faculty had been less-than-friendly, Ms. Patterson, a stout, fifty-something veteran who taught next door to me, had quickly taken me under her wing and showed me the low-budget ways to turn prison aesthetics into a somewhat cheery classroom. The Friday before my first day, she moseyed about my room making recommendations, calling me "Kar-en" in a slow, sing-songy voice reminiscent of the grandmother I'd never had. "Come on, Kar-en," she'd sung. "We'll get this done before six." We pushed desks around and bleached the faces of them nearly bone white, and though the ghostly gray remnants of the nasty graffiti remained, the task of preparing my class had become hers. I had a friend. Sweat poured down her face as she scrubbed.

Now, on this September morning, the cinderblock walls already sweated from the Baltimore humidity. Posters had fallen down over the weekend. I re-tacked *Southwestern is a Better Place Because YOU Are Here*. The rest of the room looked orderly, the desks joined together in pairs, the chairs neatly pushed under each. The yellow streamers on the vinyl shades looked like lemon icing on sickly beige cake. On the desks, I could still make out all the FUCK YOUs and fellatio cartoons.

The students would be here soon. Out the window, I watched them stroll up Font Hill with backpacks slung low on their spines, or with notebooks curled into their baggy jean-pockets, or with empty hands and fat headphones covering their ears. They walked past that gargantuan cemetery in singles, in doubles, in loose crowds and in loose clothes (on the males) or tight clothes (on the females). They walked past the tombstones of Baltimore's white male elite. The son of John Quincy Adams. Francis Scott Key. *Oh say, can you see.* Mr. Scott Key, by the dawn's early light, I see tombstones and my tired future students through urine-tinted windows.

With only a few minutes before the gigantic clock on the wall read 8:45, I felt it most poignantly: the nerves. They were nowhere near butterflies in the stomach. They were electric bricks. They sunk. They zapped. They made me want to keel over.

Ms. Brown had laid out the plan for us. Homeroom would last as long as it needed. This could mean a half hour or two hours. With our classroom doors open and with forty names on our rosters, all of the teachers would wait and see who would show. Showing would take a while, the administrators had said. Showing could take two hours.

At the time, I didn't understand why the administration needed an indeterminably long homeroom. It seemed a waste of time. Wouldn't "seeing who showed" take ten minutes? But the administration was gearing up for a messy first day due to the school's "zone" status. As a zone high school, Southwestern had to accept any kid living in a certain geographic area. Unknown kids would appear at the top of Font Hill, giving names the school's registrar didn't know but citing addresses that indeed fell into Southwestern's zone. Maybe the school had lost the kids' names. Maybe the kids had moved over the summer. Maybe they'd planned on going elsewhere but those plans fell through. When they arrived at the scheduling room—a nearly emptied classroom with large, gray computers that looked like they'd been pulled from an office in 1985—the students would need schedules, which, in that room, would take a while to create. Maybe two hours.

That wasn't the only potential glitch. Plenty of kids whose names were on the rosters, maybe a quarter of the names, would never show up at all. Who were they? Phantoms of Baltimore? Veteran teachers offered two explanations. One: those kids were sitting on the stoops of their homes, staring into the windows of other row homes, holding babies or nickel bags or just pushing their fingers into the holes of their pockets. They were kids staring at the other sides of their streets. Or two: they were standing in a line on another side of town, waiting to register at a better Baltimore school, one that wasn't just for any "zone" kid, one with schedules already printed for every student by computers designed in the past decade. At this other school, the teachers told the students they were *special. Baltimore elite. Only such-and-such percent of the school's applicants were admitted this year. The other such-and-such percent had to go to those zone schools, and aren't you glad you avoided that terrible fate?*

"You know," Ms. Patterson said to me, her usually high-pitched voice suddenly dipping deep into her throat, "they're afraid to come here."

"Really?" It hadn't dawned on me that while I'd been afraid to assume my post at the Terrordome, some students might also feel the same. But Ms. Patterson said the kids had been warned all their lives about Southwestern. If they'd made it all the way to eighth grade, if they'd gone through all the trouble of attending school, if they'd worn the white and blue graduation gowns at thirteen (because in west Baltimore, graduating middle school was a feat worth celebrating with all the grandeur of any high school or college diploma), did they really want to throw their hard work away by ending up at Southwestern? Shoot for the stars, and in Baltimore there were two: City or Poly, otherwise known as Baltimore City College High School or Baltimore Polytechnic Institute. These were the elite magnet high schools where the kids had to apply, where the test scores were soaring, where the administrations maintained order and a college acceptance letter was an expectation. Or, if your grades aren't that good, go to Mervo or Carver or another vocational school, where test scores were slightly below state average but still not bucket-bottom and where the incidents of violence were also roughly below average and teen pregnancy not quite as common as a cold. Go anywhere else but a zone high school. Stay away from those zone high schools. Noelani's roommate, a teacher at West Baltimore Middle School, which fed into Southwestern, would later tell us that the teachers at West Baltimore used Southwestern as a threat. *You keep acting like that*, they told disobedient kids, *and you'll end up at Southwestern. Is that what you want?* Southwestern apparently was a pit of no returning. Southwestern, according to Baltimore's own teachers, would determine one's disgrace. It broke my heart that the city's message to its students was essentially this: *the road we've designed for you will let you down; seek detour.*

So students did, they sought a detour. And if they found none, if the dreaded default became their only avenue, they arrived at the steps of Southwestern, registered or not.

By some stroke of luck, I didn't get assigned a homeroom. I could wait out the unknown time in my empty classroom. I sat at my desk and tried to review my lesson. But with the plastic chair pressing up against my thighs, and my sprawling metal and green desk before me, where my three-ringed white binder contained three pages of lesson plans and a whole lot of nothing else, I got itchy. I stared at a canary yellow poster that listed my five rules in bright red marker, *Listen to Your Teacher*, etcetera. The paired graffiti desks looked like vacant marriages of *Lil' Bone* and *Lakeport* (nickname and housing project, respectively). The circular, big-numbered clock looked out from above the chalkboard like Baltimore's patient eye. I got up and headed for the halls.

Noelani, Amy, Ellen, and Brooke all taught in the same hallway on the other side of the building—"the low side," people called it, because the room numbers were lower than on the side I taught on, known as "the high side." The four of them stood outside their classroom doors. Noelani held a clipboard against her chest. Ellen folded her hands behind her back, her shiny black loafers pointed outward. Brooke had a hand on her hip and leaned on one leg, jutting the other hip out. Her eyes darted up and down the empty hall. Amy seemed the most authentically *teacher*, though I couldn't quite place why. Maybe because she had two years on us—instead of thrusting herself directly from college to TFA, she spent time in Malawi, Africa, where little kids called her *Madam* and stood up when she entered the room.

The bell to mark the start of the day had rung five minutes ago, and the hallways were virtually empty. A few kids passed us—a small girl with her binder clasped to her chest, another boy with an empty backpack strapped to his shoulders. His nose pointed at a folded paper in his hands. Now and then he looked up to read the numbers above the doors. I peered into Noelani's room and counted three kids scattered in the seats. Their heads slumped forward or their eyes shifted from the doorway to their desks and from their desks to the clock. They were on time.

Noelani angled her clipboard at me. Her roster had thirty-some names on it; only three were checked. "Where are they?"

Slowly, more kids came down the halls. A group of guys meandered in jeans that bunched and gathered at their tan boots. They wore black T-shirts that hung to their knees. They had no books or binders. Papers were folded up in some of their back pockets. They looked at Ellen on one side of the hallway, then Noelani and me. One grinned. They didn't slow down or speed up.

More and more kids rounded the corner and headed our way. With each new bunch, I expected one or two kids to stop, look up at a classroom number (maybe Noelani's), look into the face of the adult at the doorway (maybe Noelani's), and walk through the door. But none did. They just kept passing at idle speeds. I felt like that yellow-beaked bird in the children's book, the dazed and baffled creature that asks every sort of animal if it is his mother. *Are you my student?* I wondered. Are *you?* What about the tiny kid with the T-shirt down to his ankles, the one who doesn't just walk down the hall but skips from wall to wall in zigzags, his hair-braided in pig-tails like Pippy Longstocking, his face grinning like the Joker? Will *he* be my student?

The hallway had gone from silent to street-like. We were privy to a student-run block party. Hardly any kid entered a room. They stopped, they mingled, they checked us out.

"Look all these new teachers up in here!" a male voice called out. A group of boys had stopped between Amy, Ellen, Noelani, and me. They were shuffling around, lingering and swaggering, lugging that heavy denim that bunched at their shins and feet.

"Aw, yeah!" One kid looked Amy up and down.

"Get to class, young man," she said without a flinch.

Another kid cocked his head toward Noelani and me and grinned. "Low-side gonna be off the *hook* this year!"

Hands slapped low-five, side-five. Fists pounded fists.

"Hey, Teach."

"What's your name, Teach?"

Will you be my student? I felt my throat sink into my gut. Why weren't these kids in their classes? How could we "raise the achievement gap" of kids who wouldn't get into their rooms.

"Get to class, gentlemen," said Ellen, whose normally chirpy voice had suddenly grown deep and stern. She now seemed taller than five foot two; her shoes seemed more ass-kicking than shiny little loafers.

"Get where you need to be, boys," said Amy, reminding me that these kids were indeed just boys.

"Move it," said Brooke, who'd quickly adopted what would be her confrontational style.

Noelani caught on, and added almost sweetly, "Let's go now."

I tried to channel my inner-teacher, but nothing emerged. I watched the boys look away. They started down the hall again.

"Teachers," broke Ms. Brown over the intercom, "we request your patience, at this time, as we are still, disseminating schedules."

News had somehow passed from administrators to teachers that time was running short and that some students simply wouldn't have schedules today. If they arrived at our room with a note, we should just let them in.

This spelled more disaster for the hallway where, like a capsule pipeline, word spread fast. In minutes, when Amy or Ellen or Brooke asked other meandering kids, *Where are you supposed to be, young man* or *young lady?* they now responded, "Don't got a schedule."

I looked back through Noelani's door. Still only three kids sat there, looking like they'd done something wrong, waiting for someone to find them in their purgatory of fluorescent lighting and set them free.

Noelani glanced down at her clipboard again. "Where *are* they?" she asked a second time.

The answer was clear, but it hadn't dawned on her. "They're out here," I said, and nodded to the halls.

• • •

Amidst utter chaos, the principal finally made his tired voice known over the loudspeaker. Students should get to class, he said. This is a place of learning, he said, not a mall. But the voice was sluggish and unconvincing. The kids didn't respond.

I'd already gleaned that our principal was not a man of inspiring disciplinary power. He first presented himself at our faculty retreat, a full day of meetings held in a conference center. Dr. Jefferson was a tall man, maybe six-four, with broad shoulders and light-brown skin, and though he looked like he was capable of possessing a commanding presence with the kids, when he opened his mouth, his words held all the energy of a limp noodle. "Our students present us with challenges," he said flatly.

"But we are ready, to meet those challenges with quality instruction." His monotone voice gave his motivational speech the same vigor that a person reading the phonebook aloud might have.

After students spent another twenty minutes or so testing out the feel of the hallway, dawdling by the classroom doors of new and old teachers, calling out the names of faces they knew, and after all the students who were ever going to settle in their homerooms that day did, the attendance was taken, the hallways settled (though never entirely emptied), and the forms were filled out. The school day officially began. The first period bell finally rang again. I received my students for about thirty minutes, then my third and fourth period students for the standard ninety.

By the time I stood at the other end of that long first day, the actual teaching had become a blur. I remembered walking up and down the aisles between the desks of students, reading from a handout I'd prepared about rules and consequences and required materials. *Bring a pen to school. Believe in yourself.* But like a guest at a stale hotel, I'd checked out of myself. When I'd checked back in some hours later, I found myself in the kitchen of my home, making squash and peanut soup for dinner, playing the fuzzy dream of the day back in my mind: I look down at students' faces, but none of them come into focus yet. Who are they? I know none of them by name or voice or good or bad habit. They are quiet. They do not accost me, and they do not applaud me. Malcolm X was read with little fanfare.

The sharpest moment in focus was this: I hold up the ninth grade English textbook and open the cover and ask what it might remind students of. They sit quietly. Some slouch, their butts nearly hanging off the edge of the chairs. Some have their chins in their hands. Some look stiff and meek, their arms pressing into their sides, their shoulders creeping up toward their ears. But none answer. So I say, "See! It looks like a door!" I close the cover to illustrate, then open it again. I nod. "A book is a door! Reading is a doorway into a new world!" I raise my eyebrows, I smile. They stare back blankly. They show no signs that they are enthralled by the prospects of visiting new lands via literature. No music plays in the background, and I win no one over. We are not in the movies.

Afterward, I moved on to logistics, like handing out bathroom passes for the semester and stressing that these were for the whole semester, that students would not receive new ones in the next five months, so they had to keep them safe and they had to use them wisely. This was one of my "systems for success," as TFA called it. Someone raised her hand and said she had to go to the bathroom, and I asked with cheery skepticism, "Do you *really* have to go?" and she said, "Yes," and I said, "Okay." And I signed her pass.

At the end of the day, I stood in my row-house kitchen and stirred soup for dinner and called the only friend I had in town, the same friend who'd told me, "Baltimore is a dirty, dirty city." Again, he was my only friend in town. With the corners of my mouth upturned, with my socked-feet on the filthy kitchen floor that my housemates and I inherited with our lease, I called him, and he asked how it went, and I said "Well, nobody said *fuck you*."

They sat and they listened and they filled out their information sheets. They were not the wild, terrorist students Tom Sypher had once depicted when he advised all five of us to "fuck with" our students. They didn't even appear to be the same kids who idled out in the halls. My students were silent. They were tentative. They were ninth graders, brand new to their rumored school. And while I didn't have the ability to process it in my kitchen, I'd later come to understand the complexity of their silence. It hid fear and uncertainty, and also personality. Silence covered themselves up and, in so doing, kept them safe. Which meant they, like me, were terrified. Ms. Patterson had been right: our kids were afraid to attend the rumored Terrordome.

I was too tired to process this. Instead I relaxed in the stirring of my soup and in the knowledge that, while I hadn't "bridged the achievement gap"—while I'd hardly taught a thing—I'd passed as a teacher, with my chalk and my rules and my lesson. And my students had passed as students, with their sitting and their facing forward. We'd filled the hollow casings of our roles; we'd looked, at least initially, like a class.

CHAPTER 4

THE PLOT OF MARIGOLDS

Three days later, Southwestern High School made the news for a massive fight that broke out in its cafeteria. The cafeteria was located far enough from my classroom to exist in another dimension, so I neither saw nor heard the brawl, but I quickly learned it wasn't your average school rumble, or at least not average for my suburban high school, where two or three kids tore at each other, got separated, and were swiftly suspended. No, this fight involved knives, at least a dozen kids, and warranted news cameras. The Baltimore City Police were summoned. According to Brooke, twelve cop cars sirened up Font-Hill, and at least six kids were handcuffed, thrown into a paddy wagon, and hauled downtown. Brooke said some of the arrested kids were hers. For the remainder of the afternoon, a helicopter hovered over the neighborhood, circling like a clumsy hawk. I looked up at the thing, wondering what it searched for, disbelieving that any violence in our isolated hilltop school could spread to the streets. Rookie thoughts.

But that same day I was on a teacher's high. The hallways had emptied, most of the teachers had turned off their lights and closed their doors, and my black boots were rubber-soled so I literally bounced through the yellow-tinted glass hall that bridged one school building to the other. I headed to my classroom on the "high side" of the second floor, feeling high on my new job at The Terrordome: my classes were going well. My students were sitting in their seats, and they sometimes even raised their hands. They called me various renditions of Ms. Kirn that involved either omitting the R in my name or elongating it Baltimore style: I was Ms. Kerr-in, Ms. Karr-en, Ms. Kahn. Any which way I was a Ms. and a teacher, and the faces of the clocks across the school now read 3:30. And it was Friday.

Two girls headed the other direction, one with her hair done up in bows. "Hi Melanie," I said to the bow-adorned girl.

"Hi Ms. Kar-en." Her voice was high-pitched and mousy.

"Who that?" asked the girl beside her.

"My English teacher."

"How she know you're name already?" The girl sounded amazed.

"She real nice."

I could not stifle the smile that spread colonially across my face. Mission accomplished: I was known, I was liked, my kids were pleasant. I bounced on, my head held high, my arms swinging back and forth. It was a strut meant to pretend the school was mine. The very school that ended its day with a knife fight, several cop cars, and six arrested kids. It was mine. All because one well-mannered student with pink pens and a purple pencil case and bow-tied hair momentarily liked me. But remember, the boots; they bounced.

As I took my last jaunty step out of the glass hallway and entered a dimly lit hall with a crumbling ceiling that exposed pipes and wires, a veteran teacher stopped me. I'd met her once before. She'd been assigned by the city to mentor the new teachers. What followed became one of my only interactions with her.

"How's it going so far?"

"Really good," I told her. I thought of hiding my confidence, but I pictured my quiet classrooms, my students' eyes on me. "My kids are really good." Unlike Brooke's kids, my kids just weren't the type, I figured, to get carted away in paddy wagons.

She pressed her shiny fuchsia lips together. "Give 'em two weeks."

• • •

Somebody wanted, but, so. The nearly new literature textbook instructed me that the formula *somebody wanted, but, so* was a viable way to teach plot to fifteen-year-olds. Kids only had to fill in the blanks. As in, *Somebody wants* something, *but* he/she can't get it, *so* he/she does something in response.

As in, new teacher *wants* students to learn how to summarize the plot of a story. *But* students engage in side conversations and not-so-side conversations and put their heads down on their desks and grumble. In fact, students have increasingly engaged in side conversations and not-so-side conversations and heads on desks and grumbling just as that fuchsia-lipped veteran teacher had predicted: two weeks into school.

After two weeks of an easy classroom where I wrote questions on the board and called on students by name to answer, and they didn't exactly answer but at least they sat up and looked at me, my students had assumed new personalities. It felt sudden, but looking back, it had been a gradual transformation—one day was a little noisier than the day before, which had been a little noisier than the day before, and so on, until something very unusual occurred, one single event that clued me in to the dynamic between my students and me, and that event hung like an exclamation mark above my job. A student tickled me. Dennis Moore had, out of nowhere, and while he was standing up, reached into the soft slope right below my ribcage and wiggled his fingers. *Tickle tickle tickle*, I think he said. I sucked my stomach taut, stepped back, and said, "*Dennis*," and there it was: a whine in the first syllable. In an effort to sound stern, I hissed the final S of his name, but my class and I had already heard the drawn, desperate vowels of Dennis' name, and my tone had surrendered what was rightfully mine: authority. "That's not appropriate," I said. But the situation was beyond salvaging—a student touched, felt capable of touching, my midriff.

"It ain't a rule," he said, and nodded to the red list on yellow poster board. "Don't Tickle Teacher" was not on the list.

"Yes it is," I said and read the second one. "Respect your teacher." He shrugged and smiled and sat down to do his work.

Somebody wanted, but, so. Teacher wants students to succeed, *but* student tickles teacher? *So* . . .

One year later, I would have taken more action. *So,* teacher lays into student with assertive speech. *You can never under any circumstances cross certain boundaries with your teacher, Dennis, and you know that. Tickling most definitely crosses those certain boundaries. My job is to teach you, your job is to learn, and in no way is touching a part of our relationship. Got that?* The class might have benefited from a conversation about boundaries, what they do for us, how to draw them when someone crosses them. But I was twenty-two, shy about my new power, maybe even afraid of it, and I hoped the students would just hand that power to me so that I wouldn't have to claim it—because I didn't know how.

Now, when the late bell rang to announce the start of first period, only half the usual kids sat at their desks, and some stood at the door peering into the hallway, and some lingered in the hall, and some were nowhere to be found. Those at their seats no longer brought their binders from their bookbags without my pleading. Their eyes fell on anything in the room other than the mandatory "drill," the daily changing task that students were supposed to accomplish as soon as they entered any classroom. The drill: it sounded military like cleaning one's rifle, or rote like lining up in alphabetical order. As a Baltimore city public school requirement, every classroom had chalkboard-space reserved for "the drill." Its secret intention was to shape the order of every classroom within the first few minutes of a period. *Do your drill,* I heard myself say over and over. *Okay, let's get started on that drill. The drill, the drill*: I saw the hardware tool dangle above my every sentence. After three weeks, not even mousy-voiced, bow-haired Melanie had her purple pencil case out or her eye on "the drill." But like a crowd eager for offshore oil, I repeated the order to *drill, drill, drill* enough that most every student achieved at least the appearance of work within ten, fifteen minutes.

Among the fiercely work resistant, though, was scrawny, diminutive Jimmy Nizbin, a white child whose antics arrested me. I stared, mouth agape, when he jumped out of his seat, ran back and forth between the walls, and made siren sounds while twirling his finger above his head. "Jimmy, what are you doing?" More sirening was his response. On his calmer days, he stayed seated but could periodically burst into three flat, forced, monotone laughs. Pah-Hah-Hah. "What's up, Jimmy?" Pah-Hah-Hah was again his reply. He grimaced. Baffled, I continued teaching. Other days, he slumped forward and drooled into his forearm. If I tried to stir him, he sneered at me from behind the arm. "The drill, Jimmy. Let's get working on the drill." He never did.

Teacher wants Jimmy Nizbin to participate in school, *but* Jimmy behaves like kindergartener with liquid-sugar coursing through his veins, or comatose patient of sedative overdose. *So . . . So . . .* insert my response to the plot twist here. But I didn't know what to do. And that was my problem. Once my students actually challenged me, I provided the intense counteraction of a barnacle. In college, I'd spent my years studying the narrative stances of Virginia Woolf, appreciating the relative plotlessness of *Mrs. Dalloway*, a book in which, let's face it, not much happens. I read the *Tao Teh Ching* and aspired to master the Taoist concept of *wei wu wei*—doing without doing. Hell, I wrote poems; I was accustomed to loving the lyricality of stillness. Of inaction. If ever I wrote short stories, my characters sat at desks and thought. Movies in which big things happened—buildings blew up or cars chased other cars—I wasn't fond of those. Needless to say, my natural disposition did not help me conjure effective remedies in moments that Jimmy Nizbin and Co. created.

So when I say that most students settled into work or into the appearance of work, I mean that among them was Jimmy Nizbin, buzzing between the desks and/or making peculiar animal noises. And I mean everyone except for the many who hadn't arrived yet. Inevitably, several more students trickled in five, ten, fifteen, thirty minutes after the late bell. Five-foot tall Letisha Clark, her hair pulled back into a small nub, bopped to the beat of the latest hip-hop hit, something about mommas and poppas running across a border. On other days, she dragged herself in and flung herself over her desk like it was the cruel daybed of her imprisoned existence. Dennis Moore strolled in after her, his eyes sometimes drooping from last night's sleep, other times popping bright and wide and mischievous, instantly scanning the room in search of someone to tease. Whatever the mood of the late kid—lethargic and cranky, ecstatic and giddy—I resented it. It was a new chemical thrown into an already volatile blend that I'd somehow managed to maintain.

Why were they late? I'd asked each morning.

"The bus," Letisha said, like it was obvious, like I should have known the bus was late, like the fact that the bus arrived late from its last stop was as common a piece of knowledge as the weather. I began to wonder if I *should* have known that the bus was late.

The new kids had stories to tell, or names to call one another; the on-time kids wanted to listen, or call back other names. They wanted to be taken away from *the drill*. Dennis sat at his desk beside Melanie and called her his boo and Melanie, who had been focused on her paper, looked up and said *psh* and, "Dennis, you crazy." She smiled—an invitation for Dennis to keep teasing—and just like that, I'd lost my best student.

● ● ●

But I couldn't afford to lose any students, and this was not just a teacher cliché but a hard fact that grew more apparent as I taught—or tried to teach—my ninth graders. Each passing day that I walked into Southwestern's opaque side doors and stood in the front of my classroom and pointed to the drill and cajoled my kids into writing something down, I learned how woefully behind they were.

In the first few weeks, I gave each kid a reading test. One by one, they sat at the small student-desk beside my big teacher-desk, and I listened to my students read lists of words aloud. Each list corresponded to a grade level, and the words got increasingly harder. One by one, they read the words. Most sped through the early grades. But they started hitting linguistic bumps at the fifth or sixth grade, and by the seventh, they were floundering. "Okay, thanks. You're all done." "How'd I do?" they usually asked. "Good. You did good," I said, and the kid got up, and I watched him or her strut back to his or her desk, and I sighed at the fact I was slowly, painstakingly proving: most of my ninth graders were sixth-grade readers or lower. Even Melanie, my brightest, was still behind at grade eight.

To boot, nearly half of Southwestern's ninth graders hadn't passed the Maryland Functional Writing Test, a standardized exam designed to assess writing at a sixth-grade level. In other words, a good chunk of our freshmen were writing below a sixth-grade level. Weekly, and under the instruction of my department head, my students wrote responses to blasé practice prompts in preparation for exam day. Write about a trip you took. Write about a meal you ate. Write about an event that changed your life forever. But the students struggled to think of ideas, to structure those ideas once they thought of them, and then to explain those ideas in complete sentences. It wasn't just labor; for them, it seemed like torture. Putting words down onto paper was an awkward, physically demanding act for them. They craned their necks over the papers and poked their tongues out of the sides of their mouths. They furrowed their brows. They clutched their pens, their knobby knuckles jutting from their hands, ready to pierce through the skin. They pushed pencil-points on the pages so hard that I heard little snaps here and there as charcoal tips broke off. What came out were short, misspelled, grammatically messy, disconnected sentences written in the blocky, inconsistent print of someone who just isn't used to writing.

Ms. Patterson taught me a pre-writing method she called "Critical Squares." "They love their critical squares," she'd said, speaking of the students. "I tell you what really helps them," she said on another day. "Those critical squares!" I thought of that gameshow, *Hollywood Squares*, in which B-list celebrities like Florence Henderson of *The Brady Bunch* answered questions about the size of one's teeth as compared to a pig's. But *critical* squares were born when a kid folded a piece of paper halfway, then halfway again, and then unfolded the paper. Voila: four boxes. One for each paragraph. Critical squares were gifts from the gods. Critical squares were the answers to below-average-writing freshmen. Students were supposed to fill the boxes with the details that would help them write glorious, organized, specific, multi-paragraph, Maryland-approved essays considered "sixth-grade level" or above.

But Ronny Williams stared at his folded-and-then-unfolded page. Ronny was a silent kid whose wide, clear, round eyes and ever-opened little mouth and two inches of fro-hair sprouting from his head all made him look vaguely, permanently surprised. He blinked a lot, but his eyes always returned to their round, alert state, like he feared he might miss something. Yet Ronny missed a lot of things, not least of which was his homework. "You don't have it?" I asked each morning, and each morning he blinked and said no.

Today, Ronny had nothing in his squares. "You can't think of anything?" I asked.

He said no. He blinked.

"Well, you're trying to think of an event that changed your life. What do you remember most? What are some of the big events in the life of Ronny Williams?"

He looked at the blackboard. He blinked. He stared. "My father left the house."

"Okay," I nodded. Now we were getting somewhere. "Do you want to write about the day he left?"

Ronny nodded.

I gave him some guidance and left his desk. When I returned, hopeful that I'd find each square filled with details about the particular day—the sting in his father's eye, maybe, or the words they exchanged, or even the food Ronny ate that day—I found instead a short list of information about Ronny's father: he drank, he never came around, he beat on Ronny's mom, he left for good. That was it. As for the actual day, Ronny had nothing to say. Nothing to remember. His memory was as vacant as his round, blinking eyes. He never filled his four critical squares.

Other students had more success with details. "He be like Jekyl and Hyde," Frank Lewis told me of his father. "He be all nice when he sober, but when he come home drunk," his lips made the *psh* sound. "Man, he a whole 'nother man."

I told Frank he had a good comparison, *Jekyl and Hyde*, and to use it in his essay.

He nodded. "I'm a do that." As I walked away, he stopped me. "How you spell Jekyl?" He looked up and waited for the letters. As I spelled the name, he wrote the letters slowly and painstakingly until that last *L*. I leaned my weight on my right foot, ready to take a step toward another student, but behind me I heard, "An' Hyde? Ms. Ker-rin, how you spell Hyde?"

Correct grammar, ordered syntax, right spelling, all of it was painful to my students, more painful it seemed than the content of their sentences. As I guided each kid to a "special event," I felt the collective weight of their sad stories mounting in the room. Renee's dad came around so rarely that she got to pretending he didn't exist. Jaleesa's stepfather snuck in her room at nights until her mother kicked him out of the house. Uncles had died, cousins had been shot, and each kid had bid farewell to at least a handful of coffins. With their grief, I could commiserate. I still felt, for my stepfather, that gaping grief-hole that hummed like some ominous cave in my chest. With their frightening fathers, I could even commiserate, as I was relieved when mine left the house when I was eight. What I couldn't feel were my students' hard shells as they nonchalantly dispatched the content. *My father beat me* or *my cousin got shot*, they reported as plainly as they might tell me what time they got up this morning.

Maybe because they were *all* telling stories like these, and they all *knew* they were telling stories like these, the actual content wasn't so difficult? It was status quo. It was southwest Baltimore. Or maybe it wasn't allowed to look difficult. I quickly learned that they were used to dealing with an endless tirade of dark shit, and they figured out how to make it as wearable as those Timberland boots they loved. So they reported with seeming ease their biggest traumas. *I'm gonna write about my cousin funeral*, someone said, and I nodded and said "Good" and told the kid I looked forward to reading it and to fill in those critical squares. But the spelling of some word got in the way. And the posture of writing caused pain. They bit down too hard on their tongues. Their necks craned over the papers in unsustainable angles. Their hands cramped after four sentences, and they shook them out over their quarter-full papers and gasped. *Gawd. Dang.* This was a classroom of fifteen-year-olds writing below a sixth-grade level: a hundred vital stories that the world should probably hear, and the inability to render them in words.

• • •

My first period and I had gotten through the drill and the students were supposed to read Langston Hughes' "Thank You, Ma'm" today. The plot was simple—it would be easy to map out. Kid tries to steal an old lady's purse. Old lady stops kid. Scolds him, takes kid inside, feeds him food, gives him money. In the end, the kid says, *Thank you, ma'm.* "Thank You, Ma'm" was action packed. "Thank You, Ma'm" would be a hit.

"Hey, I heard this story!" Dennis shouted.

"I seen this story in six grade!" someone said.

"This a *six* grade story!" Letisha said.

Books were pushed forward and heads went down as the general wave of the story's "six-grade-ness" swept the room.

By third period, I would anticipate this reaction and squelch it before it even came. "Do any of you remember this story? I know some of you have read it, and let's read it again! How great is it to practice new skills on a story some of you are familiar with!" Third period would get into it. But first period was my guinea pig. They told me, by way of their reactions, where and how my lessons could fail. I later learned that the Baltimore curriculum had put the same story on the sixth and ninth grade reading lists. Most likely the curriculum-repeat was just a mistake, but the message that mistake sent to its kids was cruel: you probably won't remember this story or, if you do, you probably aren't any better at reading it now than you were three years ago.

"I like reading things twice," I said to my first period.

"I hate reading things," someone said, "any times."

"Let's see what we can get out of it a second time."

We tried reading it aloud, and a student started us off. But when it was someone else's turn, that student invariably shouted "What?" or "Where we at?" The next kid took a few moments to find the place. He or she stared into the blocks of print in the textbook, searching for some place to pick up; meanwhile, students cracked jokes or put their heads faithfully back onto the desk, and Dennis jumped out of his seat to "throw something away," which resulted in him twirling some girl's hair, who shouted, "stop messing," and when the reader finally picked up at the right place, nobody listened. Meanwhile, Jimmy's book was still shut. And Letisha's head stayed down, her little nubby ponytail pointing toward the windows, her cheek pressed against the desk.

I started with who was closest to me. Letisha, in the front row.

"I'm tired," she whined from behind her arm.

"Come here, Letisha. I want to talk to you in private." She scowled and pulled herself out of her chair. When she met me beside the door, her eyes were barely open.

"Letisha, English One is very important." I recalled the Malcolm X lesson of the first week. "Reading and writing will open doors for you," I said.

She didn't budge.

"Letisha, you *have to* learn how to read and write."

Her eyes opened. She snapped, "I *do* know how to read and write!" Her tiredness had disappeared.

My mistake was evident, but I just shook my head. "That's not what I mean. We *all* need to practice how to read and write *better*. That's what school is for." I saw myself as an undergrad, reading poems late into the night, trying to figure out how to leap on the page like Emily Dickinson.

But Letisha folded her arms across her chest. She cast her head to the side.

"Now sit back down and stay focused on the story."

But nobody focused on the story. I stood among the rows of desks and realized I didn't have a single kid at my command. My job was to bridge a serious achievement gap. My job was to speed through my students' progress so that they could catch up to the national average. How could I do that if no one was reading, if no one even knew where we were in a story, if Jimmy was angry and refusing to work, and Dennis was up and cracking jokes the entire class loved, and lethargic Letisha was now . . . up and dancing?

Somebody wants something, *but* they can't get it, *so* . . . I'd been reluctant to respond. On paper, I'd designed a tidy disciplinary system: if students disobeyed, their names were supposed to go on the blackboard, and if they disobeyed again, they were supposed to receive a check next to their names, and after another check, their parents would be called. What about a third check? students had asked. There is no third check, I'd told them on day one. A third check and you're out of the room. Their eyes widened. Unbeknownst to them, a third check was known as: Ms. Patterson next door has agreed to take you for the day and stick you in a cubby in the back of her room.

But my rules and consequences were disintegrating as I hesitated to enforce them. And Dennis had found yet another reason to saunter toward the trash can. And Letisha, who had somehow woken up since our side-conversation, or maybe because of it, was now singing that weird song about mommas and poppas crossing some border to bring back something suspicious.

"That's it." I scraped the chalk from its metal rack and wrote Letisha's name on the board.

"What? How you gonna write *my* name?"

Most of the students' eyes were now on the board. Dennis, still standing, dropped a disembodied hair extension from his fingers. "That's a warning." She stood up straight before slumping into her chair.

I added Dennis' name beneath hers. "Dennis, sit back in your seat."

And I added Jimmy's name beneath Dennis's. "Jimmy, you haven't opened your book all morning." He didn't budge. Odds were good he wouldn't. "Everyone's eyes should be on this story."

A few names on a board meant an invitation to spar. Did I really mean what I said about all these checks and phone calls home and, as a last result, removals from the room? I heard Melanie giggle, and looked to Dennis, who was, as he rounded his chair to sit, tickling Melanie's ear with her pink feather-pen.

"Dennis! Melanie!"

"Ms. Ka-ren, he tickle *me*."

I returned to the board, chalk still in hand, and swooped my first check beside Dennis's name. There: the all powerful check was born. Watch now as students line up like ducks to cross the long footbridge across the achievement gap!

He slapped his palms onto the desk. "What you do that for?"

"Tickling others with feathers is not reading the story, Dennis. You owe me a page."

"A page?!"

"One page-long letter, written to me, explaining what you did and what you'll do differently in the future. Anyone else?" A classroom of kids glared back at me. "Now let's get back to the story."

"Why we read this story if we already know it?" Letisha called out. "I ain't reading."

I turned one-eighty, headed back to the board, and put a check by her name. "You owe me a letter too, Letisha."

She smacked her mouth, then let her jaw pop out. "For what?"

"If you earn another check, I'll call home. The rest of you, finish the story. Quietly." The thought of again initiating any read-aloud method was akin to plucking hairs from my head: tedious, painful, pointless. I told them I'd collect answers to questions at the end of class.

It was a minor miracle. Heads bowed into the books. Kids' eyes scanned across sentences. Letisha sulked five minutes but then started her page of apology. Only Jimmy and Dennis were left. Jimmy, who sat and stared into space, cawed like a crow. Dennis, who looked over Melanie's shoulder as she read, didn't touch his blank paper with a pen. He wasn't writing his punishment of one page.

. I didn't know what to do with a kid who cawed. I walked across the dirty linoleum floor and stood next to Dennis' desk. I muttered something to Dennis about writing that page. He rolled his eyes and cocked his head and looked at the ceiling. I muttered something about calling his parent or guardian if he didn't. He looked down at his blank page. I said something like, Do you understand? and he shrugged, which was a small substitution for a nod, and I turned to look at the rest of the class. To give Dennis some space. To see how the other twenty-some were doing.

Dennis Moore sat directly behind me. Dennis Moore's eyes were lined directly with my backside. I suddenly became very aware of the fabric in my pants, how it pulled across my hips, and suddenly, for reasons I could not articulate, I longed for an outfit that followed the shapeless lines of a potato sack. This time, Dennis Moore didn't tickle. Instead, I felt a small, light finger-poke on the center of my right butt cheek.

Snickers all around.

There's something called the butt-brush theory in the retail industry. Video footage confirms it. If a woman is shopping and merchandise accidentally brushes her backside, she'll leave the area and most likely the store. She won't even look behind her to see what made contact with her derrière. The theory explains my initial reaction: I wanted to bolt. Leave the area. No questions asked. Just get out. But a classroom of hormonal fifteen year olds were left to my supervision, butt-brush theory or not.

All eyes were on me. I turned around, and Dennis was gazing at some arbitrary point on the ceiling. I looked down at his buzzed hairline, his shiny brown forehead, his guiltless face. I was dumbfounded, couldn't say what I thought to say:

Dennis, did you touch my butt?

Or, *Dennis, why did you touch my butt?*

Or, *Don't touch my butt, no butt-touching in this class!*

Every option sounded ridiculous and humiliating because every option had three words: Touch. My. Butt. The kids would erupt. Joke was on me. Dennis would say no, of course not, he'd done no such thing, and this would incite more snickers. Or he might say, "Nobody touched your butt. Nobody want to touch *you*." Even my proof, that faint residual poke on my rear, was starting to dissipate, to feel like an illusion, a palpable mirage smack in the center of my ass, and I began to doubt myself, to wonder if the students really had seen anything at all, if anything had really happened to see? My self-doubt provided, I think, a safe haven. Who wants to admit that her student touched her ass in class?

"Come with me," I said to Dennis and meant business. What would I say? I didn't know. I thought I'd figure it out on the way to the hall.

The hallway was dark and empty. Sure enough, Dennis had followed. There we were, Dennis and me, standing face to face, eye to eye, the green metal door of my classroom mostly closed and the hallway surprisingly empty of the usual prowlers. I could say whatever I wanted.

I still didn't know what to say.

He stood an inch taller than my five-foot-five frame.

Out came a speech. Something like the "do you think the choices you're making now reflect your dreams?" speech, a monologue that dangled the words *diploma* and *graduation* as carrots before the uninterested kid. Something like:

"Dennis, your behavior is unacceptable. It's disruptive, it's not courteous to me, to the other students. To yourself. Do you want to graduate high school? Because right now, you're not showing me that you do. We're three weeks into school, and you're already off the graduation track. You're not here for stand-up comedy, do you understand? You're here to learn, so that in four years you can have that diploma in your hand. Don't you want that?"

His eyes were fixated on his tan Timberlands. He gave a slight nod.

"These are choices, Dennis. Everyday you can make better choices. You could be one of the brightest students in this class, but not with the way you've been acting."

I paused. Was that enough? Would he take anything I'd said home with him, along with his hormones and his afternoon hunger? Would my speech seep into any quadrant of his brain long enough to change, not just his thoughts, but the things he did and said? I didn't know. But I was running out of motivational sentences, which I'd been using as filler to buy me time; with each passing second, I was searching myself for the courage to charge him with "it," with making contact with my rear end. But that courage was nonexistent inside my overly introspective, constantly self-doubting self. My class had been left alone for a minute and a half. They were getting louder. Someone had run up to the door's window to peek at us. My time was up.

"I expect you to go in there, focus, and write that page. And tomorrow, I expect you to come on time, start your drill, and stay focused through the whole lesson." He didn't say anything. He stared into the door's narrow window the way I used to fixate on a row of piano keys or a glass of water just to find escape from a parent's lecture. How weird to be on the other side of authority. How much I wanted us all—my whole class—to smile and clasp hands and sway to some inspirational melody without me ever resorting to discipline. How naïve, how utterly amateur I was.

By the time the bell rang to end the period, Dennis handed me his one page. In it was the language of vague new year's resolutions. He said he had to "raise himself up." He had to be a better man. For his future wife and his future kids.

On her way out, Letisha also handed me her one-page letter. In between classes, I read it: "Ms. Kirn thinks I'm stupid. She dosen't think I can read or write. And she makes me read storys I know already." Letisha had addressed the letter to a friend instead of me. "So I guess I got to talk real slow to her because thats how she talks to me, like I'm slow." I looked up from the page. The kids were gone, the chairs were pulled out and edging into the aisles, the desks were no longer in their neat rows, and on a third of them rested unfinished handouts about the plots of "Thank You, Ma'm." Everyone had bolted. Faster than a woman who'd gotten her butt brushed by a rack of clothes.

• • •

Not all my classes were a disaster. By contrast, third period was jovial, upbeat, and witty. They were a noisy lot, as they came right from lunch, and I was constantly turning off lights and shushing their side-talk and sitting them down. But they laughed with me, not at me.

"Looks like you been stopping buses with them boots," Kia said one day. I was rounding the room, monitoring my students' chatty work. I looked at Kia, who was looking down at my feet.

"What do you mean?"

"They all scuffed up," said Timothy beside her.

I looked down. The toes were scratched and gray.

Kia laughed and the small boy laughed and they both looked up at me and smiled.

I laughed and shrugged. In the evenings, I went to mandatory teacher-classes and TFA professional development sessions. I graded papers, wrote lesson plans, tried to cook some semblance of a balanced meal, and crashed in bed. I hadn't had time to think of my shoes.

"Don't worry," Kia said. "I'm a bring something to fix it."

I didn't expect her to remember. What student thinks of her teacher's outfits at home? But sure enough, the next day Kia removed a plastic cap from a brush-tipped bottle and asked me to present my toes. She leaned over my feet and squeezed black ooze from the bottle, and she rubbed the black ooze onto the tips of my shoes with the brush.

"See that," she said. "Brand new." She sat up. Thin, braided hair extensions dangled in front of her face, and she grinned through them. I looked down at my matte black toes.

•••

Meanwhile, Melanie, the best student in my first period class, had recently glared at me from the corner of her eyes and muttered to Dennis, "I hate her." At the time, Melanie's comment was a blow to my teacher-ego. Looking back, it was perverse progress. I had become militant about my names and checks on the board, had called a dozen parents or grandmas at home, and those steps all tightened the ship. They didn't make the voyage much fun, though. A lot of boys still kept their heads down, their large black ski caps poking from their heads. Some did their work, like Melanie, but Letisha just sat and waited for something to strike her attention, usually a joke from Dennis. Most days, she moaned. She moaned like it was her job. She moaned at every move I made, every request, instruction, question, and each moan was an angry affront, a little stab into the thin teacher-skin I wore each day. She, too, hated me.

And Jimmy? Each day, he did nothing. His inactivity demonstrated little more than my complete ineptitude; I didn't know how to teach him.

Despite the administration's insistence that we were a "uniform-school," Jimmy Nizbin was the only kid in my first period to wear his so-called "mandatory" uniform, a purple oxford shirt with a yellow tiger on the lapel and the school's motto, *Endure and Succeed*, stitched beneath the animal. He wore it, most likely, because the administration told his mother (as it told all its students' parents) that wearing the shirt and khaki pants all year was the school rule. A school with a uniform policy, particularly one in the inner-city, had insurance against outsiders masking as students, a dangerous but common occurrence at Southwestern. A school with a uniform policy also had credibility because the policy meant the administration had its shit together. It had achieved a massive feat—every one of its kids put on the same article of clothing as every other kid. No wonder Walbrook High School emphasized, however laboriously, its full title, "Walbrook Services Uniform Academy."

But Southwestern lacked the disciplinary strength of Walbrook, a fact easily proved by the number of Southwestern kids who wore their khaki pants and purple or white oxford shirts: almost zero. Come first school day, more than half the kids still had no uniforms. Those who did quickly shed their stiff, nerdy oxfords. Whoever was left wearing the majestic purple or bright white had *poverty* written on their foreheads: their parents couldn't buy them anything else. Their parents had been told, all your kid will need this year is a bunch of collared shirts. So they stocked up. When their kid pleaded for more clothes, regular clothes, the parents shook their heads. I bought you that uniform, now wear it. The shirt made Jimmy an obedient outcast among his classes, a loner in following a dead rule.

The shirt also made him a walking irony. *Endure and Succeed* said his lapel every day, but he neither succeeded at doing work, nor could I endure him. I'd tried the "don't you want to graduate high school" speech with him while his head pressed into his arm. No, he'd said between the bent crease of his elbow. He didn't want to graduate high school. A thousand checks beside his name would never stir Jimmy Nizbin to do anything other than snicker, scream, or sleep.

So it was with good reason that I'd assumed Jimmy would resist my every attempt to assess his reading level. I called plenty of other kids' names before I summoned him to the little desk beside mine. Still, I had to figure out how he read. Maybe he couldn't do the work, a plausible explanation for kids with behavior troubles: they were so far behind that the work infuriated them, and they gave up. Of course, there were a thousand other explanations for kids resisting work: they didn't believe school would ever help them; the arithmetic or American history they learned in school didn't connect to their row-home lives; maybe their siblings didn't go to school; the arithmetic or American history they learned at school was far below their abilities and so they got bored; they were preoccupied with a cousin at home who'd just been arrested or shot. . . . I would soon learn a hundred stories for the kids who put their heads down in school and gave up. I tackled only one at a time, and early on it was Jimmy, and I was pretty certain he had trouble reading.

Jimmy sat at that little desk beside mine, his thin, white arms poking from the enormous purple sleeves of his school uniform shirt, and he actually read the words. I tried to hide my shock. He wasn't picking the dirt out of his thumbnail. He wasn't leaping up to stare out the window. He wasn't drooling into his forearm or cawing like a crow or mock-guffawing. He was reading the lists, word by word. And doing so easily. When he neared the lists for grades five and six, I readied my pencil to mark his level. But he sailed through those words, too. He read eighth grade words, ninth grade words. He passed through grade ten. At grade eleven, he stumbled on a few. He looked up at me. "How'd I do?"

"Tenth grade, Jimmy. That's amazing!" I raised my eyebrows. "You're an amazing reader!"

He smiled, handed back my lists, slid out of the desk, and went back to his seat.

I thought Jimmy's behavior would change after this moment. But the reading test was just that—a moment, fleeting and anomalous, and the knowledge it brought didn't offer me a way into Jimmy. At first, I used it as an invitation to discuss his "potential." But those conversations immediately brought the return of the old, angry Jimmy. He returned to his weird shrieks, or his jumping up and down, or his sleeping. Sometimes when it was clear he had gotten under my skin—when I scolded him or pleaded with him or sent him out of the room—he looked up at me, suddenly honest, suddenly capable of speaking a language I could recognize, and said, "Remember that test you gave me. I did real well on that test."

I nodded. I told him he did; he could read really well. But saying much more made him grumble and clam up. So I left him alone and reveled in what appeared to be his few minutes of silent reflection. He got pensive. He stared out the window and thought. It was like, for a little while, Jimmy was content to contemplate all he could be.

• • •

Jimmy's mother sat facing me, both of us in students' chairs and students' desks. She was very thin, roughly five feet tall, and missing a few of her side teeth. She wore light blue jeans and a white men's T-shirt that was as see-through as wax paper, under which her large breasts drooped to her waist. Her shoulders were narrow and her arms—the way they poked like sticks from the baggy T-shirt sleeves—reminded me of Jimmy's. Too little separated this tiny woman from the elements of southwest Baltimore; the cotton shirt and jeans didn't seem to be enough. But it was her dry, sandy, thinning hair I fixated on: it was pulled loosely into a bun. I hadn't seen a bun in this city. Even the few white women in the neighborhood sometimes braided their hair, and most of the white girls in the school just let theirs flow. But the bun spoke of another world. Someplace rural? Someplace flat and full of fields? I didn't know.

She looked down at her hands in her lap like an apologetic kid who'd been called to the principal's office. I told Ms. Nizbin about my troubles with Jimmy. At first she mumbled toward the linoleum flooring that Jimmy didn't have this problem with any of his *other* teachers, a claim that made me half doubt myself, half doubt all his other teachers. They must not have called his mother yet. Ms. Nizbin kept her gaze off me, down at the floor, the way my students did when I tried to level with them face to face. I was trying to *meet* Ms. Nizbin, one on one, in the eye, woman to woman. But she refused. What had happened to this woman, in school or otherwise, that she couldn't engage with her kid's teacher?

"He's bipolar," she finally said out of the corner of her mouth, still not making eye contact. "He has mood swings and he's just a problem child."

A problem child. The term is ubiquitous in a city school, maybe in any school. A child who's got problems. A child who makes problems. A child who, upon entering your class, becomes *your* problem. He or she will never amount to anything different, and for that, who can like the term?

"Well," I said, "the bipolar doesn't exactly explain his attitude toward school." What did I know? Maybe it did. But I wanted to talk about more than "Jimmy the medically labeled," or "Jimmy the problem kid."

"He's just down is all. He got his bike stolen." She lifted her eyes from the floor. "Some kids in the neighborhood took it. It put him in a slump. He had his bike stolen twice now!" She relayed the last sentence like it was an injustice on par with an unprovoked police beating. The exasperation in her eyes, which were finally meeting mine, asked me to commiserate with Jimmy and his stolen bike. And I sort of did, and sort of did not, because I sort of couldn't believe a stolen bike could instigate or possibly explain away the Jimmy I saw every day.

I told her, while that was sad, it wasn't exactly an acceptable excuse for his behavior. "Ms. Nizbin, your son doesn't plan on graduating high school."

"Yes he does!" she snapped. She glared at me. Now she met me. Now she was facing her enemy.

"Have you asked him? He tells me he has no intention of earning a diploma. He says he's only here until the state can't force him any longer. He plans on dropping out in tenth grade."

Her mouth turned down and her eyes squinted like she was straining to see, not really me, but something in the distance. "In middle school, his teacher told him he'd never amount to *nuthin'*." The last word was loud and curt, and when she said it she sneered at me as though, for those two syllables of our talk, I had become that notorious middle school teacher. "They put him down," she said, and folded her wiry arms across her chest and let her chin drop. "I should sue. For psychological damage," she muttered.

I doubted Ms. Nizbin would ever sue. Instead I heard, not *I should sue* or *I could sue*, but *I would sue. If I were someone else.* Someone who could meet people in this world eye-to-eye.

But if Ms. Nizbin came from a corner of the world that empowered her to shake firm hands and demand what was hers, she most likely wouldn't *need* to sue. I thought of my own mother, a former teacher herself, responding to the hypothetical scenario: I come home from school with a green lunch pail, crying, and she pries out of me what's wrong. *My teacher says I won't amount to anything.* No, even the words are too unreal to imagine. I had planned on imagining my usually docile mother storming the school and demanding a talk with a principal, which she would have done, but even that I can't see; she wouldn't have had to. No teacher of my past would have ever said such a thing. You'll all amount to decent middle-class people with decent SAT scores and college diplomas. This is what we were told. Who knows if you'll be happy, but you'll make some money for yourself, and you'll own a home, and you'll be fed and warm and well-clothed. You'll have health care. You'll have all your teeth.

Facing Ms. Nizbin, I half rallied behind the prospect of suing the school, half wondered why I had been forced to sit among her ghosts and mingle with them. Or rather, the ghosts of Jimmy, and his schooling past. I didn't realize that, like entering someone's living room by first walking through the foyer, the present sometimes had to be accessed through the past.

But Ms. Nizbin kept hitting rewind, heading farther back. "I can't hardly read and write," she told me out of the blue. "Just can sign my name. They put me on so much medication, it ruined my mind." I didn't know who *they* was. "Then they said I was re*tard*ed!" That last word was loud and curt again, and she looked me in the eyes when she said it, like she was facing those authoritative voices of the past again—the ambiguous "they" who were conflated to mean both the doctors who'd prescribed her medication and the teachers who put Jimmy down decades later. She looked away. "I got a hard time remembering things now 'cause of it."

I think Ms. Nizbin wanted me to know that it ran in the family history, and by "it" I mean, schools ruin people's lives. I'll never know if Jimmy's mother opened up to me because I listened, because I sat silent for much of our conference and gave her the space to tell her story, or if she revisited these ghosts at any and every parent-teacher conference; if, like someone stuck on a Merry-Go-Round she couldn't get off, she always revisited her pain. Either way, she seemed haunted, and by the end, I was haunted too, and not just by her stories; I was haunted by all that Jimmy must have to carry because his mother still does. By the suffocation he could feel whenever she lived his traumas through her own. By all that holds the two of them back, including each other.

But I was also haunted by the power of Ms. Nizbin's and Jimmy's past teachers. Now that power was mine. I'd inherited it from Baltimore City because, looking back on my so-called interview, I had a pulse and was willing. I gulped at my new capability to, at least according to Ms. Nizbin, ruin lives for good. Maybe it was more than a capability; maybe it was already a manifestation, and Letisha Clark would sit in this same position twenty years from now, telling her kids' teacher that when she was a kid, *they* told her she couldn't read and write, when she very well could.

•••

Another day, my first period and I had gotten through the drill, reviewed the definitions of the day's newest vocabulary, and were now in the middle of "Marigolds," which we read aloud. I had high hopes for "Marigolds." The quiet, reflective narrator built the story up to a single major event: the main character *destroys* a plot of flowers! The kids would be shocked. They'd be moved. And the kids, most definitely, did not read "Marigolds" in sixth grade, a fact I could prove from the bottom margin of each page where daunting vocabulary words like *inexplicable, ostensibly, etcetera*, were listed.

Unfortunately the students also did not know, could not pronounce a hundred more words in the story, which weren't defined by the textbook in neat bold print, which meant that, according to the textbook and to the national standards of reading levels, my students were *supposed* to know those words. *Vaguely. Associates. Elude.* One by one, kids tackled paragraphs, their previously vocal selves becoming muffled and meek. They mumbled words in monotones and strained to reach the right edge of each line, then had to scan their eyes back down and to the left side again, where they sought the brief release of a period and, once they found it, sighed. Then another sentence. And another. It was agony. No one except Melanie could get through a line without hitting several road blocks. *Tragic-comic spectacle. Reinforce. Inevitably. Ramshackle.* How were all of these words left off the official "vocab list"? How was this story chosen for my kids?

"Sound it out," I said, because that's what I'd heard teachers say, as though the student hadn't been sounding the word out, as though if they started "sounding it out," out would come the right sound, the right word, right on their tongues. Melanie could do this when she hit a doozy, and she picked up her fast, high-pitched nasally word-train where she left off. But the rest of my kids could not let this obtuse tale take over their voices, and, from time to time, someone called out,

"This story boring!"

"I hate Marigolds."

"Jimmy, you're up," I said. Jimmy's head stayed down. I called him again.

"Ehhh!" he whined, but still didn't move his head. Now I recognized his lethargic days as heavily medicated ones.

Someone else kept on reading, and someone else, and someone else, until my struggling batch of underperforming readers made it through to the end—after the protagonist little girl passes the old neighbor-woman's house and quietly hates but does nothing about the woman's marigolds, and after the girl's father cries at dinner because he cannot find a job, and after he tells his wife, no, he will not take hand-me-downs from the white people, and after the little girl goes to sleep with her palms over her ears and wakes in the middle of the night with the inexplicable impulse to tear out the neighbor-woman's garden of marigolds. In the end, all that's left is the girl's remorse and a ruined patch of flowers. But not everyone got to the end. Letisha put her head down halfway through. Jimmy kept his book shut and was making revving sounds with an eraser. *Somebody wants something, but, so.* How could I expect students to follow the story and determine the plot when the thing the somebody wanted was only insinuated through symbols and tone, and the *but* that stood in that somebody's way was a list of implied socioeconomic factors like "The Great Depression" and "southern, rural racism" and the action that trailed from the protagonist's *so*—the ruined marigolds—was an illogical, psychologically complex symptom of what she *really* wanted, and I saw all this in a heartbeat but my students could hardly pronounce the words?

Still, we had forty-five minutes, and I knew the teacher-mantra to avoid disorder: *keep 'em busy.* I assigned a writing task.

After fifteen minutes, several kids had written nothing.

"I don't know what we're supposed to *do*," a girl said with an attitude.

But I'd repeated the directions six times by now. I looked at the rest of the class. "Is this too hard for you?" As soon as I said it, I heard the huge, condescending error. The teacher-equivalent of a momma joke.

They smacked their mouths and scoffed, and some tossed their pencils on their desks. They wanted to show that they were insulted. Melanie, who had been writing, lifted her head up, looked me in the eye, shook it, and returned to her page.

"This ain't hard," Dennis said, "This stoopid."

We went through the plot together. What did the little girl want? She wanted the marigolds tore out, the kids said, and yes, of course she did, because that's what she did. But no, of course she didn't. She wanted. . . . Even I couldn't put it into words. She wanted to live in a world where marigolds weren't the only bright-looking thing. She wanted to free herself, she said as she looked back from an older perspective, from a cage she only later saw that she was in. A cage of barren, rural childhood summers. With nothing to do and nowhere to go. She wanted beauty in a world in which she could see no beauty, so she destroyed the only bit she knew.

She *wanted* the marigolds, I wanted to say. But this would sound crazy. The only real thing, the only major action this character performed was annihilating the flowers. I didn't know how to get kids to see the story's subtext. I didn't have, yet, any examples of destruction at Southwestern, didn't know that in a few months the dozens of kids who always stayed in the hallways would learn how flammable were our bulletin boards, would set them on fire with tedious regularity, and I wouldn't necessarily catch on, not right away, to the similarities between kids burning down those boards and the little girl tearing yellow flowers from the ground. Some-times when you want something from the world, you do the opposite.

Maybe Jimmy's mother was right: maybe when Jimmy said he wasn't graduating high school, he meant the reverse.

All I knew was that the story seemed impossible to explain while the students squirmed and talked, or kept their heads loyally glued to the desk.

I want to say that what follows occurred on the same day that we read "Marigolds." It might have. It might not have. I can't be sure. But the two events were close in time, so they sit side-by-side in my memory, rub up against each other like two sticks that, at any moment, might cause a spark. Might light the world up or burn it all down.

"Dennis," I called out, because he had just crumpled a piece of paper and was about to throw it at someone. I scraped a piece of chalk off the metal rack, was about to write his name down. It had stayed off the board for a record fifty minutes.

But before I could write "Dennis Moore" in chalk, Dennis leapt out of his chair and shouted, "Oh Shit!" His eyes were as wide as they could be.

I stared back at him, shocked. Why was the lame punishment of "name on board" suddenly jarring to Dennis? Had his grandmother put her foot down? No more troubles with Ms. Kirn, or else? *Sit back in your seat*, I thought to say. *And no cursing*. But Dennis's eyes were not exactly on me. They were focused over my left shoulder. He lifted his hand and pointed at the door. "Ms. Kuhn!"

A few kids screamed.

I turned to the door. Black smoke and pink flames licked through the metal vents.

"The door on fire," someone yelled.

I couldn't move.

Someone brushed by my shoulder. Next thing I knew, Dennis was stomping his boot against the door. Bang-bang-bang went his tan Timber-land boot, and the door rattled in its frame. Bits of ash fluttered into the air like dirty feathers. They floated to the ground. Dennis kept stomping until a hunk of paper, charred on one end, white and twisted on the other, dropped from the vent. I stared at it, the remnants of a paper towel.

"Dang!" said someone behind me.

"Someone light the door on fire, Ms. Kuhn!"

"Our room almost burn down."

I looked up from the paper, now rendered harmless by Dennis's fat boot, and stared back at a class that was dumbfounded and staring back at me. For once in the past week, I had their full attention. For once, we shared something. *Our room almost burn down*, I heard again. *Our* room.

Given the metal material of the door's vent, our room would most likely not have burned down. But a kid in the hallway had tried to destroy it. Some student out there hated something enough to try to destroy it. The anonymous somebody didn't necessarily hate me, or my students, our textbooks, or our convoluted "Marigolds" story with its obscure internal conflict, but something. So *tisk* goes a lighter on a random teacher's door. There it was: plot. And who had responded? Dennis Moore. I'd just stood there like a shocked figurine on a cake.

A warm seed of gratitude rose up in me, and I acknowledged a twinge of irony that it rose for the same kid who'd poked my ass just weeks ago.

"Thank you," I said to him, and he nodded his head with a quick little bow and took his seat. He didn't say a thing, not to Melanie or any girl near him. He just un-crumpled his paper, one wrinkle at a time, and smoothed it out across his desk.

After the mayhem of *holy shit, a fire,* I expected the class to return to its standard manic resistance. But they were somber. Their hostility— their folded arms, their *humphs* and moans, their enemy-stares—it had all vanished. And maybe my hostility had, too. I'd thought the resentment had been all theirs, but at a certain point I fueled it. I'd come to expect their antagonism. I never teased this class like I did third period, never tried cajoling them with humor. I met their enemy-stares face-on. Oddly enough, the fire at the door burned up some hostility. It fell away on this day like that half-burnt paper towel.

I think the fire was a tangible representation of something that had been building in me for weeks; a better understanding of the forces at work against these kids and, consequently, the forces at work against me. They'd been writing about those forces in journals and short essays; their harsh tales leaked into everything they did. Fathers who beat them. Mothers who left them. Mothers who beat them (although that was rarer). Fathers who left them (not so rare). Loved ones, dead. Trauma and poverty passed down from mother to child like genes.

And now, someone lit the classroom door on fire. Someone attempted to scald the threshold between my kids and the rest of the world. That fire represented for me what stood between them and normal lives. It was the thing—or the many things—that blocked their access to that mythically bright American Dream. As a TFA teacher, I was meant to "bridge the achievement gap," to walk my students across that chasm that stood between them and the rest of the nation's middle-class, averagely performing kids. From fifth- to ninth-grade vocabulary: that was our trajectory. But in my first few weeks, I learned that our bridge was rickety, made of decaying wood and prone to lightning bolts or simple strikes of a match. In my mind, my classroom door stayed burning, and the image corrected me whenever I forgot that my begrudging, disgruntled first period—or any class or student—was not the real enemy.

The remaining twenty minutes of the lesson were quiet. Nobody shouted. Letisha didn't sing her *border poppa* song. Dennis didn't get up to throw anything away, or if he did he *actually* got up to throw something away, and then he promptly returned to his seat. He fussed with no girl. He told no crude joke. As for the rest of the students, the tops of their heads were tilted forward, and their eyes were cast downward and scanning the textbook for answers. Occasionally, they murmured to each other. They wrote things down on their loose-leaf papers. Their pen- and pencil-strokes were soft, unsure, like feet on eggshells. Like how my voice felt as I guided their answers from above the desks. *That's right. Good job.* We were gentle. We were uncertain.

When my students attempted, however incorrectly, to answer those questions—about a girl who ruined a patch of flowers or about some other vocab-dense tale—I don't think they were just doing work; I think now they were answering a challenge. And this time the challenge was not made by me but by some random, mindless, angry kid at the door. A kid with a paper towel and a lighter. A kid who tried to wreck something as that girl in our story had, who wanted a whole field of marigolds for her own but ruined them instead. Maybe our pyromaniac also wanted the thing he tried to ruin: a beautiful, accessible, ever-swinging door, one that opened to some bright, sunny, blue-skied future.

CHAPTER 5

WHEN THE STATE WALKS IN

If you scanned a sheet of Southwestern High School statistics, you'd see underneath the bolded headings, such as Student Population, that the school had a total enrollment of about 1,600, that (Ethnicity) 86 percent of our students were African American, 13 and change were white, and a small fraction of a percent were "other."

These are rather benign digits. But you'd also see under Population Per Class that the school had 604 freshman and only 206 seniors. This fact might spark your mental alarms. While it took three English teachers—Noelani, me, and Ms. Patterson—to instruct rowdy classes of ninth graders all day, only one teacher taught the senior English curriculum. Ms. Ellis was in her fifties, moved about the hallways slowly in sensible two-inch stacked heels, never raised her voice, or her eyebrows. When handed a memo that announced some outrageous policy that the rest of the teachers derided, Ms. Ellis just shrugged. She'd been around the block, she'd seen it all in Baltimore City. Her kids—those few that comprised one third of the original entering ninth-grade class—all had the same quality: steady, patient, unfaltering. It took a special quality to reach the "Senior Year" benchmark in west Baltimore. After all, hundreds of their peers hadn't made it with them. When I passed Ms. Ellis's classroom, it was only ever half full, and her kids—looking like fully grown men and women—spoke in low tones and had their books out. Sometimes I wondered if, when they glanced around the half-empty room, they remembered all the other kids, the ones who'd dropped out along the long way.

On that stats sheet beneath Economics, you'd also read that half our kids qualified for free or reduced lunch. The sheet wouldn't tell you, though, that nearly all the students would have qualified if they hadn't been too ashamed to snag the form from the front-office counter. "They're embarrassed to be seen with it," said Ms. Brown in an extraordinary moment of candor, and she nodded to a stack of blank documents that asked students to report their households' incomes.

For Academic Performance you'd learn that forty percent of all ninth graders hadn't passed the basic writing exam, that sixty percent of all ninth graders hadn't passed the basic math test. Because these were called "functional" tests, this meant that, according to Maryland, about half the students were not. Not "functional," that is. And you've already gotten a glimpse of what "non-functional reading" looked like in my first period. None of these statistics met what the state considered "Satisfactory."

Nor did Southwestern meet the "Satisfactory" standard for Attendance Rate, which was about sixty percent. A significant minority of names on my rosters never showed, or showed only for the first few days, and another significant minority of names faithfully attended each day. But the bulk of my students graced the building sporadically. Some popped in for a single weekly appearance, baffled by whatever I happened to be teaching that day. I was reminded of that adage, *You can never stand in the same river twice*, but in this case, I never taught the same class twice. Eventually, I got to be a good enough teacher that my lessons built on the previous ones, but this skill worked against my students and me, as I would say, "Remember yesterday, when . . ." and look out at the classroom but realize that "yesterday" featured Donte, Denise, James, Shonday, and today features Dezmon, another Dante, and Shon*tay*, the twin sister of Shonday, but not Shonday.

Neither was Southwestern "Satisfactory" in the category of School Climate. For the school to have possessed a "Safe and Orderly Climate," it had to reduce its number of proposed suspensions for disruptive behavior by eighty percent. Eighty percent. The school attempted to achieve this by not suspending its students when they engaged in disruptive behavior. That the school was considered neither safe nor orderly was evident to any visitor who, after trudging up the stairs and through the halls, always asked me, "Are you bet*ween* classes." "No," I said once to a suited white woman, and added, "This is second period." Her eyebrows rose.

The halls were crazy. No matter the time of day—morning or night, during class or between—the halls were never empty. Kids were always roaming, loitering at the corners, swaggering down the hall or up, lingering in the stairwells, smoking or stacking liquor bottles up the steps. I once found a group throwing dice against the wall and laying money down on bets.

Some walked the halls like it was their jobs. They acted like the halls were just dimly lit, locker-lined streets of their familiar neighborhoods. These kids we called hallwalkers. And because the halls weren't all that interesting, the hallwalkers innovated ways to amuse themselves. One morning my first period students jolted in their seats as a sudden spate of pops and pows and cracks erupted just outside our door. Gun shots? No, too flimsy-sounding. Papery, even. The next morning, the same bursts startled me but not the kids, and within a week, none of us budged when we heard the noise. We were all accustomed to the daily lighting of fire crackers.

From my room, I'd heard more than I'd seen. The fire crackers, yes, but also basketballs dribbling down the hall. Shouts of "Holy Shit, he got a gun!" followed by the pounding of boots on the run. When I went to the door, I saw nothing but a blur of kids rounding a corner. On another day, I'd heard the incantation of that then-popular song, "Who Let the Dogs Out?" and a voice saying, "Woof woof." This was followed by a four-legged creature's claws prancing on the floor, the jingle of a dog-collar, and another set of boots running as someone called out, "Pit-bull!" Later, the kids reported that there was indeed a pit-bull in school that day. Their wide eyes and smiles said they genuinely delighted in this fact.

I'd also heard the chalky ceiling squares fall to the floor with a smack. They broke like crackers, if crackers were two feet wide and one inch thick. When I went outside my room to see, a book or a backpack usually laid on the floor covered in dust, evidence that some kid had projected the heavy object at the tile and jarred it from the ceiling. Ms. Patterson often poked her head out of her classroom, too. Once, the air was coated in white chalky bits, and Ms. Patterson coughed and shook her head. The ceiling had asbestos, she said. We were all breathing asbestos, she said.

But those ceiling squares would fall on their own, too, completely out of the blue. I remember once a kid walking obediently along—his heavy backpack an indication that he actually took books home—and *whack*, a giant square fell from the Southwestern sky, almost directly in front of him. He looked at me as if to say, *You see that? You see where we learn?* When I looked up at the ceiling, I saw the innards of the school's plumbing system, the dust-covered pipes, and I knew I'd see those pipes for as long as I worked here—nobody would fix that tile. Because nobody had fixed any of the tiles that had fallen to the floor.

So many hallwalkers roamed the school during any given class period that Ms. Brown regularly got on the intercom to ask, "*Teeech*ers! *Why* are students in the *hall*ways?" She whined the question desperately, her perfectly articulated, nasal voice crackling through the intercom. This interjection was, depending on my mood, either humorous or infuriating in its pointlessness. None of us teachers had the answer to this question, which seemed more like an existential riddle than an answerable inquiry, and even if we *had* an answer to the question, none of us could respond, the intercom-system being (as intercom-systems go) fairly standard in its one-way-ness. While Ms. B demanded to know why all these students were meandering the halls, her teachers were busy manning and womanning their first priorities—their students—who *weren't* in the hallways, who were present for class which had become that much more unruly due to Brown's interruption.

Back in Houston, a TFA teacher had told me that she always kept her classroom door open to foster "openness" and "trust." I listened and nodded and imagined I'd do the same, that I too would leave my door open as a literal and figurative "opening" of trust and mutual respect and progressive do-goody-ness between me and my future kids. By the time I got to Southwestern, I decided that veteran teacher's school wasn't nearly as low on its state standard of "Safe and Orderly Climate" as mine. If teachers at Southwestern left their classroom doors ajar, hallwalkers poked their heads in and sometimes barged right into the room, harassing the teacher and/or the students. Sometimes the harassments were harmless, as harassments go, and other times not so much. I forget what a kid once said to me one day, but I slammed the door so hard on him that the door knocked him in the face. "Oh!" I heard him say as the small windowpane whacked him on the forehead and the door reverberated on its hinges. When I confessed my offense to Amy, Ellen, and Brooke, they nodded, and one of them said, "Yeah, we do that all the time."

As the first weeks of the school year wore on, our climate grew increasingly chaotic, and the administration seemed to possess as many proactive strategies as a rock garden. On the eve of Halloween, I'd been told to prepare for an all-out war waged by the students. Your car might get keyed, faculty informed me. You could become the target of rotten eggs. Better wear something you don't mind getting dirty. And whatever you do, don't poke your face out of your classroom. Not even for a second. No matter what's happening in the halls. Just stay in your class.

I listened. I stayed in my class and taught an elaborately planned lesson on Edgar Allan Poe's "The Raven." My students drummed on their desks to Poe's trochaic octameter as we read, *Once upon a midnight dreary / while I pondered, weak and weary . . .* We chanted the stanzas like rally-criers empowered by the Gothic. Then we watched Bart Simpson's reenactment of the poem on VHS. After that, we all scanned the metric feet of our names like dutiful poets mastering iambs, trochees, dactyls and anapests, and I was proud. The goal of the lesson was to convert my kids into poetry formalists. And to keep them from throwing eggs at me.

But Brooke was obstinate about combating school chaos, a courageous trait that earned her my undying applause and a face full of egg. While shouting at hallwalkers to *Get to class!* she got struck in the head by not just one but two and then three raw, yokey ones.

What had the administration done in preparation for this pre-declared war on order? Its principal (who daily parked his car in a special carport so it was well protected from vandals) had himself a sick day. The master of our school, the embodiment of the rule, the decider of all discipline decided not to show, a choice that made me realize something: our administration was partly responsible for our school's disorderly climate.

Last among the relevant statistical categories was Special Education. Five hundred of our 1,600 students received some kind of Special Education service. They'd been labeled with ADD or ADHD or dyslexia or other diagnoses that made learning difficult, more difficult than usual for a student at Southwestern, which, let's face it, wasn't all that easy in a place where firecrackers were daily bursting.

My little room number 3536 was deemed the ninth grade English "inclusion" classroom, which meant that more "special needs" students than average filled my rosters; they were "included" into a mainstream learning environment. Looking back, the school's choice to give a completely greenhorn teacher this role seems either idiotic or just plain cruel. Not so much cruel to me as cruel to those kids who needed special attention. Kids with learning disabilities needed extra help, extra time, extra expertise, and I, like any brand-spanking new teacher, had none of these in high reserve.

But this role meant I was assigned an "inclusion specialist" to work with, and Ms. Nelson had been in the city school system for over twenty years. I had high hopes for our mission together. Her short black hair was bleached yellow on top, and because the male hip-hop-pop star, Sysqo, had just made himself famous for not only "The Thong Song" but the same incidental haircut as Ms. Nelson, my students called her Sysqo. She ignored this.

I haven't mentioned Ms. Nelson in my classroom yet, not due to some sloppy narrative omission but because her presence didn't make tremendous difference in my day-to-day teaching. Before we even met our students, Ms. Nelson insisted that we work fifty-fifty in the classroom. I thought this meant we would collaborate on lessons. This meant that she would assign herself a task for the day, and by the day's end, it would be completed.

"Your bulletin boards need decorating," she said one day. The four-by-four foot squares of cork were crumbling, the recycled bursts of someone else's champagne moment. But because a third of my students didn't come to school and a third were busy talking or sleeping and because I didn't know how to teach anyway, I did not care about underdecorated cork boards. My response was, "Why?" Why couldn't I have crappy bulletin boards for a while? Beautiful bulletin boards wouldn't solve my concerns.

The next day, flower-patterned contact paper covered every square inch of the boards, which were framed in multicolored streamers. Bubble letters headed each. One said, *Great Work*. Another, *Vocabulary*. Ms. Nelson worked quickly and neatly and then sped down Font Hill with her sister, also a special-ed teacher in her fifties, where they went somewhere to smoke cigarettes and eat fast-food sandwiches. If she returned at all, it was two hours later and the kids sniffed her smoke-filled clothes.

"These desks, they need to be cleaned," she said one day.

"They were cleaned," I said.

"Don't worry. I've got stuff at home." She looked down at them and put her hand on her hip. "Kirn, these are some trifling desks."

The next day she brought chemicals strong enough to peel off the skin on our hands, and by the day after that, the once-beige desks were bleached bone white, the sharpie-marks now the faded gray ghosts of vandalism.

"These posters are good," she said of the three I picked up at the store with my own money. "I've got more at home."

And more she had. The next day every other foot of cinderblock wall-space had its own shiny, laminated poster.

I didn't understand Ms. Nelson's ways of helping. Twenty years of experience, and she had no unit plans to offer? No disciplinary suggestions? No lessons or "best practices" to share? All she seemed to care about was the appearance of my room. Having the right buzz words laminated and hung on the walls. Signs decorated with stenciled red roses. All of her posters had stenciled red roses bordering the edges. Sometimes I wondered if she desperately longed for a flower delivery.

I equated her affinity for classroom decorating with my students' loyalty to expensive name-brand clothes, despite those free or reduced lunches they could qualify for. Mr. Owens, a kind of guidance counselor to the kids, had warned me that I would see an extra handful of students in the first week of October because the welfare checks came in by then. Some kids wouldn't attend school until they could get new backpacks and new shoes and new hairdos.

"Nothing'll be in the cupboards at home," Owens said, "and they'll miss three weeks of school. But they'll be dressed to the nines."

I was a low-maintenance dresser, a quality proved by the fact that my own students had to point out when my shoes needed shining, so I might have been unfairly impatient about such things, but to me, the administration mirrored the students' over-adherence to *how things looked*. If a child was labeled special ed at Southwestern, this essentially meant, not really that his teachers needed to teach him differently, but that he needed a special form that stated his problem, and he needed it photocopied and put in a file, and if he had that form in that file, then the school was providing him a service, was doing its duty of fulfilling his *special need*, because the teacher was required to go visit that form and have a copy of it and be aware that so-and-so had a special need. A special need was fulfilled by the act of documenting, in triplicate, the special need. Most schools didn't have specialists like Ms. Nelson visiting inclusion classrooms. The fact that Southwestern even had extra special education instructors was, according to teachers working at other schools, over the top. Really amazing. Oh, wow, they told me. That's great. Even if that extra instructor slipped out for two-hour lunches while her students—kids like Jimmy Nizbin—bounced off the motherfucking walls.

While I can say nothing in defense of Ms. Nelson's frequent AWOL status, I did gradually learn that the culprit of her self-appointed tasks was not vanity. There was a reason for her pious devotion to posters.

● ● ●

About a month into school, it suddenly struck my department head that she wanted to see all the English teachers' lesson plans. I felt I was in the clear. For every lesson, I typed up a document that contained goals and objectives and materials and engagements and drills and procedures and assessments, and I slid this document into a plastic sheath and slid the sheath's three holes through the three rings of a binder that, on its cover, said *Lesson Plans*. I was meticulous about it. I didn't know how I could teach without, at the very least, a plan, however wrong it went in real time. When another new teacher saw the binder, he was mesmerized.

"So you put all your lessons in there? For each day?" The thought had never occurred to him. "I think I'm gonna do that, too!" he nodded and smiled and looked like I had offered him a map to the fountain of youth. I envisioned his desk covered with scattered loose-leaf papers. He had been thrown into his position with even less preparation than I had. The guy must have been drowning in his new role.

Apparently he wasn't the only one without a daily plan. Upon hearing the news that our lesson plans were up for administrative scrutiny, most of the English Mother Hens (as Noelani and I affectionately called the teachers in the English Department) bustled between each other's classrooms to complain about the unfairness, to discuss the nerve of that woman, Ms. Wallace, our department head, checking up on us like this, like we weren't grown. And after they'd sufficiently confirmed how unjust was this new policy of lesson-plan-checking, they returned to their classrooms, shut their doors behind them, and sat at their desks so they could "get that lesson plan book done." Some halted instruction to accomplish this task. Let me be plainer: some teachers had to stop teaching lessons so they could write lessons they were supposed to have taught.

On the official day of lesson-plan review, I readied myself for bits of praise as the only glorious thing about my teaching was inspected: my religious commitment to a binder. I stood in Ms. Wallace's office, which was also the English department's book room, and I watched her flip through several weeks' worth of attempted lessons. From floor to ceiling, books lined the walls, and I scanned the titles, found dozens of hardbound copies of *To Kill a Mockingbird*, *A Lesson Before Dying*, *Animal Farm*, each novel neatly in rows and surrounded by clones of itself, ready for a whole class to read it. I reveled in this, the abundance of great books, and reveled in my job, the disseminator of great literature, upholder of the American literary tradition, the fosterer of . . .

Ms. Wallace shook her head. She looked up at me from her desk. She whispered, "Ms. Kirn."

Her short, black hair frizzed away from her face like it had been blown by a great wind. Her eyes got so wide that the dark dimes of her irises were fully revealed, not the slightest bit eclipsed by her lids. She looked shocked, literally.

I pulled the bottom of my button-down shirt with both hands and felt it straighten around my shoulders and across my front.

"Where," she said, again in a whisper, "are your *state standards*?"

Where were my state standards? I had a lesson for every day. Each lesson had a goal, and each goal was written in the required "behavioral" format, which meant that the goals began with the obligatory phrase, "Students will be able to," and then finished with a measurable action like "identify the five elements of characterization," and each lesson had an "authentic assessment" at the end of the day, which meant that each day I collected work from my students that asked them to perform the skills that matched the goal. The puzzle that is a lesson plan took me weeks to learn, and learn it I did, and what I'd forgotten were three integers separated by periods. Ms. Wallace wanted one point three point two. Or two point five point four. These digits corresponded to what the state called "Core Learning Goals and Indicators." They meant things like, *Students will demonstrate the ability to respond to a text*, and *Student will demonstrate the ability to control language*. In my mind, you couldn't possibly teach the subject of English without hitting at least five standards, every day.

But because I didn't list them on the lesson plan, I wasn't achieving them. Because they weren't written, they didn't exist. Where were my state standards? she asked like I'd committed a crime. Put your hands above your head. Admit your offense. Behind Ms. Wallace was a small window that showed the tombstones of Mt. Olivet.

"Each lesson *must* correspond to a state *standard*." She continued in her whispering tone. Though Ms. Wallace sat at her desk and I stood in front of her, she tilted her head so far back she actually appeared to look *down* the bridge of her nose.

Teaching state standards was a perfectly reasonable expectation for a teacher. I was a rookie, and mistakes were inevitable. I had never known, though, that the little digits had to be listed on lesson plans. But this was only my initiation into Ms. Wallace's style of schooling. On another day, she wanted to see my gradebook. This time, I didn't expect praise, but who could screw up a gradebook?

"Ms. Kirn." The same shake of the head, the same shocked face, the same question as though it were the affirmation of a crime. "*Where* are your *func*tional *test* scores?" I said *um* and crinkled my eyes and waited for her to explain this not-yet-divulged necessity of my job, this totally unexpected way that I'd fucked up the keeping of attendance.

Again, she spoke to me in that hard, slow, breathy whisper. "Beside each student's name, you Must. Write. Their scores. From the functional testsss." She made the word sound like a *tsk*. "How will you ever know who still needs to take the functional tests?" She raised her hands from her desks, palms up, like she was feeling for rain.

Ms. Wallace here was referring to a testing-day phenomenon I had not yet experienced. On the day of a "functional test," normal school-day procedures essentially shut down as a huge percentage of students were supposed to sit in designated rooms and take the latest version of the same test they'd taken since sixth grade. The kids who still hadn't passed often said they had, and refused to go. They refused to feel stupid, not to mention bored, for yet another three hours. The kids who had passed often said they hadn't, and left class and became, for that day, hallwalkers. Functional test days made the school more dysfunctional than normal.

Our gradebooks needed to keep students' scores straight so that we'd know who was lying, either way. But two months into the job, I didn't know this. Ms. Wallace ran Noelani through the same rigmarole, and our department head either liked baptizing her new teachers by fire, or she'd forgotten what it was like to not know something; that is, several years in that small office, surrounded by all those unused novels, completing paperwork in triplicate, might have taken away her compassion for the unknowing mind, might have erased her tactics to steer the mind like a ship into knowing, which was after all what we did as teachers. Sometimes I think she forgot how. I left her office baffled. Why, out of all the things I'd gotten right, did she narrow in on one missing component? Why *was* the appearance of our classrooms and our gradebooks and our lesson plan binders so crucial, much more crucial, it seemed, than the substance of our teaching?

Because the many nasty statistics of Southwestern High School—the low attendance, the high rate of suspensions and violence, the low level of academic achievement—all put our mammoth school on Maryland's shit list. I don't mean to sound metaphorical. The shit list was real, and had an official name: *Reconstitution-eligible.* Maryland had a list of schools it determined were eligible for reconstitution, which was otherwise known as, *Your school is so bad, Baltimore, that if you don't clean it up, We, The State, will take it over.*

The longer I taught at Southwestern, the more I smelled the fear of The State, which motivated everyone's hyperattention to appearances. My special education teacher, who had state standards laminated and red-rose-decorated on my walls. Ms. Wallace, as she looked for those standards on our lesson plans. Mother hen Ms. Patterson of next door, as she bustled back and forth between classrooms, asking teachers about their meeting with Ms. Wallace. Everyone was afraid of the higher-ups above them, who were afraid of the higher-ups above *them,* and this fear, which motivated peoples' fine attention to detail, stopped with The State, who teachers and administrators talked about like a malevolent god. The State could destroy whole families of people with floods or plagues or something. What will The State do? When will The State come?

One day The State paid an official visit. The visit was predetermined for weeks, and administrators reminded teachers with anxious regularity. *The State is coming The State is coming.* The administration listed the several things The State would want in each of our rooms: Core Learning Goals on the walls, Lesson plans on the teacher-desks, bulletin boards plastered with examples of "excellent" student-work. Get those Core Learning Goals on the walls, they told us. On the day the state comes, have an actual lesson plan and place it prominently on your desk. Staple cleanly written student-work to the bulletin boards, and staple them at measured angles and spaced evenly apart. Staple tests with red A's written in the top margins. And please, everyone, did we say this already? On your desk, have a typed lesson plan. Preferably in a plastic cover. That corresponds to state standards on the state curriculum. All hail The State.

It turned out that four well-dressed, exceedingly quiet, clipboard-toting people comprised The State. Each walked the halls of the school alone. Each held a pen; each held that clipboard rib-high and facing upward like a little desk so each could write something upon it in an instant. Unlike other visitors, none looked afraid for his or her life. Each seemed composed, bored even. Their gazes oscillated between whatever was right before them and that clipboard. Three were female, one was male. All looked meek and intellectual and tired, the man especially, who had a concave chest and wore wire-rimmed glasses. They all, including the women, wore suits.

But what struck me most about "The State"? They were white. All four of them. And not just white in the way I was white or any visitor could be white or a few other teachers—Brooke, Ellen, Amy—were white. On the day that The State lurked in and out of classrooms, I saw and felt what everyone else had feared, what so much of the school might have, at first, seen in me: an other, and not just any other, but a white other with a clipboard. Someone who, however meek in physicality, could wield incredible power, could check boxes on a form and write us all off and deem us incompetent. "Reconstitute" our school. Which meant most of the administrators would lose their jobs.

Regardless of the pre-State-visit-pom-pom cheers and rigmarole, the school resented the evaluation. It was a similar resentment that Patterson had for Ms. Wallace when Ms. Wallace made us turn over our lesson plans, only The State stopover bonded even Patterson and Wallace. It bonded all of us, and on the day it visited, we occasionally stood outside our doorways during planning periods and whispered, *Did they come to your room? Yeah, your room?* A hush fell over the school. Even the students—who were told over and over, *The State is coming The State is coming*—were relatively quiet that day, seized by surprising docility. I was stunned that a bunch of geeky white adults could arrest my kids' normal antics. But my kids were being judged, and by a predominantly white, predominantly middle-class suit-wearing institution that was nothing like them, and I didn't realize this would intimidate them so.

This judgment by which Southwestern's kids were hauntingly humbled was also why I think my students put so much attention into looking good, sometimes waiting weeks for those welfare checks to materialize in the mail so they could buy one hundred-dollar shoes and elaborate hairdos before first appearing in school. Not for sheer vanity's sake, as I'd quickly assumed, but to avert any quick judgments from outsiders, from strangers, from what the kids called "haters." Haters: those people who could size up and dismiss in a heartbeat who you were and how you lived. This alertness to fast and unfair verdicts was what I think also caused so many classroom teachers to talk more about the looks of their rooms than the content of their instruction. Our school was a shit-hole, and teachers did their damndest to cover this up. Why? So nobody could assume that shitty school meant, well, shitty school. I too had grown unnaturally proud of small physical things, like my yellow streamers that adorned those beige, pen-marked, ratty shades. Like my black and white postcards stapled to the shades, among them the Virginia Woolf profile that west Baltimoreans still believed captured some great-grandmother of mine.

Plus, it's easier to fix form than content. When The State comes for a day and has a hundred classrooms to visit, it will only spend a few minutes in yours, and if you look good and tidy and ordered in those few minutes, The State will check all the right boxes on that clipboard and you'll be in the clear. At least until next year, when The State comes again, because next year your statistics for attendance and suspensions and expulsions and functional test scores will be just as bad as, if not worse than, they were in the year that The State deemed you unsatisfactory. Because attention to form over substance cost us the substance that might have actually changed us. This is an incredible claim to make after only teaching at Southwestern a month or two, and it wasn't one I could even articulate in those first few months, but I started seeing evidence of it every day.

One day in the middle of first period, I got a knock on my door. One knock on the door was never a small feat to handle, as I juggled a hundred demands simultaneously during any given lesson: a new kid who suddenly showed to school; a student's hand raised because he wanted to go to the bathroom; another student shouting that she wanted to go to the bathroom; the firecrackers snapping and popping in the hall; an announcement from Ms. Brown, asking teachers yet again, "Why are there students in the hallways?"; a cluster of kids with their heads down and another cluster of kids completely off-task and a few quiet kids looking up at me pleadingly to get the room under control so they could learn, and someone, always someone banging on the door. When I looked up at it, I usually only saw dark eyes and a ski-cap pressed into the little window glass, which quickly disappeared. Just another hallwalker. But one day a young woman stood at the entrance. She wore jeans and a T-shirt and smacked her gum and I couldn't tell if she was a student or a staff member. She looked to be about twenty. She told me I was needed downstairs.

Downstairs? "For what?" Behind me, murmurs from the class grew louder. Ms. Nelson was missing for the morning.

"An IEP meeting," she said, as though I should have known about this. As though I had been informed of a schedule of IEP meetings or that I knew IEP meetings even existed. IEP's, I only knew, were Individual Education Plans, written for special education students. "One of your students has an IEP meeting now. You're required to go." I looked back at my class. How could I leave them? "Don't worry," the woman said. "I'm gonna watch your class while you're gone."

She stared back at me from purple wire glasses and chomped on that pink gum. How reassuring, I thought. I left my class, along with a perfectly reasonable lesson—something I'd spent hours on—which would get crumpled up into a ball and tossed into that institutionally large, army green waste can.

At the meeting, I sat through thirty minutes of form shuffling and then I signed a form that told me Raymond White was emotionally disturbed, which I already knew, and everyone agreed on something that I can't remember, something like the signing of the form, and when I returned to my classroom, the kids were sitting quietly in clusters, playing cards or braiding hair. We, the faculty and staff of Southwestern, had traded thirty minutes of instruction to twenty-some under-performing kids, and we'd traded it in for pristine paperwork.

For instances like this one, I was unforgiving about any and all hints of vanity at Southwestern, even while I might have perceived the emotional needs they filled. "Thanks so much for the help," I said to Ms. Nelson after she covered those bulletin boards. "Wow, my room looks so much better," I added, because it did. But deep down I still thought that, out of all the things to work on, she had spent her time on drivel. *No wonder*, I'd thought, because I was young and earnest and internally blunt but externally silent. *No wonder our kids are three grades behind.*

After the last staple had gone into the red border that outlined the board, she smoothed the contact paper with her manicured hand. "There. That'll keep 'em off our backs." It was morning, right before first period and, as punctual as the school bell, someone set firecrackers off just outside our door.

CHAPTER 6

BARELY PASSING

Coach Powell was a light-skinned, middle-aged man with a gravelly voice like low-grade sandpaper. I'd heard he had a proclivity for flirting with the young teachers. At the school's pre-year retreat, I'd seen him corner a new teacher who'd just graduated from a local college. Powell got two feet from her, lowered his eyes and mumbled something, and she'd smiled and shrugged and backed away. "He creeps me out," she said to me later and nodded in Powell's direction.

Still, I wanted to like Powell; he undertook the challenge of coaching both football and basketball. Though the swampy football field paid tribute to an era of Southwestern Sabers' ferocity that had long gone, and though our team was usually under-outfitted and under-conditioned (panting at halftime, their tongues hanging out as Powell preached), Powell's pursuit of a bona fide athletic program was admirable. Ours was a school building toward which a funeral-parade of teachers' cars inched up Font Hill just five minutes before the bell rang to begin the day; only ten minutes after the final bell rang, these same teachers would have left right along with the kids if the administration hadn't enforced a new rule: stay in the building at least ten minutes after school ends. *Don't you teachers have lessons to plan?* they asked. *Or copies to make? Or something?*

Among this "not-one-minute-past-I-have-to" atmosphere, Powell stayed late. Well after the other faculty had left, and upon a torn-up field behind the penitentiary-style school, Powell taught his boys football. On the indoor basketball court during winter, he drilled them in lay-ups. During the day, he taught something, though I never knew what. The unknown subject seemed less important to him than his coaching, a priority that was evidenced in his daily attire of swishy athletic pants and matching swishy zip-up jacket.

Powell showed up in my doorway one day while I was seated at my desk, planning a lesson. "Hi, Ms. Kirn," he said in his gravelly voice and smiled. He walked into my room, his each step embellished by the swish of his pants.

80

He said he wanted to discuss Marcus Gordon, one of the guys Powell planned on coaching for basketball season. "How often does Marcus come to class, Ms. Kirn?"

When the big, broad-shouldered, high-towering stranger named Marcus entered my room for the first time, we were well into the fourth week of school. I was put off by the man-child's physique. *Really? You're a ninth grader? And really, after a month of school has passed, you're now my student?* He was missing two of his front teeth and wore heavy gold chains around his neck. I led his man-sized body to a desk and wondered if his legs would fit beneath it. As I figured out how to catch a kid up on almost a month's worth of school, Marcus sat quietly. "You've got a lot of work to make up," I said. "Yeth, ma'am," he said in a surprisingly high-pitched lisp. But his courtesy was more surprising: people at Southwestern rarely said "ma'am." "You're really behind," I warned. Still, he nodded. He studied the several weeks' worth of handouts that I gave him and we laid out a plan for catching him up to the rest of the class. "I'm a do my work, Mith Kuhn."

"So he comes to school?" Powell asked.

"Sometimes."

"But when he comes, does he do his work?

I nodded. "*When* he comes."

"So then why did you give him an incomplete on his report card?"

"Because," I said, "he missed three straight weeks in a row and many more days after that. And he never makes up what he misses. Actually," I started wondering why I hadn't given him an F. "Mathematically, I think he earned a fifty. I was being kind with the Incomplete." I was still holding out for a mini-miracle, waiting for a flood of Marcus's "make-up" work to pour gloriously onto my big teacher-desk.

"Ms. Kirn," said Powell, now taking on the condescending tone of some cross-examining TV lawyer. "What do you give a student who never shows up to your class?"

This was a good question. It seemed to me that if students never came a single day, they should get zeroes, as they'd done zero work and come zero days. But on report cards teachers weren't permitted to give grades lower than fifties. Numbers like "twenty-seven"—hardly a mathematical anomaly at Southwestern—would make a final passing grade of sixty mathematically improbable because on the next report card, the kid would need the rare digits of a ninety-three in order to get credits for the class. While fifties to my mind were for kids who did fifty percent of the work, or got fifty percent of the work right, fifties at Southwestern were reserved for "no-shows." Powell's question had a required answer. "I give him a fifty," I said.

Powell's cheeks lifted. His eyes relaxed and the concerned crow's feet at their edges diminished. He looked like he'd figured out a checkmate, and I hadn't realized we'd been playing anything. "How can you give both of these kids fifties? The kid who never shows, and the kid who sometimes does his work? How is that fair to Marcus?"

I felt a little square centimeter of skin pinch between my eyebrows. Powell was suggesting that because a "fifty" was dispensed upon students who had never entered the school building, a kid who did from time to time make his appearance known should at the least get a "sixty." And therefore be eligible for basketball season.

At Southwestern, the passing grade of sixty was often all kids hoped for. *Did I pass?* they asked me. *Am I passing?* But "passing" didn't necessarily mean "learning," and "passing" wouldn't move students from a sixth- to a ninth-grade reading level; in fact it wouldn't "move" students at all, other than out one grade's door and into the next, where they'd now read *tenth*-grade material at a sixth-grade level. All "passing" indicated was that the kid complied minimally with the rules of being a student. She came to school. He listened to instructions at least sixty percent of the time. She turned in completed work at least sixty percent of the time. He knew to staple the rough and final drafts of an essay together, however ill-structured or error-filled or off-topic, and hand it to me. One big block of loopy cursive text, one long stream-of-consciousness chunk where even the word *writing* was misspelled—*that* was, according to our standards, "passing." Because the work had been completed. Do work, any kind of work, and you should pass.

At the end of our poetry unit I'd asked students to write analyses of single poems. I'd laid out my expectations: three-paragraph essays summarizing meaning, dissecting tropes, identifying and analyzing tone and mood, and reflecting upon the poem's connection, if any, to the students' lives. Marcus, who happened to be present, handed in a response to Ralph Dickey's poem, "Father":

> *I think the meaning of this poem is to tell people if you see your father beating on your parent you should do something to help because he probably going to try it on you. I like this poem because this is how my father was doing to my mother and I could not stop him.*

I had built a three-week unit to culminate in this project. During the three weeks, my students and I read poems, illustrated poems, acted out poems, sang poems, wrote about, talked about, thought about poems. We'd listened to music to examine how musicians could create moods just like poets. We'd identified and written similes, metaphors, alliteration, and a heap of other poetic tropes. But Marcus hadn't been present for most of this poetry boot camp. For random efforts such as the above two-sentence response, which is admittedly heartbreaking in its content, and which elicited wells of compassion in me for mammoth, sweet-voiced Marcus, Coach Powell wanted Marcus to pass ninth-grade English.

I don't mean to minimize Marcus's response. Students at Southwestern had an excruciating time with the role assigned to them—the whole student thing—and this showed as they walked up Font Hill with nothing but maybe a bunch of papers folded long-ways and shoved into their back pockets; it showed when at least five students in every class said they had no writing utensil, and I had to develop a system of bartering—their bus passes for my pens. Their resistance showed even in the way they sat. They let their legs sprawl out into the aisles, and I tripped over their Nikes and Timberlands. When I made them keep their legs under the desks, they gave the position an earnest shot. They tucked those legs beneath the table-top, and I pushed their chairs in so that they sat tall and faced the front, and then they looked at me like I'd just forced them into a girdle. Sincerely distraught, they said, "But it *feels* weird." By the end of the period, they pushed their chairs three feet away from the desks again, slid their butts to the edges of the chairs, cast their arms across the backs, and let their legs extend into the aisles, and this position would let them stare easily at the ceiling or the person next to them or the small slit in the doorway to peep at whoever roamed the hall—whoever refused even the basic rule to *enter* a classroom. But the position didn't enable them to look easily at the board or their books or me. Even the physical position required of a student felt awkward.

At the end of a day, I'd once found Ms. Gueye standing in the hall-way with a sweat-glistened sheen over her brown face. She was a veteran teacher of two decades who had just moved to Baltimore from Boston, and she taught in the room beside mine. She said, almost trance-like and stumped, "These kids aren't ready for me." She looked back into her room. Desks and chairs were scattered and empty. "They haven't come ready to *learn!*" She shouted the last word through the empty hall. I wondered what had happened in her room that day. I imagined her pacing between the desks, asking questions that she'd used successfully with her New England kids, ones about *Julius Caesar* and Shakespearean language, only to be met with angry murmurs, curses, or heads dropped into the crooks of elbows. Her only results seemed to be her own face, wet as a sprinter's on a treadmill.

Because of our kids' resistance, I could sort of understand the school's urge to reward even minimal gestures—the worksheet with just over half the answers right, the long stream-of-consciousness chunk of an essay handed in, if not on the exact due date, at least not three weeks late. These were not givens here. Still, with such low expectations, learning felt like a charade. The kid did a dance to show me he could pass, and I was expected to unhook the rope that blocked one grade to the next like some bouncer at an elite bar and wave him in. TFA's first lesson at the summer Institute was about high expectations. Keep the bar high, they'd said, and your kids will rise to meet the bar. Keep it low, and they'll continue to under-perform, getting surpassed year after year by their middle-class counterparts.

I could have offered that philosophy to Coach Powell when he insinuated that I pass Marcus for sometimes showing up. *Is that the standard we have for our kids, Coach? Should we wave them on from grade to grade because they sometimes sit in their seats? And if that's our standard, coach, is that because we think they're not capable of anything more? Is that how low our opinion of them has dipped?* Those were the words I now wish I'd said. But I was new, overworked, afraid to make waves, and trying to plan a lesson. So what I really said was, "Marcus is smart. He just needs to come to school. Every day."

"Well, if he's smart," Powell started defensively, but then he stopped. His scratchy voice managed to get soft and sing-songy, and he asked me (the way grown-ups sometimes ask their kids if they're big boys or big girls now), "Are *you* smart, Ms. Kirn?"

I stood up from my desk. I brought both arms to my chest and crossed them. I said yes.

"Well if *you're* smart, and *he's* smart, and you're the teacher . . ." I stared into Powell's face, all freckly and light, those faint crows' feet wispy around his eyes. ". . . then you need to find some way to pull that smartness out of him. Right?"

I pressed my left hand into my hip, but I didn't say anything. I didn't know what to say. Smartness suddenly became a long silk scarf in my mind, one that magicians pull yard by yard from their wide open mouths. If I was smart, I had to pull smartness out of Marcus. If I couldn't pull it out of him, then I wasn't smart.

Powell bid some cordial farewell. I stood with that hand on my hip and waited for him to leave my room.

I was insulted, yes, and partly because of that question: was I smart? Nod in reply, and I'm overly confident. Shake my head, and I'm a self-deprecating limp. It felt like a trap, one into which I had no choice but to fall and Powell could watch. The interaction stayed with me longer than it should have. *I don't tell him how to coach his players*, I thought for days after, *even after they lose nearly every game. Plus, for real, what* does *that man teach?*

Looking back, Powell seemed pretty smart himself: he perceived an inner sore-spot of a new, impressionable teacher and jabbed at it. I was a twenty-two-year-old who, before she came to Southwestern, thought she knew something about the world. Thought she could parlay some wisdom to a few classrooms of kids. She'd gotten straight A's since she could sing the alphabet; had always made not just the honor roll but the honor-honor roll; had been among the top 20 in a graduating class of 400; was captain of the track team; was Best Newspaper Ad Designer of Sixth Grade and had won herself a plaque for that one, as well as another plaque for best poetry at her university, and a medal for completing a half-marathon. Ten seconds faster per mile than she had planned. She didn't, as a rule, fail at the things she tried.

But the longer I taught at Southwestern, the more I found myself failing. Quiz grade after quiz grade, kids got fifties and sixties. Noun to verb, adverb to preposition, nobody could identify the parts of speech on a test. No matter how high or low the bar, my students on average failed to meet it, which meant that I failed them. The identity of the person I felt I was—the faithful achiever—was stripped from me, day by day, in great painstaking hunks like bark from a tree, and on any given afternoon I was left standing before my students, feeling bare, hemming and hawing and headachy. If I were to have graded myself, I would have given me an average well below fifty.

• • •

And then there was Takira Webb. Tall and lanky, with the swagger of a ballplayer, she dressed like the boys and wore a bandana around her head. On our first day together, she sat in the back of the room, so tall compared to my other ninth graders that half of her body poked out from the group, and because her eyes seemed to pierce mine with stunning clarity, I thought she might be a challenge. A rebel. Ready to make some mayhem in this final period of the day.

But no. She sat attentively the entire ninety minutes. When I asked questions, she answered with strikingly high vocabulary. When I instructed students to write something down, Takira's handwriting was the small, penciled font of perfection—each letter the same proportion, each hovering just a millimeter above the line. And the sentences weren't fragments or mazes of run-ons, they weren't riddled with odd spelling or grammar errors. They were artful, complex. She came to class motivated to learn, and she could easily interpret the subtle plot of a story like "Marigolds." When I gave an assignment that would take the other students a full class period, Takira would finish it in half the time and then look at me from that back row, wondering what was next. What else did I have for her?

She was an anomaly. So what was she doing here?

"Truancy," she told me in her cool, easy voice, a voice laced with a touch of lethargy. She'd gotten kicked out of Poly—Baltimore Polytechnic—for her bad habit of sometimes staying in bed. For days and days and days, she'd go through phases of not responding to the morning alarm. She'd hang out at home while her mom was at work. And at an institution like Poly, where 99 percent of the kids pursued higher education, the administration could afford to mandate a 90 percent attendance rate, could throw kids like Takira out. They wouldn't tolerate an aloof, lackadaisical student, regardless of how bright she was.

Takira carried herself differently than the other students at Southwestern. She walked around the chaos of the school like she was used to it, like she was better than it, and like it couldn't touch her, a quality her height afforded her. While five-foot nothing kids were hiking their sweatpants up with one hand and throwing firecrackers or breaking ceiling tiles with the other, nearly six-foot Takira looked down on them like they were fools, her eyelids ever so slyly low on her irises, and she swaggered by. When she sat in class, she addressed the other ninth graders like they were her rascal little cousins. "Quit acting like you're grown, son, show some respect." She never shouted. Her voice was suave and chill, almost effortless. And the remarkable thing, the kids listened to her. Though she lived *in* west Baltimore, she didn't seem to be *of* west Baltimore.

It was obvious that Takira was college bound. In fact, at sixteen, she should have been in tenth grade, but she'd failed ninth grade English on account of her poor attendance. It was my job, my thrill, really, to challenge her each day that she came. Sometimes I gave her more challenging analytical questions to answer in class instead of the usual comprehension ones I'd assigned to the other kids. Sometimes I gave her separate vocabulary lists to study, ones on the SAT-prep lists. But often my challenges came in the form of side-conversations. With Takira, I had genuine intellectual conversations, the kind that, as a senior in college, I'd always imagined having with my future students.

"Takira, you've got no evidence for this claim." We each sat on the tops of student-desks one afternoon, munching on some chips I had leftover from lunch, hunched over her paper. The final bell had rung, the rest of the kids and even most of the staff had fled the building. But Takira wanted help with an essay. Not an essay for my class, mind you. In fact, I had no idea why Takira was writing an essay that delineated what she called "Afrocentric and Eurocentric" styles of thought and behavior. For about a week, she'd been carting around a book with *Afrocentric* in the title, maybe Molefi Asante's *The Afrocentric Idea*, and now she was attempting to synthesize her ideas.

"Where's your proof? A paper's gotta have proof."

"Because, you know how white people are always uptight about being on time? And black people are more chill? They're more laid back and late. No disrespect, Ms. Kirn."

I scrunched up my face. Takira was collapsing her terms, making muddy waters of her argument, and replacing real evidence with stereotypes, all classic moves in freshman composition papers—college freshmen, that is. I'd spent three semesters as a writing tutor for college freshmen, and Takira's paper was bringing me back to those days. "Yeah, but that's not evidence," I told her. "You need concrete proof."

She leaned back, said, "Aw, maaan," then looked up at the ceiling. I dug into the bag for another chip, then looked back into her paper, peering into it like I did with those freshman papers. I was hunting through the claims and evidence to find a genuine thesis, to help a writer see for herself what she was trying to argue, to help her figure out how to argue it better. In other words, I was in nerdy teacher heaven. I was doing something that I was good at, something I was trained to do. And Takira was genuinely challenged.

• • •

But again, Takira was an anomaly among the Southwestern crowd. In my grade book, beside her name was a long row of A's. Beside other kids' names, rows of 50's, 60's.

Davon Green was another stellar kid, not because he was as academically advanced as Takira, but because he was genuinely motivated to be a good student. He protested whenever he didn't receive a gold star, which added up to extra points in my gradebook. He squealed when I threw his name on the board, which I rarely did because, for the most part, he was a delightful though rambunctious kid. In other words, Davon bought into the rules of school the way I did as a kid, the way the best students do. We had the kind of student-teacher relationship that made me eager to come to work. "Ms. Kirn, you gonna watch me play football tomorrow?" he asked me while he worked on an essay during class.

"Sure, I'll be there."

"What're you gonna do if I score a touchdown? You gonna give me extra credit?"

"No," I said, "but I'll run a lap around the track for you."

The next day I sat in the stands with Amy and Brooke, watching five-foot-four Davon look wobbly in all his heavy gear, and miraculously, the kid scored a touchdown. "Ms. Kirn!" he called from the field and grinned. "Where's my lap?"

But the culture of "just passing" still rubbed off on Davon, and he too measured success as the other students did. "Am I passing?" he'd ask with regularity.

I raised my eyebrows. "We don't ask if we're passing," I said, "because we want to do more than pass, *don't we*?"

"No, we don't," Davon said, probably because my first-person collective pronoun was sort of creepy and because Davon swore that just getting to the tenth grade, however low his grade, was all he cared about.

Still, I waited for Davon to revise his question because I wouldn't answer *Am I passing?* Sometimes I had to remind him of the question I *would* answer. Eventually, in a voice as dull and pained as if I were making him say *I like to wear dresses*, Davon asked, "Am I ex*cell*ing?"

I smiled wide and clasped my hands. "Why, Davon, I'm so glad you asked!" Then I dropped my smile. "Unfortunately, you are not excelling, as you only have a 65 percent average."

"So I'm passing?" he said, smiling, and I nodded, and our theatrics were over until two weeks later when he wanted to know again, was he passing?

But Davon could do better than pass, and I wanted the entire school to expect more from him and the rest of its students than the small word *here* at role-call.

I'd learned that other teachers had high expectations, like Ms. Gueye, but plenty of others, like Powell, did not. Take my special ed teacher, Ms. Nelson. She'd started declaring that she couldn't help certain kids. The kids she could not help happened to coincide precisely with the kids she was designated to assist. "He won't learn," she said about one boy who perpetually plopped his head down. Then she said the same about another, and then another. "I can't teach him. Some kids you can't do anything for." But those kids were the very reasons Ms. Nelson was in my room. The list of kids she could do nothing for grew longer each day until the only person she helped on a regular basis was a soft-spoken white kid named Alex, who was polite but woefully behind. She leaned over Alex's page and read questions aloud to him and watched him write down single-word answers with big, sometimes backwards letters.

Otherwise, Ms. Nelson opted to bide her time by glossing through Avon catalogues in the back of the room. That, or making more posters. And afterward she left the room for a smoke-break, which sometimes extended into a fast-food run and then a stop at a store, and she'd return in time for fourth period, which was easy to teach because it contained Takira and only ten other kids, and it contained no special ed students.

Then there was Ms. Jones, a sluggish, middle-aged reading teacher who always heaved and gasped in the morning once she got to her classroom at the end of the hall. She taught for three weeks in the beginning of the year, then called out sick ever since. The school had to scramble for a permanent substitute. I assumed Ms. Jones was gravely ill, but in the hallway one day Ms. Nelson and I heard a terrific screech from Ms. Jones's room, and Ms. Patterson said, "*That* situation," and nodded toward the door. "That's just not right."

"She's sick, though, right?" I said.

The corners of Ms. Patterson's mouth tightened. In the low, husky voice she adopted for straight-talk, she said, "She isn't sick. She pulled the same thing last year. Called out ill most of the year. Left her kids without a teacher. It's a shame." Ms. Patterson kept her squinting eyes on the door of Ms. Jones's room. "She has so much sick-leave, she doesn't care. She just sits at home and collects her paycheck." Abruptly Ms. Patterson returned to singing basic sentences in her high-pitched cheer. "Okay, Ms. Karr-en!" Another teacher was headed down the hall. "We just keep hanging in there, okay!?" We both went back to our classrooms. The next year, Ms. Jones did the same: taught for three weeks, then called it quits.

By November, teachers were calling out "sick" with suspicious regularity. Southwestern never had enough substitutes to cover even the average sick-leave, which meant that when a teacher called out, classrooms sometimes went unsupervised, which meant that they became pockets for hall-walkers to infiltrate and convert into playgrounds for all kinds of crazy. But substitute or not, the kids didn't learn anything on days that their teacher called out, and the kids passed the time playing cards, or sometimes destroying the room. Noelani had been absent once, and she hadn't known the cardinal rule of an educator's sick-day: lock everything up. Everything. Every book, supply; everything you hope to see the morning you return. When she returned, staplers were missing from her desk and posters had been torn off the wall and ripped in half. All her textbooks, which had been stacked along a table, were strewn around the room. Their fresh bindings were cracked. Their edges were worn a few years in one day. The kids apparently had a pillow fight with ten-pound literature books. Days later, we found one splayed open on the roof below her room. The rest of the year, we watched it soak up the seasons—February sleet, March rain, May sun. Its fat, withered pages became the measurement of the year.

Ms. Patterson told us that the vandalism was students' revenge. "If you call out sick, they'll let you have it." She said the students felt abandoned. I thought that sounded too self-congratulatory. My kids couldn't possibly feel "abandoned" by me. They rejoiced whenever a teacher called out. They constantly complained that I didn't give them *enough* free time. Why would they punish their teacher for receiving a whole free period?

One day in my third period, students were brainstorming reasons why Juliet should stay or break up with Romeo. They were writing each reason in a box and listing persuasive details under each reason in each box, but I had just told the whole class that they still had one other activity to complete that day, and two girls—Sandra and Kia—each looked up at me from behind the veil of their bead-tipped braids, and they scoffed. They looked like I'd just asked them to pee in their own shoes.

"Ms. Kirn," Sandra said. Her worksheet was half complete. "You be trying too hard to be a good teacher."

Kia nodded. "All this *work!*" Kia turned her palm up and waved it above her desk like a magician attempting to make *all this work* disappear.

About once a week, I heard the question, "Why don't we ever have a free day?" Other teachers gave free days, my students insisted, a fact I could prove by the number of times I heard the squeaky wheels of the TV/VCR cart as it rolled down the hall. I glanced out my classroom door to watch the electronics pass by, followed by the tired-looking teacher who trudged forward, pushing. Most every teacher seemed to take the liberty of a free day on occasion, some more than others, and it wasn't some educational documentary that they screened but a feature film like *Big Momma's House.* "The kids just love that movie," said Ms. Patterson with a giggle. From time to time, she let them watch it. When she said this to me, I hoped my inner cringing didn't show—because I loved Ms. Patterson but *how could she?*—and I went back to my room where I pressed on with another pedagogical attempt to teach my kids something like *how to identify the basic parts of speech,* which, despite their insistence that they'd reviewed since fifth grade, they still couldn't do. How much easier it would have been, how much happier we all would have felt watching comedian Martin Lawrence don his enormous, red grandma dress and fat suit instead of figuring out how *enormous* and *red* and *fat* qualified nouns, so were adjectives; no, not adverbs; no, not verbs. *Adjectives.*

My kids' constant whining about how much work I gave them often led to conversations about how little work they got in other classes. I was the bad parent; other parents were better. "Mr. Sypher let us listen to our headphones," someone reported. "Ms. Jenkins, she don't even teach. She just sit at her desk. We play cards in that class." "That class off the *hook!*" someone shouted from a few desks away and smiled. But inevitably, as the kids relayed info about other teachers, listing who let students do what and who only taught sometimes and who didn't teach at all, their tones went from appreciative to disparaging. So-and-so never did her job. So-and-so didn't even know the answers to the math problems himself, so how's he gonna teach anything? So-and-so bought drugs in the neighborhood, I swear Ms. Karen, someone see him on the street corner just yesterday, buying drugs.

With each complaint, I realized that Ms. Patterson was right: though the kids bitched and grunted about having too much work to do, and though they kept up this bitching and grunting like it was in their designated job description, they expected teachers to do their own jobs, to keep teaching, to keep giving work, regardless.

Back during my summer training, all the TFA newbies took a tour of a Houston school. In one classroom, the teacher sat at a desk and flipped the pages of a magazine while students erased letters in those yellowy workbook pages that, with each rub of an eraser, lose a layer of paper. I rounded the desk of one boy and peered over his shoulder. His workbook was one third complete and mostly wrong. He put his pencil in his mouth and chewed. He looked up at the ceiling. He looked back down at his recent answer. Then he erased the wrong answer in his workbook and wrote down another wrong answer. He had no idea how to cope with questions that seemed well beneath his grade level. I heard a faint tap-tap against window glass, and when I looked out the window, a moth was banging against the glass, its wings as flimsy as the pages of that workbook, its attempts to break through glass just as futile as this kids' chance at getting his question right. The teacher just sat in the front of the room with a magazine.

But in another room, the students didn't even have workbooks. They sat at their desks with their heads down, or their necks craned toward the object of the teacher's attention: a television that hung near the ceiling. On TV, the camera captured the face of a worried-looking blonde woman, and then it cut to the face of a stern, jaw-popping brunette man, and the two were deeply concerned about a very troubling situation that required eerie music to underscore it. The teacher was enraptured, mouth agape.

When we got back to our school, my advisor, Tamika, broke down. Huge fat tears slipped over her cheekbones and dripped off her face. *How could the teacher watch a soap opera during class? While her summer school kids just sat there? How could she waste an opportunity to teach her kids? It was criminal,* Tamika said. *Criminal.*

I nodded. From that moment on, I'd thought I'd found an easy answer to education's urban-school dilemma. I'd thought I understood why most of America's city kids were performing far below their expected levels: the teachers just didn't care. That's why city kids across the nation faced the vast achievement gap that I always envisioned as a great canyon with only its treacherous footbridge as a way across. Kids were underperforming because their teachers neglected them, I'd thought.

To succeed, I had to care; care really hard; care like my entire identity rested upon the degree of my caring; care like those teachers in movies who threw away all signs of a personal life and called their kids' homes late into the night and planned lessons on the weekends and taught with such creativity that they might have earned artistic awards for their lessons.

In the fall, I'd spent a full week sick. My head was clogged, and my sinuses ached, but I hung over my students' desks and tried to explain sonnets anyway. "Why you even here?" Shiqueena asked by the middle of the week. "If you sick, why don't you take off like the other teachers?"

"Because. We have too much work to do."

Go home, I figured she'd say. *Stop spreading your disease! We need a break from you anyway.* But Shiqueena looked at another girl and said, "At least *some*one here cares about us."

If, as a new trainee-teacher back in Houston, I had been able to flash forward, to time-travel to this moment in Baltimore with Shiqueena, I would have thought: *Damn! I will be triumphant! In Baltimore, I will succeed!* After all, students thought I cared. And caring was what made good teaching, right? Caring would bridge the achievement gap because not caring was its cause.

My assumption proved half accurate at Southwestern—our kids underperformed, and the faculty sometimes neglected them, which meant the faculty was partly at fault for our kids' underperformance. That is, *not caring* partly caused the problem. But *caring* wouldn't easily solve it. What I didn't know at Institute, what I only learned in my first few months, was that you could teach your freaking heart out and still come up short.

I was no pedagogical superstar, but I tried damn hard. While another new teacher on my hallway instructed every minute of every lesson from behind her desk, droning commands about completing lesson 4.6 in a small grammar textbook from 1976, my class and I listened to Aretha Franklin's "Respect"; we bopped our heads to the rhythm and sang along to Franklin's bold, belting wail, and then tried to identify the parts of speech in the lyrics. What part of speech was *Respect*?

And to get students to write more descriptively, I brought in that time-sucking TV/VCR, but only so they could watch five minutes of *What Dreams May Come*, when Robin Williams runs through his deceased wife's painting of lush purple irises and thick green ivy and electric-blue forget-me-knots. We watched just those few minutes and then I asked, *If you were walking through that scene, what would you see? smell? taste? hear? touch? Now write those vivid details down in a paragraph.*

And to make Kurt Vonnegut's "Harrison Bergeron" come to life, I had students assume the disabilities that the story's government imposes on its above-average people. Those kids with excellent handwriting volunteered to tape their thumbs to their index fingers. Those with excellent eye-sight donned silly glasses. They giggled in their newly bestowed bug-eyes and stared back at me.

And after reading Sandra Cisneros' vignette, "Salvador, Late or Early," students served on a mock-panel of concerned community members—Salvador's teacher, Salvador's neighbor, Salvador's counselor—and discussed how best to help this poor, troubled, unkempt little kid. Counselors should visit his house, my kids decided. Teachers should tutor him after school, and neighbors should notify the state of his parents' neglect. My students argued that the community had to *care*.

But after singing along with Aretha, few students knew the answer to the question, *What part of speech is respect?* When I asked, the room went restless. *Remember? We just talked about this during the drill. What's a noun?* Someone looked at the drill and read: A person, place, thing, or idea. *So what is respect?* Nobody knew. And after watching the five-minute scene of Robin Williams slipping through a world of paint, few students' writing came vividly to life. Paragraphs of description were still, to my standards, lifelessly vague and below average. And despite the fact that we'd essentially acted out the plot of Vonnegut's story, nobody left my classroom having a keen sense of his complex social commentary. And even after reading a *vignette* and defining the word *vignette* and using *vignette* in a sentence, no student ever seemed to remember what the hell a vignette was, not on a quiz or otherwise.

In other words, despite my efforts, my students did not make the leaps-and-bounds progress they needed in order to catch up to the rest of the nation. Before coming to Baltimore I'd thought I only needed to want my students' progress badly enough, to try hard enough, to work tirelessly at the job in order to succeed. Unlike the teacher who commanded from behind her desk, I paced back and forth between my students' chairs and nearly leaped between the rows, shouting this word and that word of encouragement as I aimed to do the impossible: put my physical presence beside every student at once, including the ones that were slipping away from me, those snoring or tossing paper balls or slipping headphones over their ears. But I often felt like I was spinning dizzy more than teaching, trying to captivate the whole un-captivated audience, and trying desperately to catch my breath.

To teach at Southwestern was to face a certain degree of failure. Ellen, Brooke, Amy, Noelani, and even veteran teachers all attested to this same experience: You could design a five-week unit of multimodal lesson plans during which you taught your goals through interactive musical activities and kinesthetic activities and tactile activities, and you could then prepare kids for a test on the goals of the unit, and you could administer that test, and still many if not most of your kids could fail. Why? I didn't know. Maybe because of the low attendance rate. Maybe because of the school's and the students' low expectations. My point is this: regardless of all my effort, my *caring*, I could still walk out of the building's doors at the end of a day and feel drained, wondering what difference I'd made. How much easier it would have been to let the drone of the room's air conditioning lull the kids to sleep, and switch the round dial of an old-school television to its *on* position, and watch the dramas of very pretty, well-manicured people who were very far from this world of vandalized desks and crumbling ceilings and graveyard views.

I started to understand why my special education teacher colored all those posters; she wasn't just constructing a fortress against suspicions or bad marks from The State. She was running from the demands of failure. How was she to reach kids like Jimmy Nizbin? She didn't know so she stopped trying. How were the veteran teachers going to raise their city kids to county standards when their kids had been painfully behind grade-level since kindergarten and had been under-fed and under-read-to and only showed up to school sixty percent of the time? Those teachers didn't know and so maybe they stopped trying too. The TV-carting teachers had typically served in Baltimore for decades; maybe they were tired from decades of failing. I saw the poster-making and movie-showing as infuriating laziness, and I still do, but I have a sliver of compassion for a teacher who wanted some quantifiable measure of success and so opted for poster-making. I too wanted some tangible proof of my hard work.

• • •

"This class off the hook!" little Timothy shouted. He brought his feet up under his butt and squatted on the chair so he could get a better look around.

Derek Hayes was rapping in the back, and a few ladies were standing around him, laughing, and Kia was gossiping and braiding someone's hair and howling at jokes, and a group of guys up front were pounding on the desks to some rhythm that didn't match Derek's rap, and every student was jittery, bouncy, loud, like they'd all had sugar shot directly into their bloodstreams, and this was nearly true, as they'd just come from lunch, which for them usually featured little more than corn chips and colas.

From his squatting position, Timothy looked left, then right, all the while beaming proudly at the chaos like he'd somehow commanded it or, at the very least, been specially chosen to exist in its midst. The class had gone ballistic and he was there to see!

I tried to get the group under control. I called out instructions from the head of the class, and one quiet girl, Jessica, strained to hear my words. I shouted; she squinted; it was useless. She and I were at opposite ends of a very long, disastrous tunnel.

"Ee-NOUGH!" The voice that came from my mouth was louder than my ears could take, and I winced at their ringing. "Get QUIET!" I felt my cheeks flush with blood. I kept shouting phrases at the top of my lungs (*stop TALKing, all eyes on ME*) until everyone turned his or head to see the teacher. The crazy, possessed teacher.

I spoke fast. Their attention wouldn't last long. "Look at yourselves! Are any of you doing what I asked?

"Do you even know what you're supposed to be doing?

"I'm standing up here, giving you instructions, and are you listening?

"What do you think I'm here for? Because I like the view?

"I'm not even *from* Baltimore."

They kept quiet. I kept going.

"I'm here for one reason." While I kept shouting, I felt the heat in my cheeks drain and the tightness in my shoulders drop. "I'm here for you." To my ears, it didn't sound inspirational; it sounded pathetic. I had moved my life for kids I wasn't reaching. "I'm here to teach you. And you're here for one reason; you're here to learn. To reach your fullest potential. But it hurts me—it makes me feel ill," I held a clenched fist to my stomach, "when I can't do my job because you act like *this*." I waved a hand around the room. "How can we do our jobs together if you act like *this*?" I paused. They still listened. "I'm just asking you to do your job. Every day. I promise to do mine, to teach you, to help you be all you can be." I'd slipped into Army recruitment rhetoric. "But you have to do yours. You have to come ready to learn."

The class stared back at me, quiet. I'd wasted my breath, I'd thought. But then Derek Hayes, my rapper in the back, brought his hands together and clapped. People near him did the same until a full-on classroom applause moved like a wave to the front of the room. It was the oddest thing: my entire asynchronous group was clapping and cheering. I'd just given a motivational speech. The sarcastic Yankee in me furrowed her brow and the tender part of me smiled sheepishly and these two made friends when I chuckled at the kids' applause.

I asked if they were with me. They nodded and settled into their seats. I repeated the instructions that Jessica had strained to hear, only now my voice was calm and their voices were quiet and the instructions were audible. And my kids followed my steps one by one, looking serene and relieved. *Okay*, I thought. *Now I've got them.*

In a movie, the director might end the scene here. For about five minutes, I conducted an amiable class in which I guided earnest kids through an activity. But the door to the classroom opened. As I turned from my now attentive and obedient third-period group, Ms. Grant, an assistant principal, stormed into the room. My special ed teacher followed her. I hadn't noticed Ms. Nelson's absence. She'd left sometime after Timothy had called us all "off the hook." She might have left during my speech, but she was in and out of the room so often that I hardly paid attention.

"What. Is going on here?" Ms. Grant spoke in a bold, haughty alto.

My special ed teacher looked at me, nodded toward Grant, and said, "I went to get some help."

Some help? *Where was help when the door got lit on fire? Where is help everyday for Jimmy, whom you said you can't teach?* An unruly class was my responsibility, not Ms. Grant's, and any administrator knew it. Ms. Nelson, in her weakness, had sold me out.

Ms. Grant laid into my kids. Without having seen the behavior she was reprimanding, she made sweeping generalizations about how badly they acted, about how ill-prepared they were for school, about what would happen to them if they continued in this way: suspension, expulsion. Grant's was a speech, not about my student's potential, but about their inherent disobedience. The message was not, school is to fulfill your God-given potential. The message was, school is your God to obey. With every word from Grant's, my kids looked more insulted. They *humphed* and crossed their arms and stared at a random spot on the ceiling; or they raised one shoulder, cocked their heads toward it, pushed their lips out, and sneered. In just a few seconds, they became untouchable statues, frozen into moods of disgust.

They didn't deserve her reprimand; they'd shaped up after my first scolding. But if, after shaping up, they were only attacked again, this time by someone who threatened to kick them out of school, then why should they maintain their new work ethic? I mourned the classroom mood that I'd worked hard to acquire. I'd felt I'd bared some piece of my soul to my students and, if even for a few moments, I'd gotten my kids to buy into their education, however broken was myself and the institution that provided that education. Now here was Ms. Grant, assistant principal of that very institution, erasing my motivational I-care-about-your-potential message with an angry, tired diatribe about how terrible my kids were.

• • •

Third period returned to amicably rowdy in the days that followed. On one day, the students wrote poems and read them aloud to the class, and when it was Derek Hayes' turn, he read,

Ms. Kirn, Ms. Kirn,
she teach from the heart.
At the end of the semester,
we'll surely be smart.

On went the rhyming quatrains, praising the glory that was my try-hard self, and when he finished the kids called him a suck-up but most grinned back at me, and I took this as a peace offering.

Still, the encounter with Ms. Grant became an apt symbol for how Southwestern operated. No matter where you went or what you tried to do, you bumped into an unexpected opposition. Enemies manifested in unlikely places. I was getting on Marcus Gordon's case about regular school attendance, meeting his shrugs with reminders about his grade, his dreams, his future, only to have Coach Powell take Marcus's side. *Why does he have an incomplete? Pass the kid. Just pass him. Aren't you smart? Can't you pass him?* I had schemed up a lesson for my slouching, disengaged first period, and this lesson involved extra copies, and Ms. Wallace said, No, I was not allowed to use the copy-machine because it was for administrative purposes only. I had finally gotten my third period to buy into the impor-tance of staying focused, only to have Ms. Grant crush it with her tirade. Maybe this was why failure at Southwestern was so ubiquitous: a person could finally get a little victory with one group only to have it quickly taken away by another. The longer I taught at Southwestern, the more I saw that the storms, the ones Ms. Brown warned us that we'd weather, came not just from the students but from the faculty, the staff, the entire school. Somehow, we all created the mess we taught and learned in.

The opening stanza of Derek's poem rung in my head for months after I'd heard it, especially the second line. *She teach from the heart.* In a place as volatile as Southwestern, where the students, the teachers, the department heads, and the administrators all pushed against one another to form little cyclones that tore through the halls and stairwells and classrooms each day and left debris in their tracks, it didn't seem wise to "teach from the heart." It seemed terribly naïve. One's heart seemed too fragile a thing to plop in between the storms.

• • •

On a day that I first smelled the pungent aroma of pot all through the stairwell, I had a surprise visitor from a kid's father. He'd gotten Domi-nic's report card and he wanted to understand why Dominic was doing so poorly, not just in my class, but in all classes.

Dominic was one of those students who came regularly and sat at the desk and hardly did a thing. He didn't cause trouble. He didn't make progress. He failed quietly.

"I can't understand this," the father said to me.

I braced myself for a talk similar to the one I'd had with Powell. I thought the father might ask me why I couldn't just give his boy a sixty.

But that's not the road we went down. "Dominic came from a private school!" his dad said. "He got all A's! Now he comes *here*," Dominic's dad lifted the palms of his hands up and looked around, "and he gets D's? And F's?"

Dominic, an A-student? I was flabbergasted. I described the Dominic I knew, a boy who fooled around quietly and feigned to do work but never turned in an assignment, never even seemed to care whether he was "passing" or not. As his father listened, his nose moved almost imperceptibly back and forth, left and right. He shook his head ever-so-slightly at the discrepancy between the boy I knew and the son he had.

When I was finished, he turned his head and looked at my doorway. He nodded to it. "It's crazy out there," he said. He'd never seen anything like it before, he said. He looked back at me, incredulous, and asked, "Who can learn in a place like this?"

The words echoed in my mind: *a place like this*. What kind of place had Southwestern displayed to Dominic's dad today? A place where kids smoked pot in the halls? Gambled in the stairwells? Drank Smirnoff Ice? Set doors on fire? I bit my bottom lip. Dominic was once a high-achieving kid at an academically competent private school. Within twelve weeks, he was just another anonymous face, a statistical failure at Southwestern, a kid I'd thought didn't care. Here was proof that Southwestern hadn't always inherited failing students, as some teachers assumed; it had *created* them. This sad cause-and-effect was why newspapers like the *Baltimore Sun* labeled schools like Southwestern "drop-out factories." Like a conveyor belt of assembled parts, the school churns out its drop-out students.

And yet, every now and again, an anomalous, impressive kid like Takira Webb or Davon Green appeared on that conveyer belt. *Who can learn in a place like this?* The question rang in my head. Takira could. Davon could. But as for the majority of our kids, which of the elements were mostly to blame for their failures? The low expectations of the teachers? The students' low expectations of themselves? The chaos in the halls? My conversation with Dominic's dad began a longer one I started to have with myself: what was to blame for our kids' constant failure? Where could I point my finger? At the principal? Ms. Grant? The State? Myself? Like the tenderfoot teacher I was back in Houston when I thought the entire solution to the plight of urban schools was simply *more teacher-effort, more heart, more care*, I was still looking for one answer, one easy solution, so that maybe I could march onward toward my teacher-victory. After we promised to have weekly phone conferences, and after I shook Dominic's father's hand in farewell, I watched him head back through my classroom door. His shoulders hunched forward. He scuffed his shoes across the floor. He headed slowly back into the chaotic hallway.

CHAPTER 7

HAPPY HOUR

On Fridays at five, we—Noelani, Amy, Ellen, Brooke, and I—all sat in the dark, wood-adorned pubs of Baltimore's gentrified neighborhoods—Fells Point, Federal Hill—and drank porters and lagers from pint-glasses, half-believing each sip would coax our minds away from that big school on the hill. But sip after sip brought us right back to Southwestern.

"One of my kids drew a picture of me sucking his dick," Brooke said one happy hour.

By now, our mouths did not gape for nothing. The four of us sat and stared unblinkingly at Brooke.

"Which one?" Amy asked and took a swig.

Brooke drew out the name with a sneer. "*Tray*-von."

Amy nodded. She too taught Travon.

"On his test." Brooke said. "Instead of answering the questions, he draws a picture of *me*! Sucking his *dick*!"

"Well," I said, looking into the round, amber surface of my beer. I did not know Travon. "At least you know Travon is a visual learner."

The four of them burst into laughter. I knew it was in bad taste to laugh at one's own joke, but I couldn't help my lips—they budged into a tiny, one-sided smirk.

Four months ago we would not have laughed at this. Four months ago, my fellow teachers and I would have been appalled by such degradation. And four months ago, we would not have even known the teacher-speak we were mocking—*visual learner, learning modalities, core learning goals*. Since beginning our stints in Baltimore, we'd spent our Saturdays and weeknights with dutiful, earnest "veteran" teachers who taught us these terms in Johns Hopkins graduate courses. Our instructors no longer taught in the city. They believed that the answers they gave us would solve the dilemmas of a school such as ours. We learned, for instance, that kids should anticipate what might come next in a story, that prediction was a healthy habit of an active reader, and that to foster this habit in our students we could give them not just regular rulers so students could slide the straight plastic strip down the page as they read each sentence, but transp*ar*ent rulers so that students' eyes could subconsciously collect information from the lines that lay below the line they were reading. It was ingenious, an important tip in the pedagogy of reading, and we left class knowing that even if we knew where to acquire such rulers, even if we had the funds to purchase a transparent ruler for every kid we ever taught, we would not buy them. Not tonight, or the next night, or the next. Because our minds were preoccupied with other things, with unusual, perplexing instances we hadn't envisioned back in September, ones that the textbooks we carried to our night-classes did not mention, e.g. there was not a-one classroom management tip on how to handle a student who draws a picture of his teacher sucking on a student's genitalia.

We laughed because by now we knew that our administration would do nothing about Brooke's kid's infraction, that to "write it up" on the official "write-up" form and send that form to the main office would be like flushing fifteen precious minutes down the drain of a seat-cracked, cigarette stained Southwestern toilet. We knew this because we'd tried it; the forms were like those lone lost socks at laundry mats, and we saw neither them nor signs of them again. We assumed that, because the administration ignored these relatively minor challenges to our authority, it had bigger fish it sometimes fried. We did not know exactly what our administration fried, but the principal and assistant principal made it clear, with the ever-growing bags beneath their eyes, with the way they walked down the hallway like they were trudging through foot-deep mud, that they were tired. Very very tired.

And so were we. So like the kid who tossed her book-bag into the school's easily breakable ceiling tiles because it was a way she could exert some force in the fortress that was our high school, we met problems such as ours by tossing at them our teacher-talk, a language that would hardly solve what, along with our one-hundred papers to grade, we carried home each weekend.

Also, we laughed because it was true: Travon was most likely a visual learner.

By the time the city's leaves had fallen and the ground had frozen and the light-gray cloak of the winter sky had muted the sun, we'd learned that our school had, as Brooke once said, "a million things wrong with it," and that nobody—not the administration, not The State, not the Johns Hopkins experts, not even the policy-makers who wrote this new thing we'd studied in class, this proposed "No Child Left Behind" thing—nobody had the solutions. According to the several page document ensuring that no child would be left in the ambiguous playground of "behind," schools such as ours would be penalized when our kids fell short on state standards, and being that our kids were typically three grade levels behind, they *would* fall short on state standards, and the penalty for leaving children behind was losing federal funding for those very kids that were officially deemed "behind." It was asinine, absurd, a scene from a Beckett play. We highlighted passages of the policy in class and made raging marks in the margins and talked about how the policy would adversely affect our schools, our classes, our kids, and we wrote letters to politicians encouraging its withdrawal, or its veto, or whatever word the policy needed for its destruction, and we went home at nine P.M. to sleep, feeling that our voices were useless, that raging wouldn't help, that no suit-wearing D.C. politician knew or cared to know about the people in our crumbling school on the hill beside the cemetery.

So in the face of constant failure, what my fellow Southwestern teachers and I learned to adopt was not just humility, but an indifference to and a willingness to make light of what outsiders might consider alarming. We were hyper-desensitized.

And sometimes we were angry. It wasn't just a vibe among us Southwestern teachers. TFA gathered its Baltimore teachers together for monthly professional development meetings, and you could feel the collective shift in the room. No longer were we the cheering, energetic do-gooders we'd been back in Houston. We were jaded. Battered and bruised and sufficiently hazed, we now understood why Wendy Kopp had said of our first day applause, "I love this. This is when you're still thanking me instead of *blam*ing me!"

Now we checked our wrists a lot during the two-hour TFA meetings, which sometimes involved inspirational talks, and sometimes involved content-specific "break-out sessions," and often involved a lot of necessary paperwork to process our Johns Hopkins loans, but which rarely escaped our complaints. Among the cafeteria tables, I heard teachers mumble beneath their breaths that TFA wasn't making good use of their time. To be fair, I often thought TFA couldn't have won our approval regardless of what it offered. Our jobs were too hard, our time was too short, our patience too thin. We were tapped. We didn't complain because the sessions weren't on some level valuable—they were—but because we were all too strapped for downtime. Sleep seemed more vital. A precious hour at the gym or in front of the television seemed more vital. But another hour about learning strategies? Our overburdened brains were too full. After a full day at the kinds of schools we taught at, and with another full day ahead of us tomorrow, we couldn't handle any more "professional development."

Normally we didn't see our founder after Institute, so any blame a TFA teacher might have felt toward Wendy Kopp went unheard. But one evening Ms. Kopp herself came to a coffee shop in Baltimore to promote her new book, *One Day*, and when she outlined her plan to expand TFA into ever more regions, one teacher became irate. Her hand shot up among the tables, and she demanded to know why TFA didn't put its increased funds into helping its existing corps members, who were floundering, she said, rather than spreading funds thinly across increasing numbers. I was shocked by this teacher's response—I'd always believed she was doing fairly well at her school. Kopp defended her plan.

Were we floundering? Yes, that's probably the best word for us. Noelani told me that she was the only one of her roommates who didn't cry at the end of each day. My roommates weren't fairing much better. "I hate it, I hate my job," one of them said to my surprise. "I hate my kids." She was matter-of-fact about it, and there was no changing her mind. As soon as she came home from work, she shed her slacks and button-ups for athletic gear and left the house with a duffel bag. Another roommate was furious at TFA for dropping her into a school all by herself, with no other corps members for support. When she came home, she headed straight for her room, lay on her bed, and laughed at the television for comic relief. I liked her. But she was planning on leaving at the end of the year. The last of my roommates tried to make the best of her middle school gig, but with six classes of forty middle school kids, she was drowning in paperwork and daily fending off paper ball fights. Her sunny demeanor I'd seen when we'd met in Houston was now eclipsed by cynicism.

I was better off, it seemed. High school students proved far easier to handle than middle schoolers, a fact I'd figured out after hearing my roomates' horror stories. To boot, my students had written a poem about me and Takira Webb was a crown jewel in my day. Also, I tried to maintain my humor. "Life is Funny!" read a handwritten sign on the pencil box in my desk. I'd taped the saying beside a picture of nuns hula-hooping. "Why you write that?" a student once asked me. "Because. Life *is* funny." When Noelani and I drove together, I tried to make her laugh by rewriting Stevie Wonder's hit, "Heaven Help Us All." Instead of Wonder's lyrics, I sang, "Heaven help the kid who can't spell the word 'street,' heaven help the teacher who can't keep that kid in his seat. . . . Heaven help the kid who's twelve years younger than his mom, heaven help Ms. Brown, who can't stay off the intercom. . . ."

• • •

But when humor didn't work, and anger got me nowhere, I sometimes accidentally adopted obliviousness.

"Ms. Kuhn," Calvin Young once said to me with a slow shake of his head. "You're awareness is, like, forty percent."

Calvin had just caught me in a recurring moment: a bunch of kids had suddenly stopped what they were doing to glance up at me—their mouths shaped into little O's, their eyebrows raised. "Oooh," they said and waited for me to respond, to what I didn't know. I'd missed some foul play, some crude slang, some *thing* that I was meant to penalize. But I couldn't penalize what I hadn't seen or heard. I thanked Calvin Young for his assessment, and told him that his math teacher (a.k.a. my happy-hour pal, Ellen), would be proud of his use of percentages. Calvin's wide lips wrapped around the lower half of his face, and he beamed in pride.

"I'm passing Algebra," he said, and I nodded and assured him that I believed him.

I also didn't much pay attention, for instance, to the violent incidents that occurred beyond the walls of my classroom, between the walls of others' classrooms, like the fact that some kid threw a chair at that tired, young, light-skinned science teacher down the hall. As for Ms. Patterson's insistence that we were not safe in our rooms, I just shrugged. "One of these kids goes ballistic," Ms. Patterson said, "and we're in deep trouble. There isn't anybody around here to help us." This fact was easily proved any time a teacher hit that red emergency call button on the wall of his or her classroom—the secretary answered twenty minutes later, if at all. When she stayed late to grade, Ms. Patterson checked with Ms. Gueye or me beforehand. Were any of us going to be around? Nobody should walk out of this building alone, she warned. Not now that it was dark by five. But unless Ms. Patterson was around, I left the building alone anyway.

"Those metal detectors they be using," Calvin Young once said. "They don't work, Ms. Kuhn. People be bringing guns into this school. Knives. Everything." He said this without the characteristic drama that exaggerating kids would use to list the number of times they'd been arrested or shot at, and because he was so dead-pan, so tired even in his listing of weapons, I believed him. He'd seen guns in the school. The kids around him nodded in agreement. They looked up at me, but they didn't expect me to make the weapons disappear.

Here's another small but relevant instance of the obliviousness I'd adopted: by the end of the semester, I was singing back to Letisha's *border pappa* song. She squinted and pressed her brows together but her lips turned up at the corners. "Why you sing that, Ms. Karen?"

"I like it," I said, and bounced to the beat in my head.

I had finally heard her favorite hit—"Cross the Border," by Phillies Most Wanted—on MTV. The chorus was catchy, and a Spanish guitar played the melody, and some kind of island-style percussion kept a light beat that made me want to bop my head and shimmy around. I sometimes did little jigs now in front of first period, where Dennis had by now ceased all tickling and butt-touching and actually completed the requisite sixty-percent of his work, and Jimmy, from time to time, even produced a sentence or two. In the song, a male voice called a female voice "momma" and asked if she'd run across the border for him; the female voice called the male voice "poppa" and told him yes, she'd run across the border for him. It was catchy. What a cute song, I'd thought. I nodded my head to the beat and thought of Letisha and smiled at her quirky taste, and I did all this in part because I didn't realize that "Poppa," a.k.a. some bossy misogynist slacker, was asking "Mamma," a.k.a. his submissive and eager-to-please pseudo-girlfriend, to go fetch him some drugs from Mexico and smuggle them back into the country. Cuz he needs 'em. And he needs 'em tonight. Who knew a light-hearted, wispy urban romp through Latin rhythm could be void of moral fiber? The song's message, coupled with my oblivious dancing, probably explained Letisha's wrinkled brow and squinting eyes during my solo tribute.

"You crazy," Letisha said as I bounced my every step around the room, whisper-singing the lyrics.

But here's the thing: she smiled back. Letisha, who'd once hated me, now had just a pinky-toe on my side. Obliviousness seemed to help me out. Letting things go was one successful coping mechanism I'd found. Laughing at Brooke's kids' artwork released some kind of chemical that I needed in order to go back into work on Monday.

• • •

By the end of my first semester, I was doing alright. My kids and I had found a mediocre equilibrium between crazy classroom and sane one, a fair compromise between learning and under-achieving. I planned lessons every day, and my kids sort of met me a quarter of the way, and I tried to swallow that this could be called "passing." I'd managed to make my students read every single word of Shakespeare's *Romeo and Juliet* and managed, somehow, and despite the archaic language, to get them hooked into the story. They translated Shakespeare-speak into west-Baltimore dialect; they acted out scenes of Mercutio and Tybalt fencing; they drew every major event, including the moment Juliet sips her sleeping potion, and they collaboratively arranged these pictures into chronological order so that the metal chalk rack beneath the board was one long, tragic graphic novel. Watching them argue about the fundamentals of the canonized classic made me smile.

"No, no," Derek Hayes protested and leapt from his seat. "Romeo kill Tybalt *after* he get married." He grabbed the illustration of one tights-wearing man stabbing another tights-wearing man. He moved a few other illustrations down like cars in a toy train, then placed the illustration in a new spot.

"Oh, right, right," said another kid.

My students wrote persuasive mini-essays against gang violence, and they found Baz Lurhmann's version of the play legitimately "hard," and for these facts alone, I considered myself a bona fide English teacher.

One afternoon, the social studies head, Mr. Barnes—who normally wore his face in a stern grimace meant to tell both kids and teachers, *no monkey business*—popped his head into my classroom. His face lifted into an unusually full, bright white smile. Barnes, smiling? He said, "I hear you're an excellent teacher!"

When my shoulders fell back a little and my chin lifted and whatever furrows in my brow lightened, I realized I hadn't been praised for my job all semester.

"Who'd you hear that from?" I asked immediately, and then regretted my lack of chill suavity before stoic, always cool Barnes. But I had to know: who were my teacherly admirers? Wallace? The English Mother Hens? The principal? And how many details could I draw out of Barnes to retain this brief high?

But this was Barnes I was talking to. His smile dropped, and he turned his six-foot-something bulky frame away from my door. But just before he resumed his grimace he said, like the answer was a minor chore, "Just from around."

I'd been told I wouldn't last or that people had bets on whether I'd last. I'd been told I needed to write my objectives differently and have those test scores in my grade book and those standards on my lesson plans. So this new comment was like reaching the zenith of some distant, treacherous mountain. By now, I'd held my own for nearly a semester, which won the hard-earned, scrutinizing respect from fellow teachers. And I'd toughened up enough to crack jokes about infractions that would have deterred me back in June, when I signed those TFA papers and promised two years. *A kid drew* what?! Now it was all sort of old-hat. I could handle it, I thought. I thought I could handle pretty much anything.

At the end of each day, I wandered the classroom and cleaned up the little reminders of what I *hadn't* completely handled. I picked up the paper balls that were crumpled under chairs and beside the wastebasket, into which kids had, despite my protests, tried and failed to make b-ball points with their worksheets. Papers that had too many mistakes—that required too much erasing—became makeshift basketballs. The kids' had figured, *Fuck it, chuck it. Do over.* Then they'd sat at a desk with a new, blank page in front of them and wiggled around in their chairs.

At the end of the day, I also swiped the blank pages from the desks, the ones that some students had abandoned. I fixed the symptoms of my kids' wiggling too: I pressed desks together so they neatly met one another in communal groups of four, so that the four corners made perfect, perpendicular lines, tidy seams of desk-tops. It was my own *do over*. I made the desks straight. I made the day retrospectively perfect.

One day had been especially imperfect. That day I was too busy asking my students to name four ways a fictional character comes to life. I'd asked my kids to list *dialogue, appearance, internal thoughts, actions*, reminding them that while we don't have access to others' internal thoughts in real life, we do when we read fiction, because the writers let us know what's going on inside the heads of the characters. On this day, I did not know what was going on inside the heads of Serena Ryan or Angelique Bell, who sat in a group together. All of the sudden, their desks split from a neat, four-cornered arrangement to a wide rift. The girls stood up from their chairs. The metal legs scraped across the floor. I heard the *oooh* and *oh snap* of the kids nearby, who turned their heads to watch or, feeding off the sudden burst of energy, jumped from their chairs, too. And there was Serena, tiny, wiry, dark-skinned Serena with the corn-rowed hair. She was flaring at the nostrils. And there was Angelique, soft, curvy, light-skinned Angelique with the chin-length spiral extensions. She was shouting *bitch* and *mother-fuckin'* something. I rushed to their cluster of desks. When their arms flew at each other, I stepped in. Because they were girls. Because Serena was just barely pubescent. Because Angelique was usually kind. Because they were each a few inches shorter than I, at least twenty pounds lighter than I, and because I figured I could handle this; I could keep them, I thought, from their brute force, which couldn't be so brutish, I thought, given their sizes. I stepped in, literally, between their bodies that wanted, with every inch that they had, to maim each other. To hurt. To beat and bruise. To *bang*, as the kids said. *Betty banged Bobby*, wrote Letisha one day when I asked for an alliteration. Or was it *Bobby banged Betty*? I stood in the center of Serena banging Angelique banging whatever else was stupid enough to stand in the center. Me. A body pushed me left, an arm shoved me right, and as quickly as I'd stepped in, I stepped out.

Angelique, for all her prettiness—her full, pink-lipped smiles and her almond-shaped eyes that plainly batted at the boys—Angelique shoved Serena against a table, straddled her, and pushed her neck into the ground. Serena was smaller, but fierce and fast. She pulled at Angelique's spiral twisted extensions. She clawed at Angelique's face. There was, it seemed, no technique to their fighting. They were a wrestling ball of claws and whacks and pummels. What they lacked in modus operandi, though, they more than made up for in spirit and force. I felt both when I'd stepped foolishly into their fight. And over what? A bottle of perfume oil, I'd later learned. To put on your neck. To dab in your hair. To make you smell like a queen.

How did it end? I don't remember who came in the room—the school police? Mr. Owens? The tired, light-skinned, thirtysomething science teacher at the end of the hall? How did anybody know? When, weeks ago, a drunken gang of young men rolled into my room with a bottle of liquor, no one had showed. *'Sup, Teach*, one of the men had said. They were all stumbling. They all reeked of alcohol. They wore ski caps. I said, *Please Leave*! They did not leave. The tallest man drank from the bottle; a swish of liquid funneled down the bottleneck and into his mouth. They were four staggering towers at the front of my room, each well past his high school years, each having a trip at the top of Font Hill, and if they had a bottle of liquor, I reasoned, they could have anything else. A knife. A gun. My kids just sat there, mouths hanging slightly open. I pressed the red call button repeatedly beside the front chalkboard. I ran outside my room and scanned the unusually silent hallway for help. Nobody answered. Nobody showed. After a minute, the men stumbled out, as willfully as they'd entered.

But somehow, and not long into the two-girl brawl, two men yanked Serena and Angelique from each other. I don't remember who. Within seconds, each man held a struggling girl in a back arm lock. The girls kicked and strained and pulled their torsos away from the men like sails, but they couldn't break the arm locks. They finally relaxed into the grips. They panted and stared at each other. Angelique's normally perfect hair was a newly teased nest of frizz. The neck of Serena's T-shirt had been yanked down, and the shirt now looked several sizes larger than before. They were taken away to the main office. The girls were suspended from school. I wouldn't see them for the standard three to ten days.

At the end of that day, like any other, I straightened the desks. I threw away abandoned worksheets that remained flat on desks or had been crumbled and thrown somewhere. I scanned the floor for anything else I could straighten. Anything else I could toss into the industrial green waste can. Any other way I could erase the day.

I found one ropey, stiff hair extension lying on the grimy floor. It was a black snake of coarse wires in my hand. I chucked it into the trash bin.

But Serena's perfume oil—I didn't throw it out. I stuck it in my desk drawer. I didn't know why. Maybe because it seemed a shame to chuck something so precious, something that had made two girls tear at each other. Before I closed the drawer, I picked the bottle up again and unscrewed the small white cap, thinking the aroma would amaze me. But the sour musk made me scowl.

"It's not your fault, Kirn," said a man's voice. Mr. Owens stood at my doorway wearing his winter coat, readying to leave the building.

"I know," I said, lying.

Fights broke out daily at Southwestern. It wasn't my fault. But I'd believed I'd created a classroom that was impervious to them. Ours was a *positive learning environment*, I'd thought. I'd *facilitated a classroom of success*. This was more teacher-speak I'd learned from JHU and TFA. I was such a *facilitator of collaborative learning*, I'd thought, that if a fight ever descended upon my classroom, I would eradicate it before it took root. But I'd stepped out of Serena and Angelique's brawl, and I'd done it as fast as I'd stepped in. I was haunted by both choices. The stepping in captured my foolishness. The stepping out, my cowardice—or at the very least, my ineptitude.

If I had been someone else, could I have kept my girls from beating on each other? If I'd been a broad-shouldered man with a deep voice and a low, solid, steady center of gravity? The kind who, when he walks, resembles a human wall moving down a street?

If I'd been from another place, from around my kids' way? If I hadn't grown up in a remote suburb of Philly where the two-garage, three- and four-bedroom houses were twenty feet apart and the neighbors worried about the greenness of their yards—*were they green enough?*—and the yellow buses stopped kindly at corners to take us to school where hardly any fights broke out but once a year, and not over a vial of perfume oil. Over what, I don't know. I'd never seen one of those fights either.

I'd never seen a fight.

If I had ever seen grown people fight on the west Baltimore corners, which my students reported with nonchalance, would I have known what to expect and how to stop a brawl? Would I have caught the crack in the desk arrangements, in the girls' relationship, before it split our room in half?

I stepped in and believed I could save them.

The sentence sounded remarkably like my entire endeavor at Southwestern. It was winter. I was tired.

Whenever I opened my desk drawer, I saw the small brown vial of perfume oil roll down the metal and tap the drawer's wall, and in those moments, the perfume was like a talisman I would never use. It was a reminder that, though I taught in west Baltimore, I didn't understand west Baltimore. The things my kids found important, I didn't comprehend. The ways they could destroy themselves, I didn't anticipate. And I couldn't necessarily stop them. The vial was a sign of my incapability, and of my wish that the longer I kept it, the more capable I'd become. The longer I hung onto it, the more what happened between Serena and Angelique would make sense to me, and so wouldn't happen again. But knowing the perfume would stink up my desk, I never unscrewed that cap.

CHAPTER 8

DO OVER

Fuck it, chuck it, do it over. Southwestern High School's academic schedule echoed the sentiment in my students' crumpled paper-balls of frustrated work. In January, teachers got all new classes; kids got all new teachers. Goodbye rowdy third period with loquacious hair-braiding Kia and free-style rapping Derek. Goodbye lethargic first period; goodbye *border-poppa*-loving Letisha, whom I grew to appreciate, and goodbye can't-keep-his-hands-to-hisself Dennis, who indeed kept his hands off me after that single butt-touch. Hello new semester; hello fresh start. First-year teachers from other schools were envious of our ability to wipe the board completely clean.

Most of the first day of the second semester went as expected: classes of kids were reserved, mute, albeit only to size up their strange new teacher. But as soon as my fourth and final period arrived, I knew I was meeting a new breed of difficulty.

"'Sup, Teach," said a tall, skinny kid who jutted his chin toward me in a reverse-nod. He said "Teach" like the title was in quotes. *What's up, person who's supposed to be my teacher? What's up, woman who thinks she can make me sit in a chair?* He sat on top of a desk in the back of the room and stared at me straight on.

In walked a short kid made shorter-looking by a T-shirt that reached his calves. His hair was in pigtails, and he had a skipping way about his walk.

The tall kid hopped off the desk. "Yo! Jerome. You in this class?" They smacked hands and grinned and then laughed.

A Regina King look-a-like appeared at the door. She was taller than most of the girls I taught last semester, and her hair was done up in braids that sprouted from her head like a fountain. She leaned against the frame of the doorway, stuck her hand on her hip, pressed her lips out, and squinted one eye at me. When she spotted the boys, she dropped her hand and shrieked. "Boy, you *still* in English one?" She came into the room. "Dang, this class gonna be off the hook!"

When a tall teenager with jaw-length twists and broad shoulders walked

109

in, his presence was more fodder for the "off-hook-edness" of this fourth period. He looked to be nineteen. The others whooped at his entry—"Yeah, Cuz! *You* in this class?"—but he kept his eyes low and chill. His mouth faintly smirked.

When two other guys walked in, both looking at least seventeen, the group responded the same. *Yeah, Cuz! 'Sup. This class gonna be off the hook!*

The late bell rang. Though a few kids sat in the front, in the rows I'd neatly arranged, six grown-looking kids gathered in the back of the room where they shouted, howled, *fucked this* and *that*, and showed no signs that they'd comply with any such rules as sitting. I held my roster and a stack of papers that explained such rules, and small rushes of adrenaline zipped up and down my arms. This was my new semester? This was my board wiped clean? When I called out again, my voice was meeker than I meant for it to sound, and it got lost in the noise. *Show no fear*, I thought.

Show no fear—a classic teacher mantra. It seems problematic that the tips for professionals who deal with children are similar to tips for people who deal with wildlife. Regardless, any teacher knows that to show fear in front of kids is to surrender authority, is to consent to a power that students have but don't always know they have. A small, light-skinned kid who was sitting primly in the front glanced up at me. His wide eyes and turned-down mouth and arched, puppyish eyebrows told me he was scared, and not just of the kids in the back but of my possible inability to contain them. His thin arms poking from his white T-shirt made him look like he could still be in middle school.

"Everyone! Take a Seat!" I said in the most masculine voice I could find.

The tall skinny guy reverse-nodded again with his chin, and the one with the jaw-length twists turned a chair around and straddled it. The rest followed suit. They were a line-up in the back row. It was a face-off. They looked like they could charge.

Point number one on the lesson plan: Take attendance. I ran through the roster of twenty-some names, but only ten kids actually raised their hands, and all of them sat near the front. I had a bunch of kids in my room who supposedly weren't on my roster, and a bunch of names who supposedly weren't in the room. The six in the back sat smugly.

"What're your names?"

There was a long pause.

"If you're not on this roster, you can't be in here." Perhaps they'd chosen room 3536 at random from the smorgasbord of classroom options. Perhaps their presence had been a ploy to spend at least ten minutes of goof-off time before the teacher in charge made them leave. I was hoping this: maybe they belonged in someone else's room.

"Tell me your name," I said to the short kid with the pigtails.

"His name Shortie," said the tall kid to the short one.

"His name Cuz," said the short kid to the tall one.

They both laughed. This was no help. At Southwestern, every kid was Shortie, and every kid was Cuz. I looked down at my list again, saw mostly male names, and picked one of the only female names left.

"Are you Yolanda Perry?" I asked the Regina King look-a-like.

She drew her chin into her neck, frowned, and made the *pssh* sound. "*Yolan*da?" she said with disgust. "I'm *Bubbles*!" She pushed her lips out again and folded her arms across her chest. There was no "Bubbles" on my roster.

It's funny the power of a name. Without names, I couldn't employ my disciplinary system, which still involved writing names on the board. Without names, I couldn't take attendance, couldn't find out who was in my room, so couldn't move to point number two on the lesson plan: discussing classroom rules. *This* is how you behave in a class. *These* are the behaviors that are acceptable and not acceptable. Without names, I couldn't meet the kids who sat before me, couldn't know them, couldn't teach them. Offering their identities meant they were consenting to the arrangement that the school had for us, where I was not just the sarcastically referred-to "Teach," but their teacher, the person to whom they entrusted ninety minutes of their weekdays. My new fourth period was vetoing this arrangement. I'd thought I'd seen the worst of noncompliance at Southwestern, but no. Every instance in which a child freely offered his or her name was a gift for which I'd never known to be grateful.

One kid started pounding on a desk. He had short hair, dark skin, and his eyes were shrouded in dark circles. "Who are you?"

He tilted his face toward the ceiling and shouted, "I wanna smoke two BIG BLUNTS right now!"

The others cracked up.

Who was he: he was his longing for two big blunts. And who was I: I was my longing for my old batch of kids. I was my longing for anyone to help, but even Ms. Nelson wouldn't be in my class this semester, and that small kid at the front still stared at me, his eyebrows like little rainbow-arcs, in earnest belief that I might exert some suddenly believable authority.

We didn't make it through much of my lesson that day. Attendance took thirty minutes and was an all-out war. I somehow managed to get each of their names, though I can't for the life of me recall how, mostly because their instant belligerence made me flustered and spun me dizzy. I was their enemy, that much was clear, and they made the rest of the class my private, sixty-minute hell. The students were aggressive, angry, and lewd. They talked over me. They talked *about* me. They insulted me, they cursed at me. They would not let me teach my lesson. Of course, from time to time, individual kids had done all those things, but never on the first day, and never in such frightening solidarity. These kids in the back were bigger than my usual ninth graders. They all had a "been-here, done-this" attitude that led me to conclude, rightfully, that they had all failed ninth grade English at least once. In some cases, twice. The fact that they brought no pens or pencils or notebooks indicated that they were ready to fail again.

When the bell rang, I stared out the window and watched all of Southwestern's kids spread across the field, down the hill, back into Baltimore's streets. Tomorrow would bring these same kids back up the hill. The thought of tolerating my new fourth period for a full semester made me do the thing a teacher should never do, the thing I'd started to believe The Terrordome wouldn't lead me to do. I cried in school. My view of the hill and the cemetery, normally blurry through yellowish window-glass, got even blurrier through my taboo tears.

"Ms. Kirn?" A high-pitched boy's voice called me.

With a hand under each eye, I wiped both cheeks. I turned from the window. I couldn't muster a smile.

It was the small, fearful kid who sat up front. "Left my hoodie," he said cheerfully, and picked his black zip-up sweatshirt off a chair. "See you tomorrow!" He smiled.

When I forced a smile back, I felt my wet lower eyelashes on my cheeks and I wondered if he could tell. That I'd been broken by his classmates. That I was wondering, in that instant when he reentered my room, if I'd be able to last the full year.

• • •

"Throw one of them out," Ms. Gueye told me. "I had to do that once. If a student doesn't prove he's there to learn, I throw him out."

But isn't that unfair? Weren't we trying to leave *no* child behind?

Ms. Gueye shook her head at my naiveté. "What's unfair is making the rest of the class pay for one or two intolerable kids. Sometimes you have to make a statement. That class is going to run all over you if you don't."

The next day, when Mr. Two Big Blunts, a.k.a. Tremaine, walked back into my room, those dark circles still shrouding his eyes like halo-negatives, I said, "You." I put my palm out like a crossing guard. "You cannot enter my room."

"What?!"

"Not until I see a parent."

He hollered my verdict to the others, some of whom were idling outside the door. "She say I can't come in yo!"

Others were making their slow way to the back of the class.

He looked back at me. "How you gonna do that?"

I repeated Ms. Gueye's stern policy about readiness to learn.

"Man, fuck this," he said, and he kicked a chair out of his way. It hit the wall. "Fuck this, fuck y'all."

Out went the collateral damage for Operation Recover-Fourth-Period. When Bubbles and Brandon (the tall thin kid) and Jerome (the short bouncy kid with the pigtails) and Damon (the bulky near-adult with the chin-length twists) all entered, I stopped each of them at the door. I told them they were next unless they signed a contract. I made them sit. I slapped forms onto the desktops in front of them. The forms made the kids promise they'd change their behavior: *I vow to come to class prepared; I vow to respect my teacher and classmates; I vow to do this and I vow to do that. And if I break any vows, these are the consequences. Sign and date here. Return the contract to your teacher.*

"What's *this*?" Brandon said.

"This some trifling shit," said Yolanda.

I pointed out the vow to use no profanity. Yolanda made the *pssh* sound and folded her arms across her chest again. But she didn't open her mouth again. Damon got up and left the room. Yolanda and Jerome and Brandon signed the forms.

Managing the class that day felt similar to potters' descriptions of throwing a vase or a bowl. Constant pressure. Exhaustive concentration. Steady strength, with a hint of artful yielding. Except that making a vase sounds fun, and managing these kids was not. Still, I got through a lesson plan. They were pissy though comparatively quiet.

Mr. Two Big Blunts never came back to class, nor did his nearly grown-man of a friend, Damon, the one with the chin-length twists and the very broad shoulders. I never saw either of them again. This year that I taught, sixty-one percent of African American boys in Baltimore public schools would not receive high school diplomas.

But here's the truth: their absence made my job that much easier, a thought I bemoaned as a TFA teacher. Wasn't I meant to work for "*all* children"? Weren't "all children in this nation" supposed to have "an excellent education"? But in the pace of a new semester, with kids like Yolanda and Jerome and Brandon now my daily company, and with late-day planning and night-grading and new weekend classes, I didn't dwell on Tremaine, on Damon. Like a cast crumbling around me, my brittle idealism was breaking, and from under it was slowly emerging a teacher in the flesh—flawed, worn, and real. Two days after little Kenneth Peters caught me crying at the end of the day, I caught him hanging out on a stoop in west Baltimore. In front of a row home that was sandwiched between houses of boarded-up windows and doors, Kenneth sat with a friend. I was passing through in my car, heading home. It was an interesting test for a kid: sees his teacher outside of school so what does he do? Play it cool? Ignore her? Crack a joke?

I waved to Kenneth on my way by. I expected him to, at most, nod back. But when I passed him, I heard an emphatic cry. "My *teeee*cher," shouted Kenneth Peters, who had leapt off the stoop. Through the rearview mirror, I saw him running after me in the center of the street, arms flailing. I laughed and waved again. He waved and ran and waved, smiling. When the distance between my car and him got too far, he stopped, mid-street, and turned back. To his friend, who'd remained seated on the stoop, Kenneth said, "That's my *teeee*cher!"

Indeed, I thought. *I am.*

• • •

As the weeks of the semester wore on, my fourth-period kids inevitably made themselves known to me. They went from belligerent to a combination of belligerent and quirky. Yolanda blurted protests in the middle of class—*I can't be doing this, Ms. Karen. Ms. Karen, this some trifling work you make up.* But she was all bark. She rarely moved from her seat. She just sat with her shiny, curly up-do and smacked her mouth. I learned that she was secretly putty in my hands when a curse slipped from her loud mouth one day and she immediately apologized. "Sorry, Ms. Karen!" Then she played a game to see how long she could lengthen my name. "Ms. Karrrrrrren!" Once her tongue made the finale *en*-sound, she smiled and clucked her tongue and batted her eyes. I couldn't help but laugh. All her sirening seemed to be mostly for her own amusement. Perhaps because I was the rare co-female in the room, she grew to like me. When she spotted me in the hall, she shrieked and drew out my name in high-pitched squeals—*Ms. Karrrrren!*—just as she did with members of her girl crew.

Brandon, who'd recently been kicked out of Mount Saint Joseph's private school just a mile and a half up the road, was on the verge of becoming a Tremaine or a Damon. He had the skinny limbs and narrow rib-cage of a kid, but the height and arm-span and faint chin hair of a man, and his body mirrored what his personality faced: a suspension between child and adult, and an unmade decision about what kind of adult he'd be. Whenever he walked into the room, I tried to read in his eyes how the day would turn out for him, as some days he carried that hard, cold edge of indifference. But on other days, Brandon was willing to learn. He raised his hand when I asked a question that required critical thinking. Brandon was a Takira Webb: he reveled in the chance to analyze this or that. But on other days, his minor offenses—cursing, shouting something offensive, telling his worksheet to fuck itself, tossing it into the trash—these accrued quickly, and he and I didn't last longer than twenty minutes together. I still tried to stick to my name-on-board-and-checks-beside-it method, but at a certain point, whether Brandon had the official two checks or not, I said something like, "Okay, Brandon, that's it for the day," which meant that I would escort Brandon to Ms. Patterson's room. Brandon, who carried only a bent notebook to class, would calmly ask, "That's it?," and when I'd nod, he'd do the business of shoving that notebook into his back pocket and we'd exit the room together. Then he'd head for the stairwell, which was left, instead of Ms. Patterson's room, which was right.

Next among the crew was Timmy, who had the features and the loud, drawn-out voice of comedian Tracy Morgan. Timmy conveyed potential for real academic rigor, if only because he sat in his seat and sometimes ignored the back-and-forth banter and completed his work in record speed. But then he skipped out early when I wasn't looking. At around three-o-clock, I sometimes turned from the desk of one student only to find Timmy's seat vacant.

And then there was the debacle over his hat. A cherry red baseball cap. One day, while Timmy read a story along with the class, I wandered the aisles, snuck behind him, grabbed the backwards-facing bill and slid his red baseball cap right off. It was against school policy to wear hats, and in the past, this tactic of mine had worked fine. Normally a student looked up from his worksheet, scowled, and then returned to work.

"Hey! My HAT!" Timmy sprung out of his seat.

I opened the closet door. "You'll get it back at the end of class," I said, resting the hat on the top shelf.

At Southwestern, hats meant something more than head-coverings. Hats were a territory over which students and faculty regularly fought. I hated participating in the ongoing battle, in part because some students refused to comply with a hatless existence, and a fight over a head covering seemed petty in the face of the vast troubles in west Baltimore. But I'd learned my lesson early: an assistant principal once passed my room only to spot a students' offense, which thus became my offense. "Ms. Kirn, why is that child wearing his hat?" I told Ms. Grant that the child refused to remove his hat. Ms. Grant said to the kid, "Remove that hat, son," at which time the kid removed the hat, Ms. Grant walked away, and when she was well out of sight, my student smugly slid his hat back on his head. To avoid looking useless in front of students and administrators alike, I regained, if bogusly, my vigor for the hat-removing movement.

"That's my HAT!" Timmy shouted and charged the closet.

The hook of my lock was sliding through the metal handles of the wood closet door. I snapped the lock shut just before Timmy could grab at the handles. The timing was so perfect, so close, that I saw it play in slow motion. Pleased with my victory—and neglecting to remember that any sense of "victory" meant I had somehow entered a power struggle—I stepped away from the closet, thinking that Timmy would too.

Timmy grabbed the handle bars and yanked at them. He cursed and shouted and held onto the handles and flung himself away from the doors with all his weight.

I told him to stop it, to calm down.

Why did I think a closed door and a lock would mean "game over" for a student so devoted to his head garb?

Timmy continued gripping those door handles. He thrust away from them everything he had in his five-foot-eight frame. He kept up his aggression for minutes, long enough for me to wonder what Timmy would attack next should the door *not* budge, long enough to hope it eventually would budge, long enough for me to hit the emergency call button in my room several times, long enough for minutes of pacing and calmly or not so calmly telling Timmy to stop it, while nobody from the main office responded to my emergency call.

Eventually, and maybe even to my own relief, Timmy's force elicited a new rattling sound from the door. One of the handles finally popped off. Once he had access to my closet, Timmy regained his usual, stoic composure. He reached for the top shelf, retrieved his hat, put it on his head, and walked out of the room.

Twenty minutes later, a voice on the intercom replied: "Yes, Ms. Kirn?"

An hour later, I watched the school janitor assess the screws needed to fix the door, and Ms. Wallace stood beside me, offering advice in her usual dramatic whisper: "I never. Ever. Take their belongings from them."

Since that day I kept my hands off Timmy's hat, which he wore to school and to all his other classes but, as an unspoken compromise, removed for mine. He laid it at the far right corner of his desk, patted it once, and set to work. It took the removal of closet-door-hardware, not to mention his punishment of three days suspension, for Timmy and me to develop the boundaries of a normal student-teacher relationship. But develop them we did.

The real challenge of this fourth period class, though, was the fourth personality: Jerome. Unlike Timmy and Brandon and Yolanda, who were moderately interested in receiving credit for this, their second attempts at ninth-grade English, Jerome's sole purpose in coming was, it seemed, to entertain whoever was in the room. Often his jokes were about one person's private body part in combination with someone else's body part. He could hop on an endless freight train of sexual innuendos and couldn't jump off. Though he was physically harmless and always light-hearted, he was uncontainable.

• • •

Within weeks, my mouth had learned one question well, and I hardly thought about it as it rolled off my tongue. "Jerome, why are you out of your seat?"

"Sharpen my *pencil.*" Jerome raised his yellow stub proudly to prove he had one, and having one was a feat I should praise. He didn't always bring a pencil. Sometimes he brought only what he wore—his dirty jeans that sagged into bunches at his ankles, a crisp, black Hanes T-shirt eight sizes too big that hung over a white Hanes T-shirt seven sizes too big, and his ginormous middle-parted fro that he sometimes wore in pigtails but rarely in braids. He sang Outkast's "So Fresh and So Clean". He chanted the name of his housing project, *Lakelaaand!* in opposition to Brandon Ward's, *Westpooort!* He called Timmy Rogers "Titty," and Yolanda Perry "a ho," and in ways that they both somehow found charming. And everybody, including Timmy and Yolanda, who were each at least a half-foot taller than Jerome, laughed. Because Jerome was a short, comic genius.

But he rarely did anything that required a pencil.

Today wasn't much different—he'd still called Timmy "Titty," Yolanda "a ho," but he'd done so with pencil in hand. And it needed to be sharpened. And because Jerome took a liking to humping objects, and because Jerome was not so cruel as to discriminate between animate and inanimate objects (which he found equally deserving of his pelvic thrusts), he humped a whole lot of stuff on his way from his desk to the old, noisy, hand-cranking sharpener. Yolanda Perry. An empty chair. My table of poetry worksheets. But Jerome Smith had never humped me, did not on this day hump me, would in fact never hump me, and this I considered a success. Like the pencil.

Jerome cranked the sharpener over and over until the nub with which he started got even nubbier, then humped his way back to his seat. Once there, he sang again and beat a rhythm on the desk with his hands.

I eyed him.

He looked around, then eyed me back. "What?"

I eyed him again, because this was what I did when I couldn't think of anything clever to say, and because I hoped the look conveyed an air of mystery and authority instead of my actual internal state of futility.

"She looking at me like she crazy," and he glanced at tall, thin Brandon Ward, whose cut chin jetted out in permanent arrogance but whose dark eyes were intent on his sonnet handout. Brandon was having a good day. He was trying desperately to rewrite his fate, which he had so far carved this semester as a big fat *F* in my grade book.

"Jerome!" I lowered my eyes.

He lowered his back, in mockery or maybe just mimicry. He had no idea what I was trying to communicate.

"The poetry hand-out, Jerome."

"Oh!" He glanced down at the sonnet worksheet that had been lying on his desk a full twenty minutes, the one on which all of my students should by now have been working. And, by the grace of the Southwestern High School gods, most of my students in this fourth period class were, indeed, working today. Except Jerome. And because Jerome could tip the whole class any way he wanted, it was imperative that Jerome also put pencil to that sonnet worksheet.

Despite my growing reliance on them as ways to harness students' learning, worksheets were fairly uninteresting to complete. Just take the name: Worksheet. A sheet on which one puts one's work. I'd always loathed them, but my students at Southwestern had trained me to embrace them. They liked filling them out, filling the blanks, proving their work on a sheet that told them how. So despite the fact that the only thing worse than a worksheet is a bunch of worksheets, often assembled to make what the education world calls, aptly, a work*book*, I learned to make worksheets. Today, we were learning similes via Shakespeare's Sonnet #130. Nearly every line was a comparison, and students needed to paraphrase the literal meaning "in the blanks provided."

My mistress' eyes are nothing like the sun. Beside the line, I had drawn a sun. This first interpretation was easy. *His girl's eyes aren't bright. His boo eyes don't bling.*

If snow be white, why then her breasts are dun. Beside that, a tasteful cartoon of cleavage above a v-neck blouse. This one was harder.

"What's dun?" someone asked.

"A yellow-brown color."

The students loved this. "Her tits are brown! She have brown boobs!"

"Ms. Kahn," prepubescent Kenneth Peters, who often stayed quiet, tugged at my corduroy skirt as I passed his desk. He looked up at me pensively. "Shakespeare go with a black woman?"

Probably not, I told him, but reminded the class that poetry was up to their own interpretations, anyway. And so the class period went. *If hairs be wires, black wires grow on her head* became more fuel for the argument that Shakespeare's "boo" was black. *And in some perfumes is there more delight / Than in the breath that from my mistress reeks* was evidence that this whole poem was a slam on Shakespeare's woman.

"Dang," whispered Kenneth. "He saying her breath stink!"

Yolanda smacked her mouth. "P-ssh . . . I wouldn't go with him. He don't treat her right."

Jerome could only take so much of this worksheeting. He jumped out of his seat and humped over to Yolanda. "Girl, you go with me, I'll treat you right, I'll treat you *right*." He repeated this to the rhythm of his thrusts, to which Yolanda laughed, namely because Jerome was a wiry, nonthreatening five feet tall but also because there was something endearing and entirely asexual about Jerome, despite the constant pelvic thrusts.

"Jerome, stop it! Jerrrome," I lengthened his name long enough so that my voice filled the room. "Get *back* in your *seat*."

But Yolanda only encouraged him, and when I yelled her name also, she informed me that I was not to worry because Jerome was really her son.

"She my mother," Jerome affirmed as he sat on her lap.

The rest of the class laughed.

"And she my baby momma," Brandon said, pointing to Yolanda, which I was pretty sure meant that Jerome was Brandon's son too, via Yolanda, but I didn't have time for decoding. We had twenty minutes left to our ninety-minute period, and I knew "worksheeting" would never coax them back from their fabricated family tree.

"What's wrong, Ms. Kar-en." Jerome stood off Yolanda's lap. "You jealous?" He spread his skinny arms wide and took a step toward me. "You need a little love?" He broke out into the chorus of Ja Rule's "Between Me and You," which in Jerome's mouth basically sounded like this: all the freaky things that Jerome and I do, they should stay between just us two.

I'd learned enough by now to act when a student crossed a line, not necessarily one that had been clearly drawn, as lines and circles and hexagons and trapezoids were still vaguely scribbled and crossed out and erased on the metaphorical floor of my classroom. But when students crossed that line called "dignity," I knew now to act. No name-writing on the board, and no checks beside the name. What I should have done with Dennis Moore, I now did to Jerome in record speed and with zero emotional involvement.

"Out of the class, Jerome." I spoke sternly but no longer loudly because our battle was over today.

He held up his ever-shrinking yellow nub: "What? I brought a pencil! I'm gonna sharpen my *pencil*."

"Out!"

Jerome stuck his nub in his unbraided hair.

Because I also knew by now to raise stakes, to create ever looming consequences, I added, "And the next time this happens, the next time I have to remove you from class, you won't return to this room until I see a parent."

Jerome knew not to argue. He also knew exactly where to go, so I followed him out to the hall and watched him enter Ms. Patterson's room. Inside, fuchsia-rouge-cheeked Ms. Patterson was speaking high-pitched and easy, moving steadily around her quiet, controlled, orange-accented room while her students worked in their workbooks.

At five-feet-three-inches, Ms. Patterson looked down at Jerome. "This one giving you trouble again, Ms. Karen?" Ms. Patterson nearly sang the question in her melodic soprano voice, and I nodded like a student, and she took Jerome into her room. I started back toward my classroom before I could finish hearing the lecture that Ms. Patterson had begun, the "Your-mother-didn't-raise-you-like-that" lecture, the "Listen-to-me-I'm-as-old-as-your-great-grandma" lecture, the one I had tried but, at twenty-two, could not pull off.

"Titty leave," Yolanda said when I returned.

She and her classmates huddled by the door in their puffy jackets; their half-finished sonnet worksheets were scattered across desks. Timmy was not among them.

I glanced at her. "Don't call him that."

"What?"

"You know," I said.

The bell rang. The hallways cleared out in two minutes.

• • •

Back in July every green-horned Teach For America teacher had to record in magic marker his or her goals for his or her future students. We had to write these goals on butcher paper that had been tacked to a classroom wall in Houston. Heading this butcher paper were the words *Big Hairy Audacious Goal* written in all caps. Think of something big, our TFA trainers had told us, something that society believes these kids can't do! Brainstorm a wild vision of outrageous achievement! Set an enormous audacious goal, and make it big, make it hairy, make it bodacious!

I'd once performed in *The Vagina Monologues*, and my monologue was about a woman who'd visited a vagina workshop. The leader of the workshop had asked each participant to create artistic representations of her nether regions. My character had illustrated "a big black dot with squiggly lines around it," a place, she said, where "things got lost." The words, Big Hairy Audacious Goal, recollected in me that theatrical character's image, the oddest abstraction of female anatomy. Since the day with hairy goals and butcher paper, I'd always maintained a squiggly lined black dot as the target for TFA crusaders. A big, hairy, bodacious goal. A place where things sometimes got lost.

Still, I set my goal. I wrote that I wanted my students to compose personally meaningful, analytically thoughtful, gracefully written essays, and I carried that "hairy" aspiration into the classroom. That was the squiggly lined dot toward which we charged. During my first semester, I attempted to counter every big block of disorganized, misspelled writing I read. I tried out techniques like Ms. Patterson's critical squares and I had my students "freewrite" in journals, usually Mead notebooks that I stored and locked away in my classroom so that they'd never go lost and so that students would always have a safe space into which they could record their deepest thoughts. And I had students write rough drafts and revise their drafts and peer-edit their drafts.

But back in Houston, faced with that butcher paper and with a magic marker in hand, I hadn't known that a goal like "Teacher will create a hump-free classroom environment" might also qualify as big and hairy at Southwestern, not to mention audacious.

• • •

The day after Jerome's Ja-Rule song and dance, I readied myself for fourth period, which I learned would succeed or fail based almost entirely on attendance. If Brandon, Yolanda, and Timmy all came, and if Jerome showed too, the class would become a game show to see who could a.) crack each other up the most; which often included b.) acting the most inappropriately, often resulting in c.) one of them getting removed from class, but also d.) nobody getting any work done, which meant that e.) I wouldn't have taught anything. Yesterday was Shakespeare. Today, Robert Frost. My first- and third-period students, for the most part, had grasped my rhyme scheme lesson and the symbolic significance of the roads taken and not taken. But if I couldn't execute the lesson with fourth period, I would feel like another stone had fallen into the vast chasm of "the achievement gap," and I had failed to become what TFA meant for me to be: a solution.

In walked Brandon a few minutes before the late bell. He slammed his notebook on his desk. "Be back, Ms. Kahn." He walked out.

Then Yolanda, then Timmy.

Brandon returned. The other eight or so quieter kids had filed in and settled down. The whole gang was almost here. I had to remind myself of my warning to Jerome: If he didn't behave himself, he would leave and he wouldn't come back until I saw a parent.

The late bell rang and Jerome stood at the door wearing an enormous jester hat with two felt, cotton-stuffed crescent moons emerging from his head, one electric blue, the other lipstick red, both jingling at the end from silver bells.

"Out, Jerome! Out!" I pointed at the door before he even had a chance to cross the threshold. "The day didn't even begin, and you're already out." I made my way across the room, arm held straight out and index finger pointing forward.

On my way by him, I heard little Kenneth say, "What she mean, *day didn't begin*? Day began this morning."

"You know what I mean," I turned my head and snapped.

"Dang!" Brandon said.

Jerome responded with his infamous, "What? What I do?"

If I hadn't been so bothered, so immersed in what felt like a desperate cause, I would have seen the humor. A jester's hat? Where ever did he find that thing? Why couldn't I have laughed? Why couldn't I have just let the kid in? Because Jerome was like a hinge in that room, the brass piece that made the whole door swing, the joint that turned the whole class toward this or that. Toward Ja Rule or Outkast or sexual innuendos. Toward the gossip about or reenactment of cafeteria fights. Jerome could take my hard-earned fourth period and completely derail it; he was ingenious at finding ways to make all eyes fall on him. It was a bona fide gift. But his presence didn't just result in his own persistent failure; it resulted in Timmy's and Yolanda's and Brandon's as well. And poor Kenneth Peters tried earnestly each day to learn, not to mention quiet Aneesha and a handful of other promising kids. And that's why I put my stubborn, humorless foot down: because with Jerome and his big-ass jester hat in the room, he cost us all too much.

Jerome's shoulders fell forward and he headed back to the hallway, where he shuffled to Mr. Owens' office in his enormous, butt-shaped, jingling hat.

• • •

Days went by without Jerome and a parent. He sometimes came to my door to stick his lip out and plead, to which I replied, "Not until I see a parent."

Mr. Owens stopped by from time to time and asked if I'd gotten any word from someone at home. As a member of The Future's Kids team, Owens was Jerome's case manager. Future's Kids had been convicted of a crime or were deemed especially "at-risk." Owens was a rare veteran teacher who still had the optimism and energy of a new recruit. Coupled with the realism and wisdom of his years, he was a fantastic ally, and I never wanted to let him down. But I hadn't heard from Jerome's parent. It had been a week, and I felt apologetic.

"But I can't let him in," I told Owens. "I *have* to see someone."

"I know," he nodded. While I counted the days, Owens let Jerome bide his time in Owens's office.

• • •

Jerome finally arranged to bring someone named "Uncle Orpheus" into school. During my planning period, Jerome bounced through the door, grinning from ear to ear, and a taller guy strutted behind him. The man was like a magnified version of Jerome: same wild, unbraided hair sticking out in all directions, same enormous black puffy jacket. He looked about twenty-five. I can only describe Jerome's apparent excitement by alluding to my own delight at once watching *The Jetsons Meet the Flintstones*; as a kid, there was something mind-bogglingly thrilling about seeing, face to face, George Jetson (of the futuristic world of aerocars) meet up with Fred Flintstone (of the stone-age world, the one where vehicles were powered by the barefoot peddlings of Fred's feet). I spotted this same thrill in Jerome's face: two very different worlds were about to collide, or rather, two very separate spheres of his one world. He and Uncle Orpheus settled into seats, and the three of us along with Mr. Owens sat on equal footing, in students' chairs, at students' desks.

It was in the first few seconds of Uncle Orpheus sitting beside me that I noticed he smelled like liquor. When I caught a whiff, my hope for a life-altering outcome faded.

I told Uncle Orpheus that Jerome's behavior had been unacceptable and disruptive, etcetera, etcetera, and that he had to make a change.

Uncle Orpheus turned to Jerome. "Cuz," he said, with the hint of authority that an older brother uses, "what you do?"

"I was wearing *that hat*," Jerome said. "You know *that hat*, with the bells?"

"Yeah, I know that hat." Uncle Orpheus nodded.

"Yeah, you know that hat! It's a nice hat."

Uncle Orpheus smiled. "Yeah." He put his hand on his chin. "That's a nice hat!"

Jerome laughed a little and the two nodded at each other, and I imagined that in one half-minute more, they could be completely off their seats about the niceness of the hat.

"Uncle Orpheus," I said, to which he turned his head and let his mouth hang open like he was almost surprised I sat there. For intruding on their love fest, I felt like a jerk—indeed, the hat was a nice hat. Had I owned such a jaunty piece, I would never have lived another Halloween without donning full jester garb. Still, I said, "It's against school policy to wear hats."

Uncle Orpheus looked confused, then deflated. He turned to Jerome. "She say you can't wear hats in school, cuz." He was reading the situation as a misunderstanding. He was offering his intercession.

Owens weighed in. "Jerome's aware of the school rules, Uncle Orpheus. He breaks them deliberately."

Uncle Orpheus again looked confused. His eyes caught a spot on the wall. Then he turned to his nephew. "'Rome, you just need to get your act together."

Because Uncle Orpheus had nothing else to say on the matter, we all agreed to his advice. Yes, Jerome needed to get his Act together. Jerome's Act was in pieces, and if only he gathered those pieces, his Act would congeal into one whole.

I didn't know what else Jerome, Uncle Orpheus, Mr. Owens, and I could agree on. I stood up, smoothed my long skirt, nodded to Uncle Orpheus, and we bid farewell.

Owens and I stood alone together in my quiet classroom. "Woo," he almost whistled, almost hooted. In a rare moment, Owens was speechless. I just shook my head.

"Let me know how it goes," he said.

In subsequent days, I quietly mocked this pseudo parent-teacher conference between Uncle Orpheus and me. Among teacher friends, I made steady jabs at the minimal progress my long-awaited conference had made. "My good friend, Uncle Orpheus and me," I'd say to Noelani while gripping another glass of beer during a Friday happy hour. "Should I have anymore trouble with Jerome, I'll just call up Uncle Orpheus. We'll set things straight." "The achievement gap doesn't stand a chance, not with Uncle O. by my side." "Good ol' Uncle O."

But then I learned—and I don't remember exactly how—that Jerome slept on a thin mattress in someone else's room of a house in which his parents did not live, but some of his younger brothers and sisters did, and since he was one of the oldest, he sometimes had to care for them. This should not have caught me off-guard. I'd known plenty of tragic stories from kids' home-lives. I did, after all, ask them to write personal narratives. I'd already read about the drunken father, the absent father, the rapist father (why was tragedy often the domain of the fathers?), and I read about the gang-beaten and gang-murdered best friends. I wasn't naive enough to believe that Jerome's household contained two parents and daily dinners of protein and veggies. But I had never imagined no parents at all, and not just no parents, but no personal space, and only one random mattress on the random floor of someone else's home. Whose? I didn't know. I guess I assumed there was at least a grandmother who would meet with me, who would want to know about not just his behavior in school but his prospects for passing ninth grade. I realized that Jerome hadn't slighted me by refusing to bring a mom or a grandma. Uncle Orpheus might have been the closest thing Jerome had. I had demanded a "parent/teacher" conference in a world where a student did not necessarily have "parent," and Jerome had tried to find a person that might meet this role. He did his best to comply.

While he was away, Yolanda, Timmy, and Brandon would say, at random points in the lesson, "I miss 'Rome." They'd ask, "Where

Jerome?" They'd plead with me to let him in because my class was now boring, they said, without him. Once he returned, Yolanda called him her son, and Jerome said that Yolanda was his mother, and Brandon said then he was Yolanda's "baby daddy" because he was Jerome's father, and all of my students redrew the lines of their fictional family tree.

I began to see the "Uncle Orpheus/Teacher" exchange as a gesture on Jerome's part. He didn't have to bring in a guardian. It wasn't unheard of for a student to skip a semester's worth of one particular class, especially the fourth and final period. But Jerome wanted badly to be back in my classroom. From that class Jerome got something—possibly not poems or any joy or skill of reading or writing—but a kind of makeshift family of which I was only a small part.

• • •

"Your job is to select a poet from these books and find five of his or her poems." I gestured to boxes of books I'd brought from my home library. The library at Southwestern didn't have any more than a couple hundred books. Most of the metal bookcases stood empty.

My other classes had taken to the project relatively well, despite my barring Tupac Shakur as a project-worthy poet. I wanted the kids to find some meaning in a poet they'd never heard of. Perhaps because the assignment required him to get up and dig through my stuff, Jerome decided to take a gander. His skinny arm dove into a box and somehow fished out Nikki Giovanni's *Blues: For All the Changes*. On the cover, tough fifty-six-year-old Giovanni smirks at the camera with short, bright, bleached hair. Her legs are splitting the back of a chair. Her hands clasp one another and her forearms face each other. On her left forearm is a cursive tattoo that says, "Thug-life." The same words splayed across Tupac's abdomen. She'd received hers four days after Shakur was gunned down.

This, to Jerome, was the hardest thing. "You see this? Some old woman. She have a tattoo say Thug Life." He showed the hardcover to Brandon.

Brandon grabbed the book and held it closer to his face. He nodded in approval. He handed the book back and continued flipping through an old college anthology of mine. He was intent on finding a Dylan Thomas poem he'd learned in private school so he could impress me with his understanding of it.

"You know Dylan Thomas, Ms. Kahn?"

I nodded.

"*I* know Dylan Thomas," he said, and kept flipping through the book.

Kenneth Peters was delighted by the brevity of one poet's work. "These all short," he said with his face in another anthology. "I'm a do her." He turned the pages to find the poet's name. "Emily Dickinson."

Yolanda, still bemoaning her inability to report on Tupac, ran down a list of reasons why he qualified as a poet. "He write in *met*aphors, Ms. Karen." We'd spent a class period on Tupac's similes.

"I know he does, but you already know his work. The whole purpose is to learn about a *new* poet."

Meanwhile, always-talking, always-moving Jerome had been silent five minutes. When I looked over at him, he was doing the unthinkable: he was reading. He was seated at a chair with an open book. It was a strange miracle. He laughed at what he read and read it aloud. " 'The president's penis is not . . . should not . . . ought not be . . . subject to . . . public screw-tiny.'" Jerome had stumbled onto Giovanni's poem, "The President's Penis." "What's screw-tiny?" he asked.

"Scrutiny," I corrected. "Look it up."

Should I have discouraged Jerome from reading a poem about the president's penis? If he had sat in some wealthy neighborhood school, his teacher probably would have reprimanded him for it, and such a school's administrators and parents would have most likely reprimanded the *teach*er for having it. But I let Jerome keep reading. The sentence itself is miraculous: Jerome, of all people, was reading. How could I yell at him for reading? How could I tell him to stop? To choose another book? He didn't look up scrutiny, but he turned the page, read more poems. He stopped reading them aloud and started reading them to himself. For a precious few minutes, Jerome sat quiet and read poems. This older woman on the cover of her hardback book had baited Jerome Smith with her nod to Tupac, and she now kept him with her poems.

"Can I take this with me, Ms. Kahn?"

"No, it'll be here next class."

And next class it was. Jerome goofed off that next day, called Timmy "Titty," Yolanda "a ho," shouted "Lakeland!" to whomever was listening, but when I told Jerome to get Nikki Giovanni from the cardboard box, he retrieved her white and blue cover and he quietly read her for sometimes whole, fat, five-minute periods. He never wrote a single word about her. Didn't have a *pencil*. Shy, polite Kenneth Peters crafted an entire project on Emily Dickinson. Brandon Ward wrote about Dylan Thomas. Yolanda Perry's poet? Timmy Rogers's? I don't remember. I only remember Jerome on his way to grab Giovanni, bouncing this time, not humping, to the window-side wall.

CHAPTER 9

DISARMING THE ALARM

What seemed like every day, in any given minute between 8:45 and 3:15, the school's alarm system activated. While I took attendance. In the middle of the drill. In that precious second when silence fell upon my class like snow, and every kids' eyes focused. While a normally absent, usually angry kid finally read something he'd written aloud. As another student recited Juliet's last lines, the ones that had taken us four long, tedious weeks, word-by-mispronounced-word, to reach: *Yea noise, then I'll be brief. O happy dagger. This is thy sheath. There rust, and let me die.*

Yea noise: The fire alarm went off.

I can conjure up the heart shape of Letisha's mouth, the way Jerome wore his hair, the sound of the closet door when it rattled in Timmy's hands, a thousand other strange details of Southwestern. But I can't recall the sound of that alarm. Was it a mixture of bells and whistles? Did it have the two-noted undulation of a car alarm? Was it just a blaring, high-pitched, constant one-note ring? I don't know. I got so used to ignoring it that my memory has no recollection.

The alarm went off one day in the beginning of the school year, and like any sensible person I said, "Okay" and lined my students up at the door. I said "Okay" again when they were in no linear order but were loosely jumbled by the exit and itching to leave. We headed out of the room.

"*Teeechers*," we heard on the loudspeaker. We were halfway toward the stairwell. "Please, remain in your classrooms." The class and I stopped. Remain in our classrooms? Through a fire alarm? I looked up at the ceiling, waiting for the voice-from-above to explain itself. "We are experiencing, a technical difficulty, with our systems." It was Ms. Brown's slow, surreal, contraction-free diction. "Please, teachers, do ignore, the alarm."

The students and I turned away from the stairwell, which would have led us to the exit, and walked back to our classroom, perplexed and uncomfortable. The ringing was earsplitting.

When a school is on fire, you leave the building. When an alarm tells you that a school is on fire, you also leave the building. You do not need to think about these things. Line up at the door and go. But the damn fire alarm went off weekly, sometimes daily, sometimes more than once a day. If we'd adhered to its constant "technical difficulties," we would have been practicing fire drills for hours a week. The entire population would have stood idly on a grassy hill beside the school and stared at a building that was, for all intents and purposes, not burning down. Kids would have drifted south, down Font Hill, and grabbed fast food. They wouldn't have bothered making the return trek uphill. So whenever that indescribable sound rang incessantly throughout the building, an administrator got on the intercom within a minute or two and told us what we all had assumed: Ignore the alarm. Just a glitch in the system. Remain in your rooms.

One day the alarm went off and kept ringing. My students stared at the intercom box, waiting for someone to deliver the usual message. The alarm still kept ringing. I put my hand on my hip and faced the intercom too. "Teeechers," we finally heard, but what followed was rushed panic. "This is a fire drill! Escort all classes outside!"

Behind the building, the kids pushed further up the grassy hill, ascending like an audience in a movie theater. Teachers called them and asked them to keep closer and counted them and lost count of them. The boys mock-fought, and the girls called out *hay-ey*, and some kids talked on their cell phones which they weren't allowed to have, and other kids smoked cigarettes which they weren't allowed to do. But we—the students and the teachers—all found a homeostasis between lawlessness and order where each party could feel moderately accomplished in its goal to either maintain the rule or break it.

Two fire trucks arrived at the side of the building. A few firemen jogged through the side doors, strips of neon yellow reflector tape glimmering in the sun. We squinted at those doors. Why had firemen arrived for a drill? We waited half an hour, maybe longer. When an assistant principal finally waved us into the building, whoever was left on the hill descended, crossed the parking lot, and trudged back inside. With each step up the stairwell, I smelled the dry, acrid singe of smoke. When I reached my hall, a gray, filmy residue coated the air. I stood at my door befuddled by the obvious remnants of a fire, a fire that shouldn't have been followed with the word "drill." Kids coughed as they walked to their rooms in the haze.

I prepared to face the students' litany of questions. What had been burning? Why were people calling it a drill when it obviously was a fire? As a student, I would have felt entitled to the truth. But my kids only said, in a resigned, uninterested tone, "That wasn't no drill, Ms. Kuren." Their tone seemed to indicate that a lying authority fit precisely with their view of the world.

No administrator bothered to explain or acknowledge the smoke. Each one maintained the façade that we'd just had a drill. Word only came through the teacher pipeline that the fire started in a boys' bathroom. Maybe Ms. Brown hoped her use of the word "drill" masked her panic when she stood in the office and learned that, indeed, something was on fire; something had been on fire for minutes.

The whole school now seemed insane to me: an alarm was something to ignore; a hallway of smoke was a drill. But I mention the fire alarm because it illustrated a larger schoolwide issue: too many warnings of trouble at Southwestern meant that we'd developed unorthodox responses to each. Sometimes we ignored them. When the many little "alarms" set off all day like the firecrackers popping in the halls or some hallwalker suddenly slamming into a classroom door—we couldn't always react with equal fight-or-flight vigor. Our adrenal systems were overworked and growing numb. We had to pick and choose. What was dire? What needed our adrenalin rush? But the "drill" day indicated that we didn't always know when to rush in record-speed with a fire extinguisher and when to sit back and wait. In a school as broken as ours, sitting and waiting through an alarm was a gamble we felt we had to take.

The students of my fourth period—Jerome, Timmy, Yolanda, Brandon— were still like complex little alarms that set off all period long. But Brandon, the student with the ribcage of a kid and the height of an adult, was both the smartest student in that class and the brightest security-level indicator, the scariest bomb ticking and ready to go off. *Who's the foil to Mercutio? What's the significance of Frost's road not taken?* Brandon called out the answer, then looked around and smiled. "Shit, yo. I'm smart." Brandon could plow through a stint of reading aloud without one glitch, without a pause. *Eradicate. Demean.* He knew all the words, and he didn't just robotically recite them, he thought about them. How did they affect the story, his life? It was obvious Brandon had gotten an education that my other students hadn't, and I wasn't surprised when he told me that he attended a private school before getting kicked out for poor conduct. Here, where knowing sixty percent of the answers was considered celebratory passing, Brandon was easily an *A* student.

But he struggled to stay in my room without threatening to hurt someone.

It was sometimes unclear when his threats were serious and when they were jokes. In the middle of any given lesson—while I was leaning over the desk of one student or transitioning the class to a new activity—the legs of Brandon's chair would screech across the floor, and I'd hear him shout, "I'm a fuck you up!" One day, the target of his threat was little Kenneth Peters. Brandon towered over meager, seated Kenneth. Brandon was fuming at the nostrils, looking ready to pummel the poor kid. I raised my finger, pointed at the door, and shouted "OUT!"

Kenneth scrunched his face up and cocked his head. "Ms. Kuren, why you fussin? He *playin*."

Brandon laughed, tipped his chin toward Kenneth, who nodded back, and the two slapped hands. Brandon called Kenneth *shorty* and his *people* and his *son*, and Brandon sat back down in his chair. The two got back to work. I was the one left standing with a fuchsia face.

But on another day, I'd sometimes hear the same sequence of sounds— the chair legs screeching across the floor, Brandon's threat—and when my neck twisted fast toward his direction, Brandon's fists were clenched at his sides, and the breath from his flaring nostrils hissed audibly as he stood over a seated kid. Brandon's chest puffed out, his shoulders rose, and his thin body became a wall that said, *Come try me.* That wall was unfaltering even as I shouted, "Brandon, calm down," or "Take yourself to Ms. Patterson's room," or "That's it, I'm calling home." I grabbed my cell phone (no longer bothering with the "emergency" call button) and listened to an endless ringing of a line that reached to a house where nobody was home.

• • •

"His problem's his temper," said his mother in a parent-teacher conference. From the get-go, she didn't seem interested in a parent-teacher meeting. She plopped her tall body into a chair and glared at me with eyes nearly as hard as Brandon's. I smiled. She did not smile. I knew her expression well—the west Baltimore face of suspicion, the one I'd grown to expect. Just who did this barely-out-of-college white girl, this straight-from-the-suburbs English major think she was, teaching someone else's inner-city son? Brandon's mother neared six feet tall, wore a collared button-down blouse and dress slacks on her endlessly long legs. When she bent her elbow to glance at her wrist, where her watch had peeked from behind the cuff of her sleeve, she was telling me she had neither patience nor time for a parent-teacher meeting in her single-mother life. This was not a typical "he give you problems, you call me" conference that I'd had with many a Baltimore grandmother. Nor was this a conference with the non-responsive, barely *humph*ing parent who looked sideways and refused to meet my face. I'd had a handful of those too. Brandon's mom looked me straight in the eye and waited. What did I want?

I cited the upside of Brandon-Ward-as-student: his intellect. I listed the ways that he dazzled me in class, but his mom looked unimpressed.

"My son's better than this school," she said. He was "in here," she said, because he couldn't control his temper. "In here," she said, like this was a prison. Not that she wasn't justified. Remember, even the *Baltimore Sun* described Southwestern as "like a prison."

She was probably right: Brandon Ward was better than Southwestern. Southwestern's primary style of teaching only agitated Brandon's temper. He was easily irritated with tasks like copying or identifying, labeling or reciting, tasks that most Baltimore students were all too accustomed to. The five words, *Students will be able to*, began every objective on every blackboard across the city, and while some teachers completed that sentence with goals like ". . . analyze a character's motivations and write a fictional letter of advice to that character," other teachers had simpler goals in mind. I'd once passed another English classroom and seen the following goal written in chalk: "Students will be able to copy vocabulary words." For ninety minutes, that was the teacher's only plan? To have twenty-five kids copy words and their corresponding definitions? If ever I asked the class to perform simple duties like copying or defining, tasks that were sometimes necessary to achieve loftier goals, Brandon looked insulted and pushed the work aside. He seemed allergic to anything that diminished him into an ATM machine of education, where the teacher put knowledge into him, and, when prompted, he pumped it back out. While every other kid had trained me to adopt the occasional mini-lesson that featured easy tasks like copying, especially from the blue light of the projector which they loved, Brandon rebelled. I think Baltimore City had overdosed him on it.

Whether he was "too good for this school" or not, I desperately wanted Brandon to succeed here. He possessed what most Southwestern students did not: an on-grade reading and writing level. For Brandon, there was no vast achievement gap for he and I to cross. I couldn't bear to watch his attitude infringe on what, in a finely funded, challenging school, might have been his inevitable success. I couldn't bear to fail him. *To fail him*, meaning not just to give him an F, but to let him down. How could I reel him into school without hooking him in the mouth, which he would have surely pulled against, harming both him and me in the process? Like sitting still in the middle of an urgent alarm, I experimented with unorthodox responses.

One day, Brandon rose from his chair and spun his body from his desk while I stood directly behind him. As he ascended, his gaze also rose, first to meet mine and then to look over my head. Before he took a step toward wherever he was headed—the pencil sharpener, the trash can—he stopped. He was taken off guard.

"Damn," he said. "I'm taller than you."

I nodded. "It's true." He was a half-foot taller.

"I always be seeing you seated." Brandon seemed surprised, like he'd expected that when he stood up, I too would rise, and there'd forever exist two large feet between us. He squinted at me. "You *short!*"

I nodded. His pointy chin tilted to the left. His eyes got cold and sharp, and the length of his long, thin-bridged nose became a telescopic sight through which to glare at me. When he inhaled, he expanded his chest and raised his shoulders. "I could take you," he said.

This raging stance—nostrils seething, eyes piercing and squinting, flat pectorals swelled—I'd seen it from him plenty of times before, sometimes as an act and sometimes for real. The six inches he had on me made me feel diminutive. He took a step closer, shrinking the space between us, and said it again. "I could take you." With the words, his eyes grew hard and suspicious, like he'd never known me, like his world would improve tenfold if I did not exist in it. What I'd thought was a joke now felt dangerously real.

Maybe in a more orderly school my fight-or-flight response would have kicked in. Maybe I would have written the incident up and sent paperwork to an assistant principal. *Child threatened to "take me,"* I might have noted so that someone could bury the form in a file. Or maybe I would have met Brandon's threat with threat and said, *Another statement like that, and I'm calling home.* At bare minimum, I could have told him to stop creating a hostile learning environment and get back to work. In another school I might have felt adrenalin—that surge of electric fear—in at least one of the veins in my limbs.

But I didn't. I'd grown numb. To fire alarms. To vague threats. To firecrackers. To that sudden rattle of the classroom door during a lesson when some hallwalker had kicked it in. It had once made me jump.

Brandon, I think, expected a response to his heaving, alpha-male chest. Much of west Baltimore operated under a perfect one-to-one ratio of threats which escalated two for two, three for three, and on and on until someone was bleeding. Literally. This winter, a female student had instigated a female teacher somehow—the details didn't make their way up the stairwells and down the corridors of the mammoth school—but we teachers on the high side of the thirty-five-hundred level knew that the teacher ended up calling the student a *bitch*, and this provoked the student to bash the teacher's head against a blackboard. That thing on which the teacher wrote all her kids' to-do's: it was now a weapon. The teacher was okay, we'd heard, but she took a full week off. Talk among the faculty centered mostly on whether she would get workman's comp and, if so, how much? I wondered what her class was like the first day she returned; how could she face a room that had seen her get pummeled? How do you step up to the front of the class after that incident and create your ever-precious "positive learning environment"?

"It's true," I said to Brandon. "You could very easily take me." I remember the words weren't just immediate, weren't just emaciated of any adrenalin-charged energy, but tired and lifeless when they came out of my mouth. We were forty minutes away from the end of the school day.

In the moments when Brandon raged—when his face fumed and he shouted something like, *fuck this*—I don't think Brandon saw me. He saw a figure of authority I think he was practicing to hate. Or maybe he saw a figure of his past that he'd grown to hate. Or maybe I just refused to accept that, in some moments, Brandon hated me. Still, when I saw that cold glare, it seemed like Brandon had slipped into a way of looking at the world that hadn't fully taken over him. And any time his authorities pushed back at him it was an attempt to exert power over him, which only hardened him further. What if I gave that power up? What if I put it right into his growing, long-fingered hand? Said, *There. Yes. You've got the power to do serious damage. To a woman who teaches you poetry. Now what?*

"Very easily," I said. "You could take me. I wouldn't stand a chance."

Brandon's shoulders dropped. He stopped glaring at me sniper-style down the bridge of his nose. He slipped back into the narrow frame of just a boy. Not some puffed-up kid trying to be a man trying to be a thug. Now he looked at me blank as a half-awake face in the morning—the kind that stares into a bathroom mirror and pauses because it doesn't yet remember its name. I raised my eyebrows and gave him a thin smile.

I was trying to smile Brandon off the path of becoming another Tremaine or Damon—those boys that only appeared at the very first class. I was trying to keep Brandon from becoming a full-on resistor of the very systems that—however flawed—might help him move past the worst of west Baltimore's offerings for him. But the only reason I could do this with Brandon was because his rage was still a half-act.

That day, he walked to the sharpener, sharpened his pencil, blew on the tip, and returned to his seat. He looked down at a piece of paper on his desk, looked up at the board, squinted, and glanced back at his paper. His movements were jerky, sudden, and alert. The pause button on Brandon Ward's ticking bomb had been pressed. I went on teaching the kids. Five minutes later he raised his hand. "Ms. Kuhn?" he said, and then asked me one of his famous questions, the kind that told me fast cogs were turning inside his analytical mind. These were the moments that made me want to teach him.

• • •

If I'd met Brandon—or, for that matter, Jerome or Timmy or Yolanda—on the streets of Baltimore I might have thought of them as thugs. Terrible word, *thug*. Rhymes with *slug*, sounds like *thud*. Derived from the Sanskrit word, *Sthaga*, meaning rogue, the word's first dictionary definition is "a former member of a religious group in India who robs and murders." Thugs are hoodlums, gangsters, thieves, but even those words have a bit more prestige, a bit more flare than the ugly-sounding *thug*.

But *thug* was the label some kids seemed to want for themselves. Thug life. It made them look tough; it hardened them against a hard world. *Hard*, as in, *this song is hard*. Their word for *cool* or *hip* said volumes about what they valued. The boys wore those uniforms of urban male youth: incredibly long black T-shirts hung overtop of their even longer white T-shirts, very baggy jeans or sweats sagging beneath their bums and bunching around their tan Timberland boots, a black (or sometimes gray) hoodie that they could cast over their skulls to keep their eyes low and their faces half-hidden. Upon first meeting any teacher, my kids glared with piercing, cold eyes. This used to intimidate me, but I began to realize that looking the part of a thug was some kind of protection. And it always hid more interesting personalities. Maybe "looking the part" protected my kids from people like me, who spent a semester coaxing the kids' real selves from the caricature they'd created.

Timmy, once brutal and noncompliant, was now oddly personal with me. During the start of one fourth-period class, as my kids were fidgety, talkative, adjusting to the concept of sitting in seats for another ninety minutes, Timmy spotted a brown paper bag lying on the desk of a quiet girl. "Man, is it them Non-on-all nine rubbers in there?" The brown paper bags came from the nurse's office, where kids went for free condoms.

"The drill, Timmy. Let's focus on the drill," I said.

"Ms. Kuhn." He looked ready to divulge a conspiracy. "They always be givin' out them rubbers with that Non-on-all nine." He sucked on his lips and shook his head. "I can't be wearin' that shit!"

"Timmy!" I almost shouted. "You have to always, always practice safe sex!" The oddity of my reaction was not lost on me. I focused on the words I *can't be wearing that*, and completely ignored the word, *shit*.

The way a child might confess that he's having a bad day, Timmy said with troubled sincerity, "But it be making me *itch*, Ms. Kuren."

"Well," I paused. "You probably have an allergy."

The Timmy I'd met at the beginning of the semester had been hard, unknowable, refusing to reveal even his name. Now he was divulging personal if not-so-pleasant details. I could have pushed against Timmy's antics: don't talk about condoms when you should be doing the drill, don't use curse words in the middle of class. But, oddly enough, this conversation showed progress between us. Though I had my rules and I made them known, I kept my eccentric fourth period kids on metaphorical bungee chords. Each kid could move around the room more freely than I would have liked; strange behavior was tolerated as long as nobody harmed anyone else; the rules were present but not so firm as to feel like a wall nobody could penetrate, which people like Brandon and Timmy and Yolanda would have slammed up against in defiance.

I didn't always know if such a tactic was successful until I saw these students with other teachers. I watched Yolanda strut down the hallway one afternoon, passing Ms. Ryder, the reading teacher across from my room.

"You come back here!" Ms. Ryder shrieked. She slammed a foot down on the ground and pointed at a spot in front of her. Her mousey, upturned nose was flaring.

Yolanda stuck her nose in the air and kept walking. The shiny black curls of her pineapple-style updo swayed as she shook her head.

Ms. Ryder called after her again, "Get. Back. Heeere!"

Yolanda just tossed her hand up. "Whatevah," she muttered.

The woman's beady eyes widened. "You a nasty child," Ms. Ryder called out. In a throaty screech, while shaking her head back and forth, she screamed, "*Naaaaah*-stay," stretching the length of the word at least three seconds. She filled the whole hall with that screeching insult.

My mouth hung open. Yolanda passed me and laughed. "Hey, Ms. Karrr-ennn!" She sang my name and smiled.

"Hi, Yolanda." I didn't know what I was more bewildered at: Ms. Ryder's insane, totally useless, self-serving response? What good did it do, calling a child *nasty* at the top of one's lungs? Or was I more amazed by the different personalities of Yolanda that Ms. Ryder and I experienced, even as the girl passed the short distance between our doors? On our first day together, when Yolanda had given me a death-wish glare and then refused to offer her name, I'd thought I'd met a girl with potential for nastiness. But that girl had quickly vanished from my classroom, had been replaced by someone who, yes, was loud, but also courteous, endearing, funny. I'd assumed that the hard-edged Yolanda had never existed, that she'd only been putting on a show. It appeared as though, in different hands, the old Yolanda could easily emerge.

I got other clues that my slightly lenient style worked. Toward the end of one day, I stood at the board, erasing chalked words and trying to avoid the dust that fell from the eraser. Timmy stood beside me and watched. "Ms. Kuren," he said. "You should be happy."

On my other side, Yolanda was writing *Bubbles* in big letters. The final bell would ring any second. "Why's that?" I asked.

"Cuz," he smiled. "This the *only* class I come to today!"

Why would this make me happy? Timmy skipped three out of four classes? I delved into a lecture about attending all classes, about goals and high school diplomas and making something of oneself. But I got Timmy's message. In his eyes, my class was worth coming to. With Timmy and Yolanda, I'd managed to achieve the goal I'd had with Brandon: I'd reeled the two of them into English class. The final bell rang, and Timmy bolted from my side. On his desk was a loose leaf page of schoolwork, several paragraphs long. The handwriting was neat, the sentences grammatically correct, the vocabulary spelled right. I picked up the paper from his desk and let a smile spread.

• • •

But Brandon Ward wouldn't give up his thuggish mask so easily. One afternoon, the bluish-white overhead halogen lights had been turned off, the afternoon daylight shone beneath the edges of the pull-down plastic window shades, and my students fixated on the wheel-in television. They'd spent the week weeding through the first few scenes of Romeo and Juliet's archaic language and now, on this Friday, they were receiving their reward: the first twenty minutes of two iconic film versions. They'd just witnessed the opening scenes from the simple, late-seventies version by Zephirelli; the men wore bi-colored tights, the women, velour empire-waist gowns, and everyone spoke in a semi-British accent to the quaint soundtrack of a lyre. It had been a yawn; it looked dusty. Now, one minute into Baz Lurhman's modern-day version, my students were edging off their seats. Fast editing, modern rock, close-ups of glocks, and screeching, reckless cars: Shakespeare had turned gangster.

"Damn, Ms. Kuren," Kenneth said, turning his head for just a second to tell me, "This movie hard."

I was grading at my desk. "Ms. Kuren." Brandon strutted up to me, holding a Venn diagram—two giant circles, overlapping halfway. "What I'm supposed to do with this?"

"List the similarities between the movies. Right here." I ran my finger up and down the flame-shaped space where the circles overlapped. Then I touched the symmetrical crescent moons on either sides of the center. "In the other spaces, list differences."

Brandon nodded. When he turned away, I set my gaze back to the quizzes on my desk. Leonardo DiCaprio was wielding a gun, his open Hawaiian shirt blowing by the wind of an approaching storm. The TV lit my students' faces a soft blue hue. Everyone was entranced. I had a precious half-hour of undisturbed grading time. The stack before me was two inches tall.

I felt Brandon still standing beside me.

"Ms. Kuren," he said. His bright teeth flashed for a second, then vanished. The whites of his eyes diminished as he squinted. When he leaned down, he shrunk the three feet between us to just one, and he said, "I'm a kill you."

"No, you're not," I said flatly, shaking my head, and looked back at my quizzes. What a stupid sentence. Uttered to any other faculty member, and Brandon could have gotten himself kicked out of school. There was tolerance for a good many things in Baltimore City Public Schools, but—wisely enough—not death threats.

I felt Brandon lean away. When I looked back at him, he pressed his lips together, glanced to the very northeast edges of his eyes, then side-nodded, as if to say, *touché*. As if to say, *It's true. I won't.*

The whites of his teeth flashed again. "Only playin'," he said. He bounced back to his desk, the white page with the two intersecting circles flapping in his hand.

• • •

At least once a week, Brandon showed up at my door during third period, kicked out of Sypher's History class again. "He be *fussin'*," Brandon usually said with a shrug, like this was obvious, like Sypher's "fussing" should explain Brandon's appearance at my door during an hour when I didn't have to think about Brandon. "Can't I do work in here?"

Sypher was the guy who, before school had started, had told Brooke, Amy, Ellen, Noelani, and me his traumatic anecdotes, including "The Day I Threatened to Kill a Student, Who In Turn Threw a Chair at Me." As the school year wore on, Sypher continued his stories wherein so-and-so-student committed such-and-such rebellious act, and Sypher responded with his wild, chalk-filled iron fist, which in turn restored all control to him. His disciplinary style remained the same as his advice on the day I'd met him: "Fuck with them."

The teacher-pupil combo of "Tom Sypher meets Brandon Ward" made for tragic fate, to say the least.

Some days I laid my foot down. "But you're missing history," I said. "You can't stay here."

"He just gonna fail me anyway. If I come *here?*" Brandon said, his intonation lifting on the last word, "I do more work." He brought one hand toward his stomach and reached the other out toward me. "Then I pass your class. You feel me?"

The problem with a bungee chord is that it just keeps getting longer, stretching farther, wearing its elastic away until whoever jumps and hopes to bounce back might instead slam into the ground. "No," I said on some days. "I don't *feel* you."

But Brandon's reasoning was right: Sypher would fail him. My class, he could still get credit for. And if I'd said no to him, Brandon would have headed down Font Hill and not returned. He would have missed not only History at third period but English at fourth.

"I get more work done during this period anyway," he said. Without Jerome and Yolanda and Timmy to distract him, with only the seemingly insignificant ninth graders of Southwestern, Brandon could sit in the back and stick to himself.

My third-period students were giggling and shrieking and giddy when Brandon entered the room, amped up on their malnourished lunches of corn chips and colas. But as Brandon slalomed between the desks, the usually frenzied ninth graders ceased their high-pitched, kiddish noises. Their words turned to murmurs. Brandon towered over their adolescent frames. He strutted to the back of the room where he sat at a small cubby that faced a wall and did some work. He looked laughably overgrown within the confines of that cubby.

When Brandon turned something in at the end of the period, his ideas were thoughtful, his sentences varied, his vocabulary precise and impressive, and I knew I was reading work from a kid who could easily move on to tenth-grade English, where he belonged, a kid who could graduate high school, go to college. But he wasn't convinced that any diploma would do him a lick of good in the world he knew. So I was left in the position as cheerleader for a student who sometimes didn't attend my class, or who attended my class but not at the right time, or who, when he did attend the right class at the right time, sometimes threatened his classmates.

• • •

It was standardized test day, when some state or federal bureaucrat decided to sprinkle stapled booklets of grayish pages of arbitrary questions upon every school classroom like a reckless poet scatters his verse from the roof of a building. Here, Baltimore English teachers. Make your kids take these tests. Here, Baltimore students, fill in the bubble-sheets. No, the test will not ask you about *Romeo and Juliet*, which you've been reading but which we test-makers care nothing about. No, the test will not prompt you to describe Tupac Shakur's metaphors or allow you to create your own literary character in lieu of the multiple choice. You'll have sixty minutes to read passages you've never seen before and then answer questions whose true answers you will never learn because your filled-in bubble sheets will be whisked away and sent back to us, your faceless bureaucrats, and never returned to you. Now choose the right answers. You have sixty minutes. Go.

Bungee chords be gone. Brandon, Timmy, Jerome, Yolanda, had to remain seated, and *quiet*, for an hour. *Come on, fourth period*, I thought on this dread day. *Show me that the loose disciplinary choices I've made, the ones that have kept you in my room while your other teachers have kicked you out, won't render our whole class chaotic at the very moment when I have to reign you in.*

"If I catch you talking, I'll give you a zero for the day."

Yolanda groaned and put her head down. As Brandon would say, I felt her. An early summer had descended on our port city, and this unexpected heat wave colluded unhappily with "Standardized Test Day." Sitting in the room was misery. It felt like the oil-slicked, sludgy green water of the Chesapeake Bay had infiltrated the air molecules of Charm City, and we now breathed the toxic hot muck of the bay even as we sat in the poorly circulated cinderblock school. Just like the alarm system, the supposed "air conditioning system" was faulty. The walls sweated. The kids sweated. And now I'd made a daring promise: I'd tear up the test of any talker. One peep, and I'd have to reek havoc on their bubble sheets.

But my fourth period class got quiet. They faced their test booklets. Kenneth bit his pencil, then filled in a bubble. Yolanda lifted her head up from her forearm, sighed, and opened the newspapery booklet. Brandon, always eager to prove his intelligence, tore through the first question, the second, the third. Only he did it bear-chested. His brown, hairless torso looked half the width of his baggy, belted jeans.

I stood behind his bare shoulder. "Put your shirt back on, Brandon."

His white tank-top was draped across his other shoulder like a dishrag. He filled in a bubble and ignored me.

"Brandon," I whisper-yelled.

"It's too *hot* to be wearing a shirt," he said.

"You need to put your shirt on. Now."

This isn't going to end well, I thought. *Why am I making a scene over this? Why can't I just let him keep his shirt off?* And then—like those cartoon depictions of angels and devils hovering over people's shoulders, battering them with opposing viewpoints—I thought, *Because! Because kids have to wear their clothes! Because what if Ms. Grant walks by and thinks I'm even more inept than she'd originally assumed! Because what does it say about me that I let my students sit around topless? What kind of teacher does that make me? A doormat teacher. A dishrag teacher, draped lifelessly over the shoulder of some bear-chested kid. Because there has to be some boundary, some line Brandon Ward cannot, must not cross.* On standardized test day, I'd found and then drawn my line: Clothes must stay on.

I didn't hang over Brandon and wait for him to poke his arms through the giant holes of his ribbed tank top. Instead I walked away from his desk. I gave him some space. By the time I turned around, maybe his half-naked self would be clothed again.

Jerome was staring at a bulletin board and whacking himself on the head with a ruler. Tap, tap, tap, smack on his crown. I scrunched up my face and gave him the "What are you doing, get back to work" face.

"It *itch*," he whined, referring to his un-scratchable scalp. He'd recently gotten his long hair braided into cornrows. He kept banging on his head with the ruler but didn't utter another word.

I turned around. Brandon's chest was as brown and as bare as before.

I leaned over him again. I whispered my ultimatum: the shirt or the door.

"What?" he shouted. "I'm taking my test!"

Please, Brandon, I wanted to plead. *Just put the damn thing on. Just stick your head through the neck hole, draw your arms up through the arm-holes, pull the cotton down around your lanky frame, and get on with your life. Please don't make me enforce a rule that will result in your zero, which will pull you down like a mathematical brick tied to the foot of someone treading water in the Chesapeake. We are so close. We are one month away. You nearly have your English credit. You're one year closer to a diploma that is statistically improbable for you (being male and black and Baltimorean) but one year closer nonetheless. You might just make it to tenth grade.*

But no. It was too hot. The scene escalated. *Fuck. Shit. Bitch.* Brandon now meant business. This was not the mock-rage he wore when he said he could take me. I now knew the difference between faux raging Brandon and real. Real raging Brandon did not give a fuck about you or anyone else. He would pummel whatever piece of shit got in his way, so you might as well step out of it. Brandon Ward as Anger Incarnate. He stood up, fists clenched, jaw popping, eyes hard and unknowing, and shoved his chair. Its painted plywood backing banged against the desk's edge, and little Kenneth jolted a vertical inch. But we were spared any other violence: as bare-chested as when he sat in his chair, Brandon stormed out of the room, leaving his classmates and an hour's worth of work that resided in those many rows of empty little ovals.

Kenneth resumed reading the questions. Yolanda threw her head back onto her forearm, groaning. Timmy glanced at the clock and started filling in the circles at random. In between the walls of "Great Work!" bulletin boards and inspirational "Give 100%" posters, I paced. My mind was now only half present for this hellishly hot testing day. I'd worked on my relationship with Brandon for three months, had developed a tolerable connection with a kid who, yes, pushed my buttons but had also complied with my class far better than any other on his schedule. But the shirt incident confirmed a sad truth: my relationship with Brandon was not special enough to "save him," not enough for him to grant me the respect I needed in order to teach him anything. The probability that he'd stay in Southwestern another three years seemed slim at best.

• • •

"Did you hear?" Sypher found me in Amy's classroom, biting into a sandwich during my lunch break. Instead of just reporting his news, he made me ask for it.

"Hear what?" We were a month away from the end of the semester.

"Brandon Ward. He's been kicked out."

I kept eating. "How many days?"

"No, not suspended. Expelled. For good."

I put my sandwich down on aluminum foil. I thought of Brandon's grade, his shabby but solidly passing sixty-five percent. I thought of every painful day that I'd put up with his crap. "Why?" And why *now*?

"He threatened to kill me." Sypher folded his arms across his body and raised his eyebrows. He looked accomplished.

Before I could keep myself from saying it, I said it: "He didn't mean it!"

Sypher buckled his eyebrows. "I don't *care* if he meant it. I can't take chances like that. The kid threatened to *kill* me."

Of course Sypher was right. Of course, of course. A school couldn't tolerate death-threats. But as much as I knew the bureaucratically "right" answer to the situation, that answer also seemed fundamentally wrong. Brandon Ward would keep threatening, keep pushing, keep letting his tempers flare like those flames that drivers light beside a broken-down car. And whatever new school he was in would push back. It would serve its job as relentless umpire: *Outta Here*, it would say, and out he'd go. Because the school couldn't tolerate, maybe shouldn't tolerate, the behaviors of a kid like Brandon Ward.

But like that broken-down car surrounded by flares, Brandon too would go nowhere. Sure, he'd get sent to another school. Probably another high school, or maybe, if the city felt he was out of chances, the alternative school: the end of the educational line, the last straw that Baltimore City had to offer its delinquent kids. I knew a teacher there who had to hold her classes in a trailer. The school was running out of room, was getting too many lost causes from the city's high schools, was adding mobile homes to this, the very end of its long, knotted line. But how long would Brandon take before finding the boundary, the uncrossable boundary that he'd slip across one day and refuse to honor? He'd stand on the other side, facing his authorities, arms crossed, face smug, and say, "Try me." Or he'd utter those few powerful words that he'd tried on both Sypher and me: *I'm a kill you.* Out he'd go. And maybe Baltimore cared, but not enough to tolerate death threats. Who could blame them? Why did I?

Just like that, an enormous pain in my ass was gone, out of my hair, someone else's problem. Sypher was telling me because he thought I'd be pleased.

• • •

The weather got hotter in Baltimore; the hallways and classrooms were less populated with each passing day. In the spring, attendance tradition-ally slipped from sixty-something to fifty-something percent, and this semester was no different. Maybe some classes also suffered from the fate of my fourth period. Jerome Smith was no longer with us either. Some unknown kid had walked up to an English teacher and shoved a Polar-oid in her face. Between the white plastic borders of the picture was a disembodied penis entering a disembodied vagina. The teacher screamed, and the kid ran away. She didn't know his name, but a few days later, she spotted the same kid—Jerome—in the hall. "There! You!" An assistant principal was passing by. "*That*'s the kid who showed me a pornographic Polaroid." By the end of the week, Jerome was kicked out of school for sexual harassment.

Compared to our first day together, my once hard-core fourth period felt lonely. Of the six kids on that first day who gave me initial trouble, only two were left. Yolanda sighed during the lessons and held her face up with her palm. Timmy made a loud, deep-voiced joke or two, but with no one to wisecrack with, his attempts sunk like stones. And though Yolanda still called him *Titty*, the nickname seemed sad to her without Jerome and Brandon present to fuel the teasing. There were upsides, of course, to the thin attendance. Prepubescent Kenneth Peters was more talkative without the other kids, and so was Aneesha and the only other girl in the class. In fact, with only about twelve kids on the roster, fourth period quickly became the easiest class on my schedule. No one tried to derail my agen-das. Everyone was fully on board with the mission to graduate ninth grade. I felt I was genuinely teaching those that remained. This, I knew, was a version of success.

Meanwhile, in some other classroom in Baltimore, Jerome and Brandon were back to their same antics, trying to convince whatever new teacher they had that they weren't teachable, that they were hopeless, that they were thugs.

• • •

The normally day-lit windows were dark. The school was cocooned in nighttime. I imagined the Baltimore world outside the school walls, where on one side were the acres of cemetery descending down the hill, and on the other side, rows of boarded up homes, alleyways of broken glass and graffiti, and boys waiting on corners, eyeing whoever drove by. It was strange to feel, for once, safer within the school than outside of it. Belly-throbbing bass beats shook the gymnasium, which was nearly as dark as the outdoors. The space was hot and packed with kids dancing, thumping. I was so-called chaperoning. I felt crazy, hanging out on a Friday night in the building I typically fled at 4:30, but tonight was a rare, end-of-year dance, the kind of school-sponsored event that Southwestern either didn't tend to plan or, if it had planned, usually needed to cancel due to reasonable fears that the school might implode. During this year's annual "fashion show," which consisted of Southwestern's highly confident girls strutting across the auditorium stage in outfits they normally wore to school, "outsiders" came to watch—students' cousins, moms, uncles, aunts—and consequently sections of the audience broke out into fights. Something about warring territories, some old, unknown street aggression that had originated in the neighborhood and infiltrated the school.

At the dance, I pushed against the collective force of people and found a way toward a spot on a wall where I could stand by and watch.

A tall kid walked by. Jetting little chin. Lanky frame. It was against school policy for Brandon to step onto Southwestern's grounds. I called his name over the bumping hip-hop music.

He turned his head in my direction. When he looked me in the eyes, I became subconscious: the club-style music, my casual jeans. The situation had *disaster* graffitied all over it. I was no longer his teacher; the school was no longer his authority. He could curse, harass, even hurt me, and nobody in that building could dangle an official penalty over his stubborn little head.

But he could also talk to me. I wanted to hear about his new school, about whether he was passing, or even attending. Maybe Brandon Ward was perfectly fine, had learned his lesson, was thriving in some new Charm City environment destined just for him. I had to look up to meet him in the eye, and I felt meager and frail in the massive crowd. Still, I asked how he was.

When he looked back at me, his eyes weren't the crisp, round daggers I'd known in his raging moments, nor were they the sharp, dark globes I'd seen when he'd returned smart answers for my questions. His eyes were foggy. His eyelids were like heavy window shades half-covering his irises. It either took him a second to recognize me, or a second for his brain to send signals to his body, and his chin-first reverse-nod played out in slow motion. He was in a haze; he was high. "'Sup," he said, a word that seemed muddy in his mouth.

I don't know that he could have said anything else, and he didn't bother. He disappeared back into the crowd just as he'd appeared, and I told no one that Brandon Ward was back on campus, and no fight broke out at the dance that evening, and I drove home that night, wondering where the happy endings, where the redemptive narratives, where the triumphs were in this town.

II

SECOND YEAR

CHAPTER 10

THE REVOLVING PRINCIPALS

Ms. Ryder's sun-yellow gauze pants and matching sun-yellow blouse blew in the hot September wind. Beside her were walking flags of other primary colors: Ms. Patterson, stouter than Ryder, in cranberry. Another mid-sized woman in shimmering peacock green.

"Everyone's dressed in their Sunday best," said Noelani with a sigh from the driver's seat.

I was sitting passenger. Coach Powell emerged from his sedan across the parking lot, straightening a tie underneath a white collar. What was the occasion?

I'd forgotten the world of my job, and with it, all the insane details: Ms. Ryder's raspy shriek as she called Yolanda *a nass-ty child*; Powell's light-skinned, freckled cheeks as he got up close and demanded I change Marcus Gordon's grade; the U-lock slipped into place before Timmy Rogers broke open the closet door and retrieved his red baseball cap; the vent of my door that was set on fire; the ambush of drunk men who stumbled into my class, liquor bottles in hands; the unresponsive emergency call button and the first knuckle of my index finger bending backwards against it; that intermittently ringing, half-broken fire alarm; our truant principal and his bored, distant voice over the intercom. *Youngsters, please get to class. . . .*

Here it was—my job—and I sat in the car nursing the hollow resistance in my throat. It seemed that Noelani was also in a kind of stupor as we watched our well-dressed colleagues, as we remembered that this dysfunctional school was not just a very long dream we'd forgotten over the summer.

"There goes Mr. Johnson," Noelani said.

"Who?" I couldn't place the name until I saw him. A man in a deep-purple suit with tinted glasses and gold chains strutted toward the conference center. "*Lester,*" I said, and remembered the gaggle of cooing girls who encircled him in the hallway, who sometimes literally hung on his broad shoulders in between classes despite his half-hearted attempts to shoo them away. *Lester,* the kids called him, because that was his first

147

name, and sometimes he called the girls *Pretty*, as he did one day when a female student and her mini-skirt passed, and Lester told the female student she was *Pretty*. And then he added, *Pretty ugly*.

I'd totally forgotten Lester. But this year might be different. Inside the conference center our new principal waited. She'd moved from another zone high school to resurrect our statistically failing school. Maybe in the minds of all the teachers was the mantra about a first impression, and getting only one chance. But I watched those English Mother Hens—Ms. Patterson, Ms. Ryder, Ms. Someone-Else whose name I couldn't remember—all dressed in flowing, bright colors, all teetering in higher-than-usual heels and blushing with rouge and smiling and waving big to colleagues they hadn't seen all summer, and I got the sense that the church-grade attire was for themselves. For a few days, or maybe just a few hours, they could be the people they wanted to be. Before the year really began and the students arrived and the administration blundered, these teachers could be kind, even-tempered, cordial, and well-rested. Not screaming at students who'd driven them to the brink, and not calling out sick once, twice a week. Today they began anew with the cleanest of professional slates. Out with the old, in with the new—including the new sun-yellow pants-set, far fancier than Ms. Ryder's old teal one.

But Noelani and I remained parked and seated.

I'd spent half the summer visiting friends, the other half idling around heat-stricken Baltimore and taking a class at Johns Hopkins, where I learned about special education from a tall, broad white guy whose face browned as the weekends accrued. Each Monday he appeared with a more severe sunglasses tan. I shifted my attention between the remarkable clarity of this suntan-mark, and the monotony of his PowerPoint presentations.

"This is how I teach," he said of his method, which consisted of him standing at the front of a room, clicking on a laptop, then turning his attention to a projector screen, where he read from yet another Power-Point slide that contained special education acronyms—B.I.P.'s, C.O.P.'s, A.R.D.'s, P.L.P's—or another bulleted list about how we should diversify our instruction to special ed students. The only diversification of his lessons came at the end, when anxiety ensued in our big, bronze instructor as he realized he still had half his slides to go and only five minutes to click through them. I didn't mind as he sped through the remaining acronyms in rapid-fire succession. During the school-year, he was a principal of a special ed high school, and I could respect the man's need for less time planning lessons, more time soaking up sun.

While the projector screen flashed anew every few minutes, I made notes that glorified the hypothetical perfectness of my upcoming year. I would design a new management system wherein my kids would enter my classroom and immediately devote themselves to grammar and great literature because I would stamp their drill sheets with little stars or I would sticker their papers with smiley faces as long as the students were on task, and these stickers and stamps would be very persuasive. They would keep my kids on task. I would teach revolutionarily engaging units during which my students would read plot-driven, dramatic auto-biographies and value their own rich lives by writing well-crafted (and grammatically pristine) autobiographies themselves, and this unit would make them fall in love with writing, and life, and autobiographies. And in general I would be a more competent teacher because I would regain control of that vocabulary board that Ms. Nelson had dominated my first semester, the one that listed twenty-some words chosen by her, undefined and totally unrelated to anything my kids were reading. This year, this glorious year, I'd discipline myself to maintain a weekly list of words, and I'd teach the definitions of these words all week, and these words would be relevant to my students' lives and to the texts they were appreciating, and then I'd quiz my students on these words, and they'd know them, and they'd use them in real life. And it would be good. *Vocabulary, stickers, auto-biographies: these would perfect my classroom, Mr. Sunglasses-Tan.* He replied to my well-planned thoughts by pressing on his laptop, saying *Okay*, and reading another slide.

"Ready?" Noelani asked back in her car.

That word clutched at my stomach, turned it forty-five degrees like a doorknob. "'Member last year?" I stalled. "With Mr. Owens?"

"Owens!" Noelani cried. "I love Owens," she sang, and Owens became a reason to get out of the car. We could talk to Owens. Owens would moti-vate us. We'd make Owens write inspirational messages on his clipboard and hold them up to us throughout the retreat-day, just as he did for stu-dents who walked the halls.

"He could tell right away that we were new last year," she said.

"He said we both looked green," I remembered.

The more I dress like this, he'd said, gesturing to his swishy track suit on the first day that we met him, *the more my students and I get along.* On the day he'd first met us, Owens thought we were overdressed. I looked at Noelani's lap, then mine. Though we wore virtually the same ensem-bles as last year—skirts, shirts—our outfits were marked by crucial varia-tions. Soft-soled sandals instead of heels. Jersey-knit wash-and-wear shirts instead of button-up, easily wrinkled blouses.

"It's gonna be a better year," one of us said, to which the other agreed.

"We're not 'green' anymore."

"We've survived Jerome Smith."

"And Antoine McCargo."

"And Ms. Brown's intercom announcements."

"Oh my God. Those announcements."

"*Teeechers,*" Noelani impersonated.

Together, we emphasized every other syllable with a high-pitched nasal whine. "*Why* are there *stu*dents in the *hall*ways!?"

We laughed. The laughter died. The silence hung like fuzzy dice under a rearview mirror. We had reminded ourselves of the administration.

"But it's gonna be different this year," Noelani said. "With the new principal."

I said yes, and Noelani said yes, and we opened the car doors and got out.

• • •

A fellow TFA teacher had spent his first year with the principal we were inheriting, so maybe we learned the rumor from him: that when this new principal, Dr. Jackson, had trouble with her teachers, she blessed their class-room doors with holy water. I never knew exactly what "trouble" meant, but this tidbit didn't bode well with my colleagues, perhaps because it collapsed the standard boundaries of church and state, or maybe because it evoked a holier version of a door-hexing. On the upside, I reasoned that at least Jackson made proactive choices. Our old principal, Dr. Jefferson, had been a figment of the Southwestern imagination, a proverbial Snuffleup-agus of the Baltimore school system. Throughout the year, Jefferson had only occasionally commandeered the intercom, typically to give the school its surreal, far from daily "Word of the Day."

"Youngsters," began Jefferson in his reserved, lethargic, dry tone. "The word of today is: *Abnormous. Abnormous* is an adjective," unnaturally long pause, as though our principal were searching for his next cue on some sheet of paper before him. "Meaning *irregular*. To use it in a sentence, you might say," pause, "'Betty had an abnormous day . . .'" another long, awkward pause " . . . when she met the clown," pause, "on the street." Noelani and I and the other TFA teachers laughed at this. We would later tell each other how *abnormous* it was that the fire alarm hadn't erupted in three days, or how *abnormous* it was that Jerome Smith hadn't humped anything animate or inanimate yesterday, or how *abnormous* it was that no tiles had fallen from the ceiling that week. We outdid each other with mock-sentences and we laughed, but once the laughter waned, what hung between us was our collective futility, and we sighed. Something about the Word of the Day—its consistent randomness, its sentences that always contained the un-Baltimorean, other-worldly white names like "Betty," its subsequent meaninglessness to our students—seemed incredibly sad.

Now the new principal might bless our doors with holy water? To me, it seemed like a step up. I reasoned that at least Dr. Jackson made her presence known, albeit to the Lord Almighty.

Inside the conference center, Noelani and I and every faculty member sat at round tables just like last year, like we all awaited a banquet dinner that would never arrive. Eventually, a short, spry middle-aged woman stood at a podium in the front of the room. She wore her hair short, and she wore a pantsuit that tapered at the ankles and accented the diminutiveness of her flat shoes. She looked sprightly, Peter-Pannish. Her initial greetings were expected. *Good morning, I'm so and so, I'm pleased to be working with you this year.* It wasn't until her one particular line that I perked up. "*Y'all,*" she addressed us in a throaty, stern voice. "I don't know how *y'all* feel." Her eyes widened. "But I do *not* feel like playin' this year!"

I sat up. *Y'all? Playin'?* What was this straight-talk speech I was not accustomed to hearing from administrators?

Her audience of teachers *mmhmm*-ed and *alright*ed. She shook her head to the tune of their responses. She grabbed the microphone with one hand, snaked the cord through the other, and stepped in front of the podium. This was a far cry from Jefferson, who wasted the physical prowess of his six feet by clinging stiffly behind a podium; who, every time he spoke to his faculty, seemed to be reading from a script he dug up from some 1950s handbook on *How to Speak Like a Leader of a School.*

"Let's not even pretend like we all don't know why I'm here," she said. Light-footed in her flats, she darted between our circular tables like a sprite. Everyone knew why she was here, she said. She turned one way, then the other, as if to say, *I'm talking to* you. *And to* you, *over there. And way over there, in the back,* you *too.* "I'm here because this school isn't working." The older women in primary-colors, the ones whose outfits had blown outside in the hot breeze, they nodded and *mm-hmm*ed in the air conditioning. They'd been around for decades, they'd been in a lot of not-working schools, and they'd always said this school was one of the least working ones they'd been in.

"I need *you* to help *me* get this school back on track," the new principal told her staff. As Jackson made eye contact with nearly every person in the room, I realized that I hadn't felt present to my former administration, not for the whole year. They'd rarely visited my room, they hardly knew my name. Now this woman was looking straight at me, and I smiled and nodded.

"And if you do that," she paused and looked around, "if you help me, then you and I will get along just fine." She stretched the last two words, *just fine,* like butter across a slice of bread. "Do you hear me?" she asked, and after some teachers but not all murmured yes, she asked more loudly, "Do you *hear* me?" and a raucous "yes" echoed against the walls of the banquet hall.

•••

A few months before this first speech to Jackson's new faculty and staff, the alumni association of her former school voted to have its principal removed. She'd served only two years on the job. If we Southwestern teachers had done our research, we could have learned that Jackson was placed at her former school by the school district chief without consultation of two local state delegates, that in reconfiguring the school, Jackson disregarded and therefore offended these delegates, and that they then pressured the chief to fire her. A year later, Jackson was officially relocated. In the minutes of a School Board meeting just months before Jackson arrived to us at her new job on Font Hill, a few parents and alumni pleaded with the Board to keep Dr. Jackson. "I want to know," said one concerned alumna, "if there is going to be any reconsideration . . . so that we can have her continue with her mission and her vision. We really need her. . . ." Another woman, a member of the alumni class of 1948, also spoke. She'd graduated before *Brown v. Board,* when the school was one of only two Baltimore high schools that African Americans could attend. This 71-year-old woman cited the stability of a former administration as a reason that she had possessed, as a nineteen-year-old, the confidence to challenge and gain admittance to the University of Maryland's School of Nursing. "There used to be stability at one time. What is happening now that principals are leaving before they can even do what they are set out to do?"

Jackson's record had been far from perfect, though. During her first month at her former job, hundreds of students had been assigned to classes they didn't need or couldn't yet take; seniors sat furiously in tenth-grade courses and ninth-graders sat baffled in eleventh-grade courses, and other kids, refusing to waste their time, just walked the halls. Why sit in a class you don't need? Why learn from a school that doesn't care about which credits you must have to graduate? Though Jackson defended the disaster by arguing that the school's scheduler had quit in the summer and had left the products of her unknown incompetence behind, the *Baltimore Sun* exploited Jackson's first month as an embarrassment, and only after four messy weeks did each kid receive an appropriate schedule. Jackson then had to tell her teachers to "go easy on" the kids who'd missed a solid month of class; in other words, the first month of school was a wash.

What made the story unusual wasn't the scheduling chaos; it was the publicity such chaos received. "Students' Possess Irrelevant Schedules" could have easily been a headline for Southwestern. In fact, Jackson's former school looked much like any inadequate Baltimore high school, and though Jackson had called Southwestern "not working," she could have easily used the phrase to describe her former school. It had been deteriorating for years. Though it was once touted as one of the city's top high schools, it offered no advanced-level courses for its students, and according to the *Baltimore Sun*, its seniors "had a mean combined SAT score of 762." Members of the Alumni Association toured the school with the CEO of Baltimore schools, and reported feeling "devastated" by the conditions. An alumnus, one who voted to have Jackson removed, defended his vote at the aforementioned board meeting, arguing that the place needed a new start, a new principal.

And this was why Jackson now stood before us. Not just because our school was "not working," was indeed failing, not just because Dr. Jefferson was inept and we needed a new principal, but because her old community felt the same about its school, about its former principal, which was now our brand-spanking new one. And so Dr. Jackson left behind another not-so-well-working school, and Dr. Jefferson left behind our institution for another school, presumably where he made a speech about improving it, and the principal of whatever poor school Dr. Jefferson took over, well he or she got shuffled somewhere else, and on and on went the circle until it was completed and someone, somewhere, shifted into Jackson's old slot. Through our small-windowed perspective on Font Hill, we were witnessing the symptoms of a principal-shuffling phenomenon.

Among community members, the perception of Baltimore City Public Schools is far from positive. For me, this is best underscored in a documentary, *The Boys of Baraka*, about an experimental middle school in rural Kenya. For twenty poor Baltimore boys, the Baraka School is an intended detour around a disturbing statistical fate: a high percentage of African American males are shot or incarcerated before they reach adulthood. The twelve- and thirteen-year-olds spend their middle school years away, in the African bush, and make significant academic and behavioral progress. But in the middle of the film, when administrators report that, due to Kenyan instability, the boys have to complete their educations in Baltimore's public schools, the parents are wrecked. In an emergency meeting with Baraka school administrators, the parents react in all kinds of devastated ways: they scoff, throw arms up, stand up from their chairs and yell, sit and curl forward, their hands on their foreheads, letting tears roll down their cheeks. For me, the most difficult few seconds to watch are when one mother wails, in a stern alto, "When you're sending our kids to Baltimore schools, you're sending them to *jail!*" As if the line isn't hard enough for any Baltimore educator to swallow, she repeats it with heartbreaking conviction. *When you're sending these kids to Baltimore schools, you're sending them to jail!* This mother and countless parents of Charm City saw Baltimore's schools not as metaphorical ladders to the American Dream, but as bleak cul-de-sacs that returned kids right back to the poverty out of which they came.

But for most kids, that cul-de-sac was the only educational pathway they had—the city's broken schools were the city's schools nonetheless—so the district made its gestures to fix them, and among those gestures was the constant shuffling of its principals. "We've had three different principals in the past four years," said one TFA teacher of a school very much like Southwestern. "How are any of them expected to fix the school if they only stay on average a year and a third?" Maybe the city reasoned that, like a child randomly fidgeting with a Rubik's Cube, if it kept rotating the principals around and around, somehow all the pieces would click into place. A certain combination of rearrangements might produce a perfect cube; a sudden Joe-Clark-meets-Eastside-High movie-ending could appear before all our eyes. Maybe the city itself had subscribed to Hollywood pedagogy.

Regardless, Jackson seemed like an improvement. So after I spotted Mr. Owens in his customary ensemble—a dark-blue swishy track-suit—and after he shouted what would become an oft-repeated, shocked greeting to me that week (*You came back!*), and after I hugged him hello, I said to dear Owens, "Jackson seems like the real deal," to which he lifted his eyebrows high above his bulging eyes and put his lips together in a tiny o, the way someone admires a fierce knock-out. But then he said, "We'll see."

And I remembered what I loved about Owens: no one seemed to internalize better than he that the stakes of our jobs were high, that in our hands rested the futures of kids, that with any given action or turn of phrase, a teacher could win over a kid, who could then head for metaphorical Emerald Cities of success. But Owens carried this passion along with a tempered dose of realism. Jackson would have to prove herself. Owens would just wait and see.

"'Member when we met this time last year?" I said to him.

"Man, Kirn, you were so new." Owens' open-mouthed smile revealed his delight about confessing now what he didn't spell out then. "It was obvious, you know. You can see it now, can't you? In these new folks?"

We scanned the room, and our eyes collectively rested on one circular table where a few of the newest young white teachers stayed seated. This was the new batch TFA had sent. They glanced around. One woman's face was shiny, and I have to pressure myself to call her "woman" because, though she was a college graduate, her long, side-parted, glossy brown hair made her look like a girl. She didn't stand up from the table during break, and this position forced her to look up at everyone like a child caught in a world of adults' waists. A year ago, I probably looked just as green.

Resign yourself to chaos, I told these newbies. In the first few weeks, you'll develop relationships with kids, and the administration will pull those kids out of your room, and you'll never see them again. At the same time, you'll get daily knocks on your door and when you open it wide, a new student-face will appear and hold a schedule on which, sure enough, your name and your class will be clearly listed.

I expected and prepped these brand-new teachers for the same disorder that the *Sun* had reported in Jackson's old school, and not because I'd read the article, but because I'd seen the same disorder at Southwestern the year before. Despite the fact, I told them, that you'll have spent several hours with your kids laying ground rules and articulating consequences and learning their names and soliciting several diagnostics so that you're aware of the precise tragedy that is each kids' grade-level performance—despite this, your classes will change. And with each kid added, you'll have to start over again. By the second month, you might even get another knock on your door, as Noelani did, when you'll learn that one of your students who has sat in your class all semester shouldn't be there, that the kid is "special ed" and isn't allowed to be in a mainstream class, that the kid won't thrive in a mainstream environment. But to top it off, you'll be asked to change this child's failing grade because, in fact, this diagnosis was not a new discovery; it was a paperwork error. It was the school's sloppy fault that he hadn't received the kind of education he was lawfully entitled to, so the school now asks you politely to pass the child for a class in which he'd made no progress. Otherwise the school could be sued. This is what they told Noelani, and this is what they might tell you as you stand in the doorway and receive a form to sign.

Also, new teacher, you might not have enough desks in your room.

But unlike the desk-debacle of my first year, I walked back into my classroom for the first time since June and all of my vandalized desks stood present and accounted for. Under each desktop a chair was neatly tucked. My yellow streamers were still tacked to the beige vinyl shades, and my posters about similes and Maryland state teaching standards and my postcards of Virginia Woolf and Ghandi and Malcolm X all remained on the sweaty cinderblock walls where I'd left them.

Ms. Wallace popped her head in. Her black hair looped in wide short curls around her face instead of, as in last year, standing frizzed and shocked in all directions. "I used your room for summer school," she said in an unusually pleasant tone. "I made sure the kids took good care of it."

"Thanks," I said. "Your hair looks nice."

She put her hand to it, smiled bashfully, and shrugged. She'd obviously gotten a new look for the new year. "I have your rosters."

"These'll change, right?" I said to other teachers when I held them up. None of us knew then that they would not change.

The positive notes of the new school year didn't end with desks and rosters. I found myself constantly contrasting Jackson's way of operating to our former principal, Dr. Jefferson. When the students arrived—the boys waddling in their shin-length black or white T-shirts and sagging pants, the girls strutting in their colorful, well-coordinated outfits and newly styled hair—Jackson didn't pull a Jefferson. She didn't wait for the hallways to fill completely with kids before announcing something like, *Youngsters should move along to their proper places.*

No, Jackson spoke urgently. *Get to class.* Her voice was grating and no-nonsense. This was no dusty, Victorian-robotic, contraction-free and grammatically diagrammed syntax of Ms. Brown. *There won't be any playing today,* she told her kids, just as she'd told us. But to throw more heat into the command, to make the lingering hallwalkers actually move, she added consequences. *In five minutes, we'll round up any student not in class and suspend them.* A-hah! The wise promise of repercussion. Students reluctantly tore themselves away from the walls of the hallways, where they'd been leaning, and they meandered to the room numbers on their schedules.

And once the students arrived in their homerooms, the school wasn't locked down for two hours as the administration tried to figure out who was present and who wasn't, as in last year's two-hour homeroom period. The first day moved along swiftly. And though I anticipated frequent knocks on my door, wherein someone would announce a total shift to my classroom dynamic, those knocks never came. It was a small miracle. The administration was doing its job.

• • •

During the first week, while I sized up the personalities and reading capabilities of my temporarily quiet third period, the fire alarm erupted. New to the school, my ninth graders immediately wiggled in their seats, sat up, and waited for me to tell them to move out. I paused, index finger held in the air like I was checking wind, mouth gaping slightly open and eyebrows raised, expecting a fast explanation about technical difficulties from the loudspeaker. When half a minute passed and none came, I nodded toward the door and, before joining the class, grabbed some of my belongings and my black leather teacher-bag. This was most likely a fire, I thought.

The students and staff meandered out the side doors and assembled onto the long, steadily ascending hill by the parking lot. I looked up at the grassy hill and saw my ninth graders not in rows exactly but loosely gathered together and looking vaguely intimidated between the hordes of far bigger kids. *First week*, I thought. Their fear worked to my advantage.

About fifty meters away, I spotted small and spry Dr. Jackson rushing from teacher to teacher. Making sure no one was hurt? Concerned about our wellbeing in this possibly real fire? I'd never seen Jefferson outside after a fire alarm.

Jackson approached cluster after cluster of teachers, and each time, the teachers shrugged or shook their heads, which made Jackson scowl and shout before moving on to the next cluster. She was demanding something. A head count? The time? I wondered if I had whatever she wanted.

"Grade books?" I finally heard. "Teachers, let me see your grade books. Hold 'em up." She shook her head in disapproval when she got the mostly empty-handed responses.

"Grade books?" I asked another English teacher. "Why would I need my grades?" So our grades didn't burn down? The teacher didn't know. She didn't have her grade book. I pulled mine from my black bag. When Jackson reached us, I held up my shiny-covered yellow book with its cartoon-drawing of a red apple. She nodded, but when the other teachers showed empty hands, she started in on her lecture.

"How are you supposed to know who's made it out here safely if you don't have your class rolls?" She was steaming. "This is a fire drill!" she said, like it was obvious.

A fire drill! That sensible institutional practice we'd never had. The thought that the alarm signaled a fire drill hadn't occurred to most of us. Nor had the thought occurred to ink our new kids' names into our blank grade books since most teachers were still doubtful that our classes wouldn't be completely upended by the middle of the month as they were last year. Why ruin a perfectly clean grade book with names we might never see again? The habit of expecting ineptitude was hard to break.

Jackson shouted to the teachers that she was keeping score, that she knew who had been on-the-ball enough to bring a fire-drill necessity, and who had screwed up. We looked at each other perplexed, unused to the feeling, maybe, of accountability. I could see veteran Ms. Ellis, blank-faced and unfazed. She shrugged and headed back toward the school, slowly trudging toward her job as the sole senior-year English teacher. I tried to take a cue from her, but I couldn't exude Ms. Ellis's coolness. Though I doubted that Jackson kept an accurate mental record of her entire staff's grade books, I was anxious. I'd been lucky. I'd grabbed my stuff as an afterthought.

But I also had another feeling, one that dangled above me like that noontime September sun above the parking lot's steaming blacktop. I didn't feel like acknowledging it—wanted, instead, to suppress it—but the feeling was glaring nevertheless. I felt wary. Distrustful. On-guard. Regardless of my accidental brownie-points earned, we'd all been expected to comply with a set of rules we hadn't been taught. Jackson had exhibited the most basic error in disciplining, something I'd learned early at TFA Institute, something I'd been spending the better part of this week doing with my students: draw up your rules and communicate them clearly. Only then can you initiate your punishments and rewards. I was grateful for my very first official fire drill at Southwestern because it concluded a week of relative order, but during that drill I also saw what was probably obvious to any veteran on our retreat day: the power in our school now rested in the hands of someone who did not *know* our school. Jackson didn't understand the climate she was entering, one that she'd supposedly been hired to save. It was a school so chaotic that its alarm to declare its chaos was broken; it had never experienced and did not have protocol for actual safety drills; it was used to lacking accurate rosters for its kids. As a way of making it back each day, each week, each year, its teachers adjusted to insane conditions. The teachers were now accountable for the symptoms of its incompetent former administration. And this worried me. How many of our adjustments looked, from the outside, like our own incompetence, even while they managed to save us from going insane ourselves?

When everyone settled back into the classrooms, Jackson spoke over the loudspeaker again. Our schoolwide exit from the building had taken over three minutes. Had this been a fire, some of us would have gone up in flames.

CHAPTER 11

KILLING THE KITTEN

Anthony Smalls was ten baggy-jean-waddling strides away from his science class, and he was headed there. On his way from where? I never knew, but Anthony strutted in an empty hallway wearing the unofficial male uniform of sagging sweatpants and knee-length Hanes white T-shirt, looking like any lone hallwalker of Southwestern. Only Anthony did not walk the halls. Anthony went to class, hardly skipped class, even did his work in class. When he sat at his desk in English, he listened and he thought about my questions and he offered ideas. He wrote those ideas down. Some days, when I grated on his nerves, he pressed his arrogant sharp chin into the air like a smaller pubescent Brandon Ward, but the tough face was as far as Anthony went in rebellion, and it existed maybe for the same reason Baltimore boys swore never to get caught smiling on camera. Never look soft. Never look like you could be pushed around. Even if you're a very thin kid who goes to science class and likes to learn.

"No you don't, young man." Ms. Ames had just rounded the corner and now stood at the end of the hallway. "You turn right around and head back where you came from." She glared at Anthony from behind her plastic-framed glasses. She pointed down the same long hall he'd just walked.

"My class right here," said Anthony, who took another step toward the door to science, now just five strides away.

"Turn around, young man."

"But it's *right. Here*," Anthony said, taking slower steps now, thinking, *She wouldn't stop me from going to class.*

"Son," said Ames, "You take one more step and I'll suspend you. Turn yourself right around, and head back where you came from."

Back where you came from. The mantra was the administration's coping mechanism for hallwalkers who, despite Jackson's no-play talk, had done nothing this year but play Merry-Go-Round in the halls. The administration's policy was now to send them somewhere. Anywhere. It didn't matter. Usually, *back where they came from.* I think the five words spoke to a deeper-seeded desire to literally return any pesky kid to his or her origin,

159

wherever an assistant principal perceived that to be: the home, the womb, the cabbage patch of rascal souls. Please, someone, take back these kids.

Oddly enough, the method worked for Southwestern's plague of hallwalking. Instead of hollering at kids to get to class, to *get where they belonged*, which would have hardly moved the kids an inch, and instead of suspending scores of kids each day, as scores still roamed the halls, the faculty and staff members just kept them moving. The method gave the school's adults a modicum of authority. *Turn around*, kids were told, and they could easily comply with the order: they spun one-eighty and headed for another hall, another stairwell, maybe another floor. And because each assistant principal and each department head really only cared after the one or two hallways nearest their offices, any hallwalker on the move became someone else's problem. *I don't care what happens on the low side of 35*, Ms. Wallace used to say, referring specifically to the other side of our floor where the math and science teachers taught, where on Halloween Brooke's face had twice met the crack and then ooze of raw egg. *Just keep our side clear.*

The goal, aside from pushing responsibility onto someone else, was to keep hallwalkers itinerant. Officer Freeman, one of our two school police, used to reason that maybe the hallwalkers would finally get tired of their nomadic day and take a seat in a class where they'd actually learn something. He once shouted this hope to me over his shoulder before he high-tailed after yet another herd.

For these reasons, whenever an administrator saw a kid in the hallway during class time, and the kid was headed in one direction, the administrator made the kid turn around and walk the other way. Most kids did so without a protesting peep; they meandered back down the long, dusty corridor or into the dark stairwell from whence they came.

But not Anthony. Anthony probably made his *psh* face: head jerked away by a quick wrench of the neck, lips pressed and pushed out at the edges, brow furrowed. Then all at once the expression released with that punctuating sibilant *pshhh*. No way in hell Anthony was turning around, not when his class was just two steps away.

He stood at my door an hour later, narrating the incident with rhetorical fever. "Three days, she give me! I got three days suspension! For going to class!"

The school was in between classes. Other kids blurred by my periphery, but the focus of my vision was Anthony's flaring nostrils.

"That ain't right," he said and folded his arms and shook his head back and forth. Then he tilted his head up. His sharp chin pointed at me. This was my cue to concur. In another year, the boy would be several inches taller, I thought, and the chin would point down, not up.

"I'm sorry, that's, that's unfair," I said. I didn't say it with the rising tone of indignation, but with the flat sigh of factual reporting. Regardless of why Anthony was in the halls during class, he'd just been suspended for trying to *get* to class. If he had turned away from science, if he had headed back into the simple maze of halls, he'd have gotten off clean. But he didn't. The situation was certifiably ridiculous.

"This school is so *stoopid*," Anthony huffed and looked up again, waiting for my reply. Yet another cue. I was meant to agree.

It was a familiar quandary: countless kids had reported with justifiability the *stoop*idness of our school. They'd come to me exacerbated by an administrative decision that made no sense to them or to me. At least weekly I saw the same expression on different kids, the face that was equal parts appalled by injustice and exhausted from it. It was the same one I'd spotted in the kid last year who'd been hauling his backpack to class when a large ceiling tile fell in his path. After it crashed at his feet, and after the white dust of what Ms. Patterson said was asbestos rose up like chalk bits, he eyed me, eyebrows drooping but jaw still clenched; he had just enough anger left to want at least my witness, the thin meager acknowledgement from the lone adult in the hall. *See?* I felt he was asking. *Did you see that? The ceiling just fell. The ceiling was within inches of falling on my head.* I shook my head at the kid and offered an apologetic shrug, and he bit down on his back teeth and walked on.

Here was Anthony, wanting the same thing. *See this?* He wanted my witness. *How ridiculous is this?* And I wanted to say yes, Anthony, you are right. You had no reason, Anthony, to turn away from the very classroom number that's listed on your schedule only to walk one hundred, two hundred meters around the entire rectangle of the building again, which would have taken you how long? Two minutes, at least? Two wasted instruction-time minutes. And it would have put you at risk of stumbling upon another administrator, whose rules might have been as senseless as Ms. Ames's. And why? Because she misjudged you? Because this school is too big for anyone to know your ninth-grade nostril-flaring self, to know that you *aren't* a hallwalker, that you raise your hand, know the answer, do your work, and that your critical thinking is sharp as your chin, sharp enough to question wrong answers and sharp enough to reject bad rules?

But during the short two minutes remaining between now and the fourth period bell while kids shouted and shuffled past classroom doors, I didn't feel I had time to dissect or even expose Southwestern's problems. In my months of teaching, I'd become an isolationist; I'd decided I could only concern myself with my own classroom. This was an admittedly limited philosophy but one that had been paying off. Though the hallways of our school were still peppered with looming kids, and though the attendance rate was still pathetic, and though wars between housing projects still led kids to brawl (which resulted in the disappointing string of cop cars to siren up our hill), my teaching had vastly improved from last year. Like that lens in the optometrist's office clicking left and right and bringing black letters into focus, something in my teaching had "clicked." My progress was made vivid for me one day when even the most rebellious kids' faces were masked by the cover of a small book. On each book was painted a man's purple and green face. The face's enormous almond-shaped eyes were as large as his plump, purple mouth, and the thin green bridge of his nose extended up from the lime green swirls of his nostrils like a child's tree trunk. As my kids pressed their own faces into the pages of the hardbound book, two dozen bizarre, almond-eyed paintings stared back at me: Richard Wright's *Black Boy*.

Maybe they were hooked because I managed my class more efficiently—I kept a tighter ship and communicated rules better. Or maybe they were hooked because, before we even opened the front cover, I'd played Robert Johnson's raspy, foot-tapping, front-porch blues and asked students to imagine the time period in which Johnson sang. "Sounds old," they said. "This from back in the day," they told me. They scrunched up their faces; they weren't used to scratches of record-playing. But after a few measures, my students nodded their heads just slightly to the rhythm of Johnson's guitar. Or maybe they were hooked because of the relatable content, which was why I chose Wright's autobiography over some of the ninth-grade textbook's selections. Once we cracked the binding of the book, they found the short, dramatic scenes riveting.

"Dang," a student said after someone had read the opening scene out loud. Young Richard set his mother's curtains on fire. Now the house was burning to the ground. And "Dang," someone else said when Richard's mother beat him so badly he nearly died. And "Dang" again when, at age six, Richard hung the family's kitten. Wright describes the little pink tongue of the kitten popping from its mouth.

Dang, I thought to myself. Even Joe Bryant, the big kid with the affinity for tossing paper balls, had gotten hooked. His unbraided hair stuck out wildly from behind the cover, giving the green and purple face a third dimension, making that face look shocked by Wright and the flaming curtains and the murdered kitten. Wright's was a world my students related to. The erratic rules resembled their own: authority figures can't be trusted; neighbors rob you; protectors turn you away; sometimes you have to bludgeon somebody to acquire your basic needs; sometimes the people you love—or more importantly, the people who are meant to love you—nearly kill you.

The rules were backwards enough to resemble Southwestern's. And in retrospect, how Richard coped with them, how he side-stepped them or met them head on, might have taught a lot to Anthony Smalls. Richard killed the family kitten because he was angry at his father. Richard thought the man was cruel and "a stranger . . . always somehow alien," and he wanted to relay the sentiment to his father without getting beaten. "Kill that damn thing!" said his irked dad, so Richard decided to pretend the command was the direct order it was never meant to be. After the kitten hung from a rope tied to a tree, his father bristled but didn't beat Richard, and Wright says, "I had had my first triumph over my father. . . . He could not punish me now without risking his authority. I was happy because I had at last found a way to throw my criticism of him into his face. . . . I had made him know that I felt he was cruel and I had done it without his punishing me." For a six-year-old, it was ingenious.

But now, as I stared at angry Anthony, I didn't think of this story. And I didn't commiserate about how fucked up was our school; I quickly reasoned that if I agreed with Anthony, if I said *yes the school is "stoopid,"* I'd only validate that his was a deeply flawed, morally questionable institution, and why should he comply with its flawed, morally questionable rules? I *needed* Anthony to comply with Ames because I needed him in my classroom. Anthony was a sharp kid, sharp enough, I reasoned, to hear what I really said, a lesson I believed was wise and life-changing and which he'd remember forever upon ever:

"Sometimes you're not going to respect people in positions of authority," I said in what was my best attempt at an even-tempered, sisterly voice. I thought of his first job, of his first manager who might not manage any fairer than Ms. Ames. "But unfortunately, they're still in positions of authority. And that means you have to learn how to handle them," I added, "without hurting yourself."

"No!" he shouted. "No you don't." His protest was immediate. His head titled farther back, and his arms tightened across his chest. I was now the target of Anthony's nostril-flaring. "Don't go turning this around on me!"

"I'm not. I'm saying," I paused. How had this backfired? "Sometimes you're going to be smarter than people in authority . . . and even if they don't deserve to be there, they still hold power over you . . ." But he'd already turned his head to the side, and I was talking to his small, angular profile. ". . . and because they can do real damage if you let them get to you . . ." I continued because I couldn't let up. If he didn't learn this lesson, it could break him. "You have to learn how to handle them, those powerful people above you, so you don't bring harm to yourself."

Anthony let a few seconds pass and then turned his face to mine again.

"Why would I walk," he said slowly, squinting, "*all the way* around the building, when I'm already *at the door*!?"

The students watch us, all the time, wrote Theodor Sizer and Nancy Faust Sizer. Their book, *The Students Are Watching,* was one of the most eye-opening I'd read at Johns Hopkins. The Sizers argue that a school teaches as much by its design as by its teachers' lesson plans. A school's rules and policies, its consequences for breaking rules, its arrangement of desks and chairs in a room, even its intercom messages—everything about a school communicates lessons to its kids. *We must honestly ponder what they see, and what we want them to learn from it,* write Sizer and Sizer. *The students are watching.* The concept is enough to paralyze any well-meaning educator.

On this day, Anthony might have learned that following orders was hailed higher than applying logic. He might have learned that, like some grunt on a frontline, his obedience was more valued than his mind. That he was not someone to listen to. Not someone to be trusted. Not someone whose words or ways of seeing the world mattered enough to influence the powers that be. Anthony didn't need my agreement to confirm what he'd already seen. Our school's actions spoke louder than any confirmation I could have offered.

Another bluster of kids passed. The bell had already rung. I knew I should say *Get to class* or something that would assert the very order that the school failed to keep. But I couldn't bring myself to utter the words, maybe because I couldn't bring myself to fulfill my role as enforcer for an institution whose consequences had transgressed a good kid. I still had no answer for Anthony. Why would he walk all the way around the building when he was already at the door? The question was beyond answering. Of course he wouldn't.

Anthony huffed at my silence and turned his head, eyeing the long, emptying hall.

"Gotta go," he said. "I'm *Do Not Admit.*"

In the morning, if the paperwork got filed right and if the secretaries at the front desk updated the list of kids who'd gotten suspended today (all big *ifs*), the name *Anthony Smalls* would be listed on tomorrow morning's green handout entitled "Do Not Admit." As in, no teacher could let Anthony enter his or her classroom. Like Richard's mother who gives her son an ultimatum—either go beat down the boys who attacked you, she said, or stay out of my house forever—I was supposed to shut my door to Anthony, which meant mine was the second doorway to learning that Anthony wanted to walk through today but couldn't.

"See you in three days," I said as little Anthony waddled away in his enormous, floating white Hanes T-shirt like a grounded, cotton cloud.

• • •

If, for the hour, or the day, or the week, Anthony no longer viewed me as a member of his team, I reasoned that it was a small and selfless price to pay for the potential gain. Maybe in the privacy of his home he'd swallow my message—that we couldn't let the "stoopidness" of our school get the best of us, that succumbing to our anger toward authority could do us harm, that we had to find more creative ways of coping with a morally corrupt authority when the ticket that authority offered was ultimately what we needed.

But damn, how I wanted to admit that, yes, Anthony, your school was stupid. More than stupid: insane. As proof, I quote the school psychologist, who, in explaining the behaviors of a manic kid named Nick Lowery, once said, "He's not crazy. He's actually very sane. And very bright. It's just his way of coping with an insane system. He looks around him and sees how F-ed up everything is. And that's why he reacts the way he does." When he wandered the halls, Nick left behind a string of expletives. He resembled the ragged, worrying, ghostly people that passersby see on streets and avoid because, while the strangers mostly mutter to themselves, who knows when they might lash out. Nick shook his head back and forth at his private thoughts or his inaudible grumbles, and he walked in a daze punctured only by sudden, panicked outcries. I'd once seen him stop in the middle of a hall, turn to the nearest adult, and tell her, "Shit, I still got weed on me. Shit!" he cried. "I gotta bounce!" The teacher stood stunned, and Nick charged away, oblivious to the norm he'd broken: randomly confessing a crime to one's authority.

According to the psychologist, Nick had a genius IQ. This fact troubled me. Were genius students driven crazy here? Was Nick's behavior a way of coping with his insane world? At least Anthony's way of coping was lucid indignation, and focused rational protest. Had I been him, I don't know that I would have conjured up any other way of dealing with Ms. Ames, whose voice always strained through the weary pipes of her nasal lethargy, whose eyes were foggy and fatigued behind those enormous tinted lenses, whom I did not respect in the old administration and whom I did not respect in the new. Her decisions were rash, her power exerted haphazardly and usually to prove (to herself or to someone nearby) that she was still capable of wielding control over a building that was very much out of control.

And that was the problem: despite our new principal, the school was still failing. The cranky machinery that was Southwestern had initially gotten a quick tune up with Jackson's arrival, but it did not steer the mega-steamship around. Our functional test scores and attendance rates and incidents of disruptive behavior were still statistically abysmal, and our school looked pretty much the same to any outsider, including The State, who still visited with clipboards on scheduled days and still hung above our heads the high stakes of a state takeover. A takeover would mean Jackson's failure. A takeover would mean she and her entire staff would lose their jobs. Jackson had brought some initial energy— the promise of a better day—and, along with that, a few hand-selected administrators to try and get that better day done. Among them was Mr. Rawls, a skinny but fierce-looking bald man who never cracked a smile and who eyed any room like a prison guard, and who terrified me, which was good, because he did the same for the kids. But Rawls was looking worn down. And by October, minus a better-controlled Halloween, which I measured by the count of eggs in Brooke's face (zero), our school was about the same. The only difference: we now had an administration that tried to do something, and those doings—those rules and whims— became increasingly erratic, perhaps *because* the school hadn't changed much, perhaps *because* what Jackson had brought would not solve in one year the problems such as ours. Someone was desperate to prove her worth, to show that her efforts counted.

In retrospect, I feel for a woman who was expected to single-handedly reform in one year what an infinity of unnamed forces had marred over the decades. As Mr. Owens once told me, the turn-around of any school requires at least four years because the building needs to empty of every student who knew it during its lawless phase. And as Wendy Kopp, CEO of Teach For America, once told me when she visited that Baltimore coffee shop, these schools also need the financial commitment of the nation, a rewriting of how they get their money so they can have the funding to fix their inevitably crumbling bits. Poor Jackson was a Band-Aid over a broken skeletal system, or rather, considering the turnover of principals, a Band-Aid over a Band-Aid over a Band-Aid, and when I look back on her efforts, I feel for her.

But while I watched or heard about kids getting caught in the web of her randomly enforced rules, I often saw how her efforts hurt. One afternoon, the school's entire power system failed—lights turned out, leaving the people in the school's inner classrooms to sit in complete blackness. As I shuffled down a dark hallway with Noelani, surrounded by a slow current of kids who also pushed out of the building, I felt a tap on my shoulder. Enough light from the outer classrooms' windows illuminated a boyishly grinning Keith Carter.

"Keith!" I hadn't seen him since last year.

Framed by the black polyester do-rag he always wore around his fuzzy cornrows, Keith's face was strikingly innocent. Unlike the boys who, when asked to smile for the camera, would keep their jaws clenched and squint their eyes—*smiling is for faggies*, they'd say—Keith didn't try to suppress a relentlessly pleasant grin. But when I asked Keith questions in class last year, he rarely knew the answers. He blinked and offered his plain grin, an expression that made his fourth-grade reading level even tougher to bear. *Kindergarten was fun*, he used to say. *You ever notice that? Why's school not fun after kindergarten?* He asked me this and then went back to his work, which was nearly impossible for him.

Now I could catch the whites of Keith's eyes flash and darken and flash as he blinked and smiled, looking unabashedly happy to see his old teacher. He resembled little kids before they realize they're supposed to portray impregnable coolness and indifference to moments like spotting your old teacher in an unlit hallway.

When I asked him how his year was going, he said "Fine. I just got suspended."

I furrowed my brow in maternal concern: the *I'm disappointed* face. Maybe Keith had finally exited that innocent stage after all.

"Mr. Johnson want help getting the TV/VCR. So I'm in the hall, going to Mr. Barnes office. But Dr. Jackson see me and suspend me."

"Did you tell her what you were doing?"

He nodded. "She just say I was cutting class."

Before I could ask another question, he added, "She give me ten days."

My mouth hung open. I turned to Noelani, whose mouth was hanging open too. Ten day suspensions were reserved for violent brawls.

"Bye, Ms. Kirn." Keith blinked and bounced away.

"Bye, Keith," Noelani called out. He turned and smiled and waved, looking delighted to bid farewell to a teacher he barely knew.

Maybe Keith was lying. If it had been any other kid, I would have been more skeptical. But Keith hadn't seemed to register his suspension as a possible injustice. It was a fact. Confusing, but not any more so than Keith's ten years of schooling. Maybe here was the reason Keith didn't find school fun after kindergarten. It contained too many unforeseen land mines. His shrug indicated an unquestioning acceptance of Jackson's decision, as though he were used to authority making no sense and expected nothing more.

The Sizers would say, Keith had been watching and his lessons were clear: though the decisions of principals were sudden and nonsensical, Keith's explanations did not matter. Only his compliance did. In this case, Keith had accepted and internalized the very lessons that Anthony still raged against. That was the big difference between the two of them. Anthony had the natural inclination to expect better, to think sharply about situations around him and, when needed, conclude them unfair.

To boot, he got mad and needed someone else to get mad, too. Keith had no interest in eliciting my compassion or convincing me that he'd been wronged. He'd shared the fact of his suspension like he would have shared the date of his birth. But Anthony was sharp in class, while Keith's performance was dulled by an achievement gap wider than I'd seen yet. Did the two characteristics—intellect and rebellion—go hand in hand? Was Anthony's critical mind a curse in a place such as ours? And what about Nick Lowery, with his genius IQ? The pattern led me to consider a disturbing hypothesis about Southwestern: sometimes the smartest students had the toughest time. The sharper their minds, the tougher it was for those minds to internalize the lessons our place taught, lessons like: *turn around, go back where you came from.* It pains me to say that Keith was clueless, but that cluelessness might have worked to his advantage. Keith didn't rage, didn't shout expletives, didn't retaliate against any affront. He just swallowed his suspension like soda and maybe thanked his lucky stars that he'd gotten ten days away from Southwestern, which had its power turned on the next morning.

• • •

Weeks after Anthony's suspension, in the middle of the class that met before his, I got a knock on my door. When I opened it, Jackson was standing on the other side. "Come with me," she said. "Out to the hall."

I turned toward my class, which was freshly amped on sugary calories from lunch, and I turned back toward Jackson, hitching my thumb over my shoulder, ready to protest. Leave my room? Unsupervised? But she was already walking away from me.

A cluster of teachers waited in the hall. Ms. Patterson, Mr. Owens, Ms. Ryder, and a new TFA teacher, Ms. Simmons, all gathered in a semicircle. Simmons looked somber and perplexed. The rest just looked impatient.

Jackson rounded out our semicircle, and we stared at her.

"Teachers," she began. "I can *not* clean up this school alone. I saw kids up and down this hallway!" She gestured toward one end of the hallway, then the other. "In front of *your* doors," she said, and pointed to Simmons and Ryder.

We stayed quiet.

"We need bodies in these hallways. Kids won't keep walking the halls if we stay in these halls. Do you understand? You've got to *stay* in these *halls.*"

I suppose I could have thought of little Richard and his father's command to kill that kitten. I could have followed his lead and said "Yes, Ma'am" to Jackson and taken her orders literally. I could have spent my days in the hallway outside the classroom while my rows of students were left unattended, where they would have no doubt dealt playing cards and turned up the volumes on their CD players and learned nothing. Well, not nothing. The Sizers, in their wisdom, interject. My students would have learned the same lesson Jackson tried to teach me: that order in the halls took priority over educating any minds. But unlike Richard Wright, I couldn't stomach the costs of such a choice; also, I would have lost my job.

Or, I could have followed Anthony Smalls's lead and outright protested. "Riddle me this, Dr. J," I didn't say. "If you think your teachers are hired as hall monitors, then who are you hiring to educate your students?"

"No," I didn't say. "I won't, in the middle of class, 'stay in the halls.' Now if you don't mind, I've got a class to reign back in and resume."

What I wanted to say to Anthony Smalls, but never did, was that I knew how he felt. I'd been caught at the hands of ignorant authority plenty of times before, as most of us have, and I usually kept my mouth shut. And that is exactly what I did in this case. I said nothing.

No, Anthony, as the noise-level rose in my third period, the class that was far bigger and louder than yours, I didn't point out the irony. I didn't ask how I could both "stay in the halls" and teach my rambunctious kids. I even kept my mouth shut about the fact that three teachers in that semi-circle actually *did* spend much of their precious planning periods out in the hall. When he wasn't tied up with kids in his office, Owens was well known for patrolling the building, holding up his clipboard high above his head, and repeating the motivational quote he scribbled onto it. Sentences like, "Let no man pull you low enough to hate him," and "If opportunity doesn't knock, build a door." Kids looked up and some-times concurred with the little Confucian clipboard. "I feel that one," they said. And Ms. Patterson actually moved her vast teacher-desk outside her classroom to grade papers, and Ms. Simmons, who was brand new and five-foot-two with a mousey, southern accent, followed suit. When kids rounded the corners and spotted the two teachers with their big desks blocking the way, they murmured a few *oh shits* and turned around. Ms. Ryder and I were hallway-monitoring slackers, for sure. We didn't use our planning periods to conquer corridor-disorder, so if Jackson wanted her teachers in the halls, if she wanted us to be more like Brooke, who became the target of eggs only because she shouted until her voice went raw that kids should *get where they belonged!* then Ryder and I deserved Jackson's wrath.

But not Simmons, and not Patterson, and not Owens. Not the people who busted their asses to do two jobs at once. Jackson's inaccurate characterization of her staff was more evidence for my suspicion that Jackson didn't know her school well enough to employ her no-play, tough-love style.

Instead, Anthony, I inhaled very slowly. I tried to control the throbbing in my temple vein, the reddening in my face. I tried to appear "part of the team" by nodding and looking totally willing to take what I thought was bullshit onus for a sinking ship. We all did this: pressed our lips together and nodded. Yes, absolutely, we all need to be in the halls. We *mm-hmm*ed, we *yes ma'am*ed, and we walked away, feigning sorry tails between our legs.

Where I come from, Anthony, this is how to handle authority: suck it up and bitch in private.

But Anthony, my problem is this: it does not work. It doesn't revolutionize a broken world. It keeps me in class, doing my job, just as feigned obedience would have kept you in class, doing your job, but it doesn't transcend the brokenness of our system. It just keeps us operating within it.

CHAPTER 12

READING *POWHITETRASH*

They were mostly black, I was white. They lived in the inner-city, I grew up in the suburbs. They knew bus systems and row homes and the subtleties of local drug-pyramids. I knew minivans and spacious isolated backyards and after-school specials starring skinny white kids whose characters popped stimulants so they could pull all-nighters. I grew up middle class, and they, my students, hovered around or below the poverty line.

And yet, the differences between my students and me were not usually the subjects of our conversations. Perhaps because I was too busy teaching. Perhaps because the differences were so obvious, we didn't need to say them aloud.

Still, we occasionally stumbled upon the symptoms like little walls between us, such as the day I told a class that I'd never been in a fight before, and the kids couldn't believe me. It was beyond their comprehension that I, a grown person, didn't at some point in my twenty-some years need to raise my fists and sock it to somebody. But I insisted. Unless you counted the times I pulled my sister's hair or bit her arm, I'd never fought anyone. Some kids took my reference to amateur fighting tactics as evidence that maybe I *was* telling the truth. Maybe Ms. Kirn really *had* never rumbled. But a few kids still shook their heads in disbelief. No way. No how. Everybody fights somebody, eventually.

And sometimes the subject of race came up during the sporadic but oddly recurrent discussions about how we cared for our hair, which went hand-in-hand with how much lotion we put on our skin, which led to some kids' shock: how could I never wear lotion? How did my skin not become ashy? And why did I wash my hair almost every day? Didn't I know it could fall out?

I must have been lying, Davon Green said, especially since my hair looked the same every day. I must have had it styled once a week.

"It's the truth," I said. I resisted turning to the one or two white kids in any given class who represented the nine percent white population at Southwestern, a sizeable percentage for a Baltimore school. Who wants to be called out for skin color? So, in the middle of a lesson, while my kids' textbooks were splayed open on their desks, I added, "I think white skin produces more oil than black skin."

Aside from making myself feel like a walking oil slick, my comment also made me realize something: I rarely announced my whiteness in class. I felt strangely self-conscious. I felt bare, and ready to cover up my hands with gloves.

"You ever notice that?" Davon continued. "Ms. Kirn hair look the same every day."

Davon was stalling. I tried to steer my kids back to our lesson plan. But he persisted with his characteristic musings. "Ms. Kirn, how come when white people get wet in the rain, they smell like dog? You ever notice that?" He looked up plainly.

Before moving to Baltimore, I would have chalked this comment up to some wise-ass affront. But Davon was sincere. He wanted my explanation. Because the question felt like a further digressive tug from my lesson, I think I just shrugged and moved on. But had I let myself engage in Davon's distractions, my real answer would have been, *No, Davon, not until coming to Southwestern and not until immersing myself in a mostly black culture, which produces completely different smells than my own, had I noticed that, yes, white people, when wet from rain, smell vaguely like my childhood pet, Benji.*

Noelani raised the topic some time later. "Do your kids tell you that white people smell like dog when it rains?"

"Yes!"

"Did you ever notice that it's true?" she asked.

I nodded.

"Weird," she said.

"I need to start carrying an umbrella," I said.

These moments were unusual, though. Race was more like an undercurrent than a topic of conversation. My kids had made note of my black Mary Jane shoes—*Look at Ms. Karen cute shoes!*—or my folded-over, ribbed, yellow socks. (Three girls had pointed and laughed at those a full minute, unable to calm themselves down enough to explain what was so funny.) But my whiteness was a subject rarely mentioned. When it did come up, I cringed due to some illogical notion that perhaps I should keep it a secret. I once stood in the hallway in between classes and overheard one of my students.

"I gotta go to Ms. Karen class," he announced. His friend was trying to keep him in the halls.

"Who that?" the friend asked.

"Skinny white lady."

On this day, the word *skinny* got my attention. I wore pale gray, flat-front pants that, for whatever reason, had me believing my hips and butt were ever-growing and massive. But the word *white* was equally arresting. It made me hyperconscious of my difference. And yet, these feelings made no sense: my kids knew I was white. Our differences were well evident. I even clung stubbornly to my locally admonished pronunciation of *Ball*-tee-more, which everyone else around me called *Bal-more*. My students coined it my "Philly accent," but the pronunciation came less from Philadelphia and more from four years in academia: I over-annunciated. As a joke, when my kids insisted that I call them by their nicknames, I sometimes repeated them in my painfully nerdy, academic voice.

"Lorrr Busterrr, is it?" I asked Davon Green when he started tagging all his work with the nickname. "Is that what I should call you?"

No, said Davon, irritated. "Lor' Busta. Bus*taaah*"

"But I think Lorrr Busterrr is too long for a nickname," I said, taking pains to sound as white as possible with all those *R*'s. "Can I just call you *Lorr*? Would that be alright?" I was feigning obliviousness, and Davon knew it. A good many of the male nicknames in Baltimore had Lor' before them. Calling him Lor was like calling Mr. Owens *Mister*.

He threw his hands over his ears. "No! No! It's *Busta*!"

"Why not Lorr? Lorr sounds good! Oh, Lo-*orr*?" I called, like I was beckoning him from outside.

I called Davon Green "Lor" so long, he secretly grew to like it. "LOR!" I cheered when he bounced into my room in between classes, even when I no longer taught him, and Davon smiled and updated me on his life.

In instances like these, I underscored racial difference as a joke. So why couldn't I breech the subject of race directly? Maybe because, despite my rapport with my students, which was remarkably good, I feared it was tentative. What if, in talking directly about race, we hit a wall that no one could find a way around? Teaching was volatile. The most obedient class period of the semester could turn into the most chaotic. It happened. Kids turned. And I knew this same rapport that allowed me to joke about nicknames and hairdos was contingent upon my students' impression that I stood on their side, that we were "in this" together, an idea that felt only half true because, each day, I was able to drive out of what my kids called "the ghetto" and to my rented, three-story Victorian row-home on North Calvert, just a few blocks south of Johns Hopkins, in a small pocket of Baltimore where white people walked their dogs on the sidewalks and went for long, slow jogs around the campus.

•••

My fourth-period class and I were in the middle of Maya Angelou's "When I Lay My Burden Down," an excerpt from our textbook that I only flinched at if white students sat in the room. Early in the story, Angelou introduces the antagonists of the piece as *powhitetrash*. *Everyone I knew respected these customary laws,* Angelou writes, referring to codes of etiquette about addressing elders and rules of uber-cleanliness, and then she adds, *except for the powhitetrash children.*

In the face of obnoxious white kids who mock Angelou's grandmother and expose their dirty, free-balling nether regions, the older woman does nothing in reply. She just hums and sways and sticks it out. And this is a lesson to Angelou, whose tale moralizes about the choices we have when faced with bullies. But for me, the biggest tension usually occurred in my classroom when my kids first read that phrase, *powhitetrash*. I immediately checked the faces of the one or two white kids in the room: Did they feel alienated? Insulted? As students at Southwestern, they were for the most part *poor*, and they were by description *white*, and would they now feel like *trash* in the middle of school?

But I'd taught the story several times, and on this day I'd taught it again twice before, and no one had ever protested. I'd started to assume that my kids instantly "got" the narrator's irony: when Angelou, as an adult, calls the white kids *powhitetrash*, she's not advocating racial epithets. She's evoking how her younger self saw them. The single-worded spelling stressed this, I'd thought, as it reflected how she heard the phrase as a child. My assumption that my fourth and final period would reach this same conclusion was so firm in my mind that Bobby Hudson's comment caught me off guard.

As soon as we shut the books, Bobby said, "Ms. Kirn, I want an apology!"

"Why's that?"

"She's calling me powhitetrash!"

Sandy-haired Bobby's brows looked stern, but he was also smiling. Among him were his unresponsive classmates. Only two girls sat together quietly in the middle of the class. The rest of the group were boys, but not like the boys in that fourth period class from last year, where Jerome Smith and Brandon Ward and Timmy Rogers engaged in a Southwestern-style game show that might have been named "Who Can Best Agitate the Teacher"? No, these new boys were aloof. Lethargic. And somewhat hostile. About a dozen scattered among the thirty desks, hanging over the desktops or lounging across the chairs with uncanny silence. So far they'd reluctantly performed their duties in schoolwork. But other than Bobby, they all seemed as vacant in enthusiasm as the room felt vacant in kids. I hadn't sparked a good rapport with them yet, but the small size had me assuming they'd be a breezy lot to teach. A calm way to end the day.

Looking at Bobby's odd combination of stern eyes and boyish grin, I couldn't tell if he was actually offended. He might have been playing, but it didn't seem wise to dismiss a potentially real concern. Still, I didn't know what to say. I might have remembered the all-knowing Sizers, of *The Students Are Watching*, who would have seen the teachable moment in Bobby's remark and would have encouraged him to grapple with the issues inherent in the text. But I wanted the "issues inherent in the text" to go away. The "issues inherent in the text" had never arisen before, possibly because I'd never had a white student as outspoken as Bobby. Because this particular group hadn't gelled yet, I didn't think we could successfully wander down the rocky road of racial understanding without hitting a few decent-sized potholes.

So, instead of letting Bobby grapple with the tension, I explained the tension away. "She's not calling them powhitetrash just because they're white." My words were rushed. I was irritated. The faster I could get this over with, the better. "She's calling them that because they're rude and disrespectful. And because they're acting like trash."

"I still want an apology!" Bobby said, and still with that mixed, dubious expression.

A couple of the other boys groaned, and there was some mumbling that I couldn't decipher.

"Hey," Bobby said, "I'm the only white person in here!" The whine in his voice grated my nerves. "I gotta stick up for myself."

Before I even thought about it, I raised my hand. "Hello?" I turned it, back-side facing Bobby, and then pointed to my face, which had been growing increasingly white in the sunless February.

"You don't count," Bobby said.

I checked the faces of the other boys in the room. They stared at me, expressionless, their arms folded against their chests.

• • •

I once walked into Ellen's empty classroom, where she and Amy were sitting at student desks, murmuring disapproval about something. "That's ridiculous," Ellen said, and Amy nodded.

"What's ridiculous?" I asked.

Since our rooms were on different hallways, the three of us always passed information back and forth, reporting who'd gotten suspended, who'd been put on "The Pip," (the dreaded Performance Improvement Plan for failing teachers), who'd set something on fire, and so on. But this gossip was graduate-school related. In their class the other night, an elementary school teacher announced that he didn't "see race" in his classroom. Ellen said he called himself "color blind."

"What did he mean?" I asked. "Like, he doesn't discriminate against any particular color?"

"No." Amy said. "He said he didn't *see* color."

Though everyone in his class remained skeptical, the teacher in question swore that he didn't know which of his fourth graders were white and which were black. It sounded like a pinch of naïveté mixed with a heap of self-delusion. Ellen and Amy's disapproval of it, though, surprised me. We too had rarely talked about race, and I'd always wondered if, upon graduating from our five-week-long Institute in Houston, we TFA-ers were meant to become "color blind." After all, in my suburban Philly world, that was the P.C. way to live; if two people stood on a corner, and one was black, and the other was white, people I knew went to painstaking lengths to identify the individuals by anything other than the colors of their skin. *See that woman over there, the one wearing the red shoes? The one with the green scarf?* Race, though it was plainer than a minor accessory, wasn't acknowledged. Even though my job as a TFA corps member made me increasingly aware of racial inequality across school districts, I'd still sometimes speculated that maybe, in addition to my comfortable and not-so-stylish teacher shoes and my purple and gold Southwestern lanyard that hung around my neck and held my faculty ID, I was supposed to don color-blind lenses before heading to work.

But if race was a part of the inequity we were fighting, then wouldn't it also become a part of our awareness? And wouldn't that make so-called color-blindness dubious? Instead of becoming "blind," I became hyperconscious. At Institute, I'd read a study that white teachers made more frequent eye contact with white students, that black teachers made more frequent eye contact with black students, and that Latinos did so with Latinos, and so on. Before I could dismiss this tendency as "racist," the study explained it as a biological instinct: humans are apt to look for recognition in the people who resemble them. The prospect of this arrested me—that I could unconsciously tip the scales in favor of my white students by making just one subtle, nonverbal, biologically inherited gesture. And I doubted that feigning "color-blindness" would garner against this unconscious discrimination. In fact, it could *perpetuate* unconscious discrimination, as the teacher refused to see not only her way of seeing, but how that way of seeing affected her class.

I didn't believe I could afford to pretend I wore those color-blind lenses. I willed myself to look into the eyes of all my students, holding a locked gaze for moments at a time, and then shifted to another face, and then another, and when that new face was white, my mind sometimes halted, mid-thought, as it wondered if the gaze was too long, too short, too something. Was I discriminating? I looked away. The chalkboard's slanted sentences reminded me of what I was teaching.

Eventually I noticed that whenever I faced a room of all-black students, I addressed them with subtle relief.

• • •

It would have been easier to teach my fourth period if the roster hadn't included the names of Bobby Hudson and Alex Fisher, another white kid in my class who was two years older (and one foot taller) than the usual ninth grader. He'd failed Noelani's class last year because he hardly showed. (He wasn't present on the day we read Maya Angelou.) Without Bobby and Alex, I would have had about a dozen males and two quiet females—all African American—and when we read about things like *powhitetrash*, that class could have collectively snickered, and I would have enjoyed their brief modicum of enthusiasm rather than sweating someone else's offense.

Also, with an all-black fourth period, David Turner could never have decided that I was racist.

"Look at that. Notice how she always hang around *his* desk?" David murmured his observation loud enough for me to hear. I was hovering over Bobby's workspace in the middle of the room.

Not far into the semester, David—a student who wrote practically on grade level, who could easily produce his insights in correctly spelled, neatly written sentences—stopped doing his work. He started passing the time by monitoring my moves. He kept a tally of evidence that I discriminated against him.

"Always helping *him* out," Samuel Chase said, who sat with David. David's mission had caught on, and a few of the other boys sometimes joined in.

"Hmm, I *wonder*," David said sarcastically, "why she give *him* special treatment."

Bobby shot a dirty look over my shoulder. When I turned my head, David and Samuel made their eyes small slits.

"Alright," I said lamely. "Let's just focus on our work."

"Why we even reading this?" said Jamal Cook from the back of the room.

My fourth period's hint of hostility grew. Minus a few friendships, like David's and Samuel's, the class did not like each other, and the class did not like me. David and Samuel had already mocked Jamal for being *too* dark. *Boy, you so black you blue*, they'd told him.

"Why is this book called *Black Boy*, anyway?" David extended the word *black* like he wanted to spit it out. Bleh! Black!

"Great question." I knew it was an agitated point rather than a bona fide curiosity, but I didn't care. "Why do you think it's called *Black Boy*?"

Students in other classes had usually gotten angry at the title too, though it took them awhile to articulate why. On a good day, they might hint that the title only let two elements of identity stand in for all that Richard Wright was. He was black, and he was a boy. And that bothered them. I figured this fourth-period class, a fairly bright albeit angry lot, could at least give words to their frustration, could air it out and maybe in the process realize the title's irony.

But David didn't bite. He scrunched his face up and scowled. "How'm I supposed to know?" He pushed the book a few inches across his desk, like it pained him to sit nearer to it than he had to. "*I* didn't write it."

Trying to take some pressure off—and attention away from—David and Jamal's antagonism, I walked to the desk of one of the quiet girls. What did *she* think about Richard's decision to kill the kitten?

But as Latrice murmured a response, I heard the screech of chair legs against the floor. When I looked up, Bobby was standing red-faced and fuming at the nostrils.

Shit. I'd missed something. What had happened? Who "started it"? What was "it" anyway? On one side of the room stood Bobby, fists clenched by his sides, ready to charge, and on the other sat David, arms crossed, his smug expression like a dare.

How did these two kids get to hating each other so badly? The tension had been building for weeks, and it originated from Bobby's disability. At first, Bobby seemed like the strongest student in the class. Unlike the aloof males, and the two exceptionally attentive but shy females, he was eager to raise his hand, and he had clever things to say. Question after question, up shot Bobby's arm and, with a smile across his shiny face, he volunteered his ideas in his chipper, nasally voice. "See that, Ms. Kirn, I'm smart." But when I asked the class to settle in and write something down, Bobby refused. Day after day, Bobby did nothing that let me give him a grade. One day, as I looked again at a blank page on his desk, he returned my gaze with sagging, guilty eyes. Too tired to muster the energy for another pep-talk or a scolding, I asked him, in a defeated tone, "Why don't you ever do your work?"

In an unusually muted voice, he said, "I can't hear you, Ms. Kirn."

I sighed. Even the smallest question had to be twice as difficult. "I said: how come you don't do any work?"

"No, I mean, I can't hear what you're saying when you tell us what to do."

I must have given him a disbelieving look.

"It's true. I have a hearing aid. I just don't wear it."

"That makes no sense. Why wouldn't you wear it if you can't hear?"

He looked away. "I'm not wearing that thing," he muttered. "It's embarrassing."

His voice was thin but angry, and something in my chest sank. The embarrassment was real. I squatted beside Bobby's desk and explained the directions yet again, not knowing that, from David's perspective, I now favored Bobby, not knowing that by kneeling down to Bobby and explaining instructions just for him, I'd stoked David's hatred for me. "Does that make sense?"

Bobby nodded. He got to work.

But when Bobby turned his paper in at the end of the day, it was half-finished, and riddled with spelling, grammar, and syntax errors that put him way under the fifth- or sixth-grade level of literacy I was accustomed to reading. I realized that in a class of clever though lethargic boys like David and Samuel, Bobby was, hands-down, the lowest-performing student. The thoughtful answers that he produced by mouth seemed nearly impossible for him to capture via pen.

Like a third of all Southwestern's students, and unlike Samuel Chase and David Turner and Jamal Cook, Bobby was a "special needs" student. When I uncovered his file from the bowels of the Southwestern filing system, indeed, two disability census codes were listed: 02, and 09. What did 02 mean? *Hearing Impaired.* That little beige hearing aid that Bobby never wore, indeed it existed somewhere in his world.

And 09? It always seemed to me the least useful category. 09 meant a student had, literally, a *Specific Learning Disability*, a description that read more like a joke than a nugget of information; the IEP never specified anything more about this *Specific Learning Disability*. Tons of my students were labeled "09"; it was a dark blanket tossed over educational anomalies growing ever-less anomalous. But special-ed experts Stephan Silverman and Rich Weinfeld are practically psychics in regards to Bobby Hudson. For 09 kids, they say, "Staff and parents may see a disparity between the student's cognitive potential as demonstrated by his verbal or spatial abilities in his area of passion, and his academic weaknesses such as written expression, reading comprehension, and organization."

A *disparity*. That's exactly what I saw. An orally enthusiastic kid; a painfully disabled writer. The juxtaposition felt, to me, like a punch in the gut. Here was an articulate kid with energy and ideas, but unable to ever write them down. For the writer in me, it sounded like a cage: how could someone live in a body that had ideas but couldn't record them?

And that was how I found myself giving special treatment to the one white kid in the classroom: because, by law, he required it. And because, agitating nasally voice or not, he sort of broke my heart.

From then on, every time I knelt beside Bobby's better ear and repeated the instructions, every time I leaned over Bobby's desk and guided him to write sentences, David, a bright and increasingly angry student, scowled. The tension between David and Bobby built from weeks of dirty looks and murmured insults. Now the culmination was here: with Bobby, ready to punch, and with David, daring him to try.

Angelique Bell and Serena Ryan taught me one lesson well enough: I was not powerful enough to step in between two warring fifteen-year-olds. But I yelled, "Stop." And I ordered Bobby to go sit at the small desk beside my larger one. And the remarkable thing is that he did. Keeping his eye on David, Bobby turned from the desk and walked toward the window-side of the room.

After making a few rounds in the class, watching kids go, one by one, back to their books, I confirmed that the pre-fight adrenalin was on the decline. I sat beside Bobby. Pretending to do something productive, lacking the focus to grade, I listened to his furious nasal exhalations and knew that this situation would not bode well in countering David Turner's tally: I'd let the white kid sit by the teacher.

But as Bobby's breathing stretched out into measured, calm, nearly inaudible whispers, he started to talk. He started to fill in some of the gaps of his vague, special-needs paperwork.

"I black out, Ms. Kirn."

"What do you mean you black out?"

"When I get mad, I don't know what's going on. I once put my fist through a board three inches thick."

Three inches seemed like an unbreakable thickness for a relatively average-sized fifteen-year old. Still, I'd been skeptical of the hearing-aid claim, and look how that had turned out.

Bobby kept talking. He said he'd been in anger management programs since he was seven. He said his dad died when he was one year old. He said he'd put three people in a hospital after they'd said something about his dad. Bobby sounded like an adolescent version of the Incredible Hulk, capable of turning green, tearing his clothes, and lifting a vehicle at the onset of a broken pencil tip. I didn't know if he was capable of putting any person into a hospital, but I did know this: whether he made his armor out of lies or truth, he felt he had to wear some kind of protection in this world. From Bobby's perspective, the world was a threatening place, which meant that when he told me about his vulnerabilities, like the embarrassing hearing aid or the anger management, a little bit of that armor came down.

This was more than anyone else in the room had done, which meant that, despite my efforts, my closest connection was with the white kid in class.

I looked out at the classroom, now officially hostile to Bobby.

• • •

Power struggles are inherent in teaching. Veteran teachers are sometimes so established (and have honed that wide-legged gravitas that says *I own this room*) that their students hand them power almost instantly. Or, like a skilled martial artist who dodges a blow by redirecting the attacker's clumsy force, they can also be adept at deflecting power plays. I hadn't become proficient at either tactic, and I knew I'd gotten caught in a complex web of power-plays spun by both David *and* Bobby. Bobby needed special attention, was legally *deserving* of special attention; but Bobby also fed off special treatment. Receiving extra praise for those unlimited hand-raises, sitting beside the teacher after times of strife—these things motivated him. He sat up taller when I said "good job." Meanwhile, the slightest evidence of preferential treatment offered David a different kind of energy, one that fueled his anger. He called out even louder that I was "racist" and tightened those folded arms against his chest. On some days, David got so angry that he sat back and did nothing all class period. In other words, my effort to help the progress of one student decreased the progress of another. Together, David and Bobby had created a web, and I was caught in the middle, and because I couldn't figure out how to untangle it, I resented them both.

Though the boys' tension never again neared a full-on fight, the tension was all I could see and made me a frustrated teacher, which made for a frustrated class. Nobody wanted to be in that room. Heavyset Malik Morgan walked into class ten minutes late each day with a black ski cap on his head and his headphones over his ears—three immediate affronts to my so-called authority. Those broken rules were like the bricks of a wall he built around himself, and each day I had to tell him to take off the hat and the headphones, and this pattern seemed a pretty apt symbol for the rest of the class. They blocked me out; I pushed back; they blocked me out again; the cycle went on.

As a teacher, I wasn't used to an unchangingly bad rapport. In other classes, my odd assemblage of kids began as cold or dead-pan or maybe seemingly angry, but they gradually warmed up. And while "warming up" didn't necessarily mean my classes ran like effective, well-lubricated learning machines, my biggest tool in my teacher toolbox was always my rapport. I let them joke about my hair, and in exchange, I teased them for their tough-sounding nicknames, Lor Busta being only one example, and these small moments proved what I believed: that the students wanted intimacy. When the boys especially buried their faces beneath the hoods of their sweatshirts or slinked past a teacher in their shin-length T-shirts and baggie jeans, they gave the impression that they wanted anonymity. Some of them did. But for many, they also wanted to be known: they wanted you to take their pictures; they wanted you to read the stories they'd written.

But David wouldn't look me in the eyes. He wouldn't use my name. I was not "Ms. Kirn." I was *She*. Or *Her*. As in, "See, there *she* sitting with him again." *Him* was Bobby. David didn't find me worthy of my title.

What does a student want? How does she get energy? What kind of power-game is he playing? These were the questions I'd learned to ask. A teacher has to find a way, not to suffocate desire, but to channel it. Redirect the game. Give the kid what she wants in a way that works to the teacher's advantage.

Maybe David was jealous. "Notice how she always give *him* extra help," he'd said, and maybe David wanted me to give him the same. Like Bobby, maybe David was that classic student-archetype, the "attention seeker."

But early on in the dilemma, I'd tried sitting beside David. How was his work coming along? What did he think of the story? He only leaned over his shoulder and said to Samuel, "She won't even get off my case."

I backed off, circled, and tried again. This time, he said, "She think I'm too stupid to do this alone."

When I sat with Bobby, I was racist. When I sat with David, I was also racist.

I eventually pulled him into the hall one day. There we stood, face to face. His hair was braided away from his forehead into tight cornrows. His lips were thin and terse. I had to explain why Bobby received different treatment. Normally, I didn't announce to my students exactly who was a "special needs" kid. *Dear students*, I didn't say. *Timmy over there has been labeled Code 10, for "emotionally disturbed." And Latrice is 08, "language impaired."* But they usually figured it out on their own. A student once tugged me down to her desk and asked, in the middle of a lesson, "What's wrong with him, Ms. Kirn?" She side-nodded to a boy near her. I told her he just needed a bit more help than she did, and before I could worry that she'd start calling him "stupid," she nodded and asked the boy if he needed her help. Students at Southwestern could be remarkably kind toward that thirty-three percent of their peers who had learning disabilities.

So I told David that Bobby required more attention, that Bobby had a special need I wouldn't go into, but that it meant Bobby was a little less capable of succeeding without help. And I told David I didn't give him the same attention because he was very capable. This was not about race, I said. This was about the kinds of learners they were.

And I told David that he was an exceptional student, which was true, but that he needed to stop letting his opinion of me get in the way of his success.

David listened to all of it, arms folded, eyes looking just slightly to my left, over my shoulder. "You done?" he said.

"I'm done."

We went back into the room.

• • •

The double-standards continued. If Bobby needed a pencil, and I exchanged one of mine for his bus ticket, David said I favored Bobby.

If another boy asked, "Ms. Kirn, can I get a pencil?" and I asked the kid for his bus ticket, David announced, "She don't trust us." *Us*, in this case, did not apply to the whole class.

As for David, if he failed to bring a pencil that day, he refused to ask me for one. "I don't want one of *her* pencils." Without a pencil, he could scrutinize my behavior without distraction.

One day while my students took a quiz, another student asked what I meant when I asked about the *setting* of a story. Setting had been a vocabulary word, and he was supposed to know it, but I budged anyway and told him, "It's the time and place."

For this, David called me "lazy." "She don't wanna write two words so she just write one and make it harder for everyone else."

It was then that I realized the beef between David and me was not logical. Even David must have seen through it. For whatever reason, he had formed an opinion of me that no counter-experience or reasoning could break. I was his lazy, racist, white teacher.

"I'm tired of her shit," he added, but still didn't look me in the eye.

How could I have taught in west Baltimore for a year and a half and not known how to win a class over? Why, suddenly now, did race become a factor in my classroom? Each day, David sat in my room as an infuriating irony: a capable student who performed miraculously near grade level but who still found an excuse to fail. This time, the excuse was me. I felt responsible to break down his assumptions, to chip away at the wall between us. Otherwise, I worried that David's perception of me, and to a lesser extent, Samuel's and Malik's and Jamal's, would, like Bobby's ineptitude at writing, imprison them. They wouldn't learn in my classroom, so they wouldn't earn their English credit, so they wouldn't graduate high school, and they'd rest their fate in the worst of statistics: on the corners, without diplomas.

• • •

Later in the year, I learned that David wasn't the only one suspicious of a white teacher's intentions. One day during my planning period, I stood in the hall with Mr. Sullivan, a social studies teacher, and Ms. Simmons, my fellow TFA teacher, and monitored halls. Together, we addressed the hallwalkers with renewed energy.

"Look who's rounding the corner."

"Is that Antoine, wasting his whole day in the halls!"

The kid in question grunted. His buddies looked away and kept walking.

"Turn around, fellas. Back where you came from."

The hallwalkers stopped, turned around, headed the other way.

"Must be a lot of learning happening out here in the halls."

Sullivan, Simmons, and I badgered them until they rounded the opposite end of the corner, passing from our sight.

When I turned, I saw Mr. Owens headed toward us, smiling and laughing. "Look at you three."

I smiled back until he said, "You're not part of the *problem*."

It suddenly dawned on me what "we three" had in common.

"What do you mean," I asked. "Part of the problem?"

Mr. Owens put his hand on my shoulder and looked down at me. "Aw, Kirn." He leaned in. "It's unbelievable. There are people in this building who think you're here to keep the kids down? People who think the white teachers are here to keep the 'black ghetto kids' ignorant."

"Who?" I asked immediately before I had the forethought to realize Owens would never betray another teacher.

Owens just shook his head slightly. It didn't matter who.

"They think I'm here, *here*," I looked around at the dust-filled hall, up at the broken halogen lights and the crumbling ceiling tiles, "to perpetuate some racist agenda?"

Owens nodded. "It's unbelievable," he said again.

"Well," I said, and took a parting step. "If you don't mind, I need to get back to my room. Gotta plan my repression of young, flourishing minds."

"Pah!" Owens laughed.

I laughed back. I laughed because it was better than shouting. Better than crying. I walked into my empty room, shut the door, and stood alone in my room of cinder-block walls and crookedly hung posters. The most prominent poster hung directly above my blackboard: *Southwestern Is a Better Place Because YOU Are Here!* it read. I'd written the slogan two years ago in purple marker on goldenrod poster board. I'd underlined the word, *YOU*, three times. I'd made it because I wanted my future students to feel significant. I'd wanted them to feel like they mattered. Southwestern was a *place*, and I was *here*, but the sign and Mr. Owens were the only voices telling me that my presence made the place any better.

• • •

Just four days later, the entire faculty had a staff meeting. Teachers shuffled into the "Media Center," the school's term for the library because the room had nearly as many computers—twenty—as it had books. I sat with a fellow TFA teacher from the science department. In retrospect, sitting with another white teacher probably didn't counter any conspiracy theories that might have circulated. Still, I hardly saw this particular teacher, who was new to the scene, so I asked him how things were going.

Adam was not a beacon of light and good news. "Did you hear about Jackson?" He had swooping, gray U's beneath his eyes, and he looked like he could splay his chest across the table and take a nap.

"What about Jackson?"

He looked over his shoulder. Jackson was chatting with another teacher at the front of the room. Adam looked back at me. "She doesn't want new TFA teachers next year."

"Who told you this?"

"Ms. Davis. Jackson told the department heads, no more TFA teachers."

It felt like a double-blow of rejection after Owens's comment. We were a movement of young people who, however flawed, dared to envision a nation where every kid could read on grade level, and we were unwanted? Why? How, after filling vacant positions and coming to work each day and doing our jobs, could we be rejected by a woman who hardly knew us, who hadn't even been at our school a full year?

The science teacher looked over his shoulder and scribbled something on the meeting's agenda. He slid the paper across the tabletop.

Because she's racist, it read. Then he drew the piece of paper back towards him.

I watched him run thick black pen-lines repeatedly through the word "racist." Line after line, he eliminated the unprintable word until all that remained was a rectangular box, deeply etched by pen-marks. It sat between us on the page, an unacceptable void.

With a sigh, my shoulders fell. But here is the odd thing: I never knew then, nor do I know now, exactly why my shoulders fell. I don't know whether they fell because I believed the science teacher—believed that Jackson actively wanted to eliminate white and/or TFA teachers from her faculty, which was entirely possible—or whether they fell because the teacher's accusation felt equally as improvable and petty as the rumor that we TFA teachers were "trying to keep the ghetto kids down," which had probably also been uttered between teachers in this same way: quietly, privately, in the awkward confidence held between people of the same skin color. In a clique defined by race that felt like an invisible cage.

I'd like to say that my fourth-period class and I had a breakthrough. But it never drastically improved. Jamal Cook dropped out of school to pursue a life on the corner, so I never had the chance for a chipper turnaround with his deep-voiced self. To his credit, perpetually late Malik Morgan had pleaded with Jamal otherwise. Though Malik always seemed on the verge of dropping out himself, I once intercepted a note from him, addressed to Jamal, that said a life on the corner would only lead to death. I brought the note to an assistant principal, who made a copy for Jamal's files. But despite Malik's persuasions, Jamal bailed, and the school didn't stop him. Bobby Hudson stopped attending too, but I was told that his mother was unhappy with the education he was receiving and she sent him elsewhere. Samuel slowly lost the enthusiasm for hating me, which gradually turned into a loose, comfortable rapport, and maybe with the loss of his partner in crime, David gradually put his personal crusade against me to rest.

By the end of the semester, our class was complacent. Far from a community of general love and goodwill, at least I no longer had to obsess over its waned hostility. All that remained of our meager class were the two quiet girls, the handful of black boys, and Alex Fisher, the remaining white kid who sat quietly in his camouflage, which he wore because he went hunting before school. The other boys didn't like to talk to him because, according to Samuel, they believed he was crazy.

"He shoot things," Samuel whispered to me. Then, as though the one begot the other, Samuel added, "He in the K.K.K."

"How do you know that?" I asked. But Samuel just shrugged. It was his assumption.

Meanwhile, Alex sat far from everyone, and when he wasn't busy doing his work or asking me about Nostradamus, he doodled regal, tall-horned deer in his margins and day-dreamed about getting back to the woods.

One day during a vocabulary quiz, I watched Malik Morgan dig a pencil into his afro and scratch his scalp. He stared up at the board of words, which included *reek, sneer, cunning,* and *sonnet,* and he squinted. He was visibly racking his brain for answers, trying to remember the definitions so he could put the right words into the empty blanks on the quiz. I sat at my desk and watched, wondering if *reek* or *sneer* or *cunning* or *sonnet* would ever appear readily in his conversations with friends, wondering if any of these words would ever really mean anything to Malik, thinking that the answer was probably *no.* I felt oddly grateful that he made a concerted effort regardless. I realized in this moment that, congenial rapport or not, my class had ended up okay. Though they hardly worked to their potential, many of these kids would finish the semester with ninth-grade English credits under their metaphorical belts.

Afterward, Malik blamed his confusion on the fact that he lost the week's definitions. David was sitting beside him, and I knew the two had become buddies.

"Why didn't you call David?" I asked.

In a high-pitched voice of disbelief, Malik said, "Naw, man." He looked at David.

"We don't call each other!" David said like the idea was preposterous.

I laughed. "Why not?"

"Cuz," said Malik. "That's gay."

"Malik!"

"Sorry, it is."

"You don't call your friends on the phone?" I asked.

They both shook their heads adamantly. "Not guy friends," Malik said.

Things quieted between the three of us as we each thought about this.

"We don't really have *friends*," David said.

Malik made his thinking face again, eyes squinting, and then agreed. "If you're close to someone, you call them your cousin or something."

"Yeah, not your *friend*." It was one of the unusual times that David's constant distaste for the world wasn't directed *at* me, just near me.

"What's wrong with *friend*?" I asked.

"Because," David said. "Everyone snitches on everyone else." He looked at Malik, who looked at David, and the two of them nodded to each other. It was an odd moment: they were buddies enough to agree that they weren't really buddies. They didn't trust each other. If needed, they'd snitch. In a paradoxical moment of confidence, David Turner said what became the only thing I ever really learned about David Turner— that he did not trust the world—which seemed to explain his worldview. "Around here," he added, "there *are* no friends."

CHAPTER 13

NORTHERN EXPOSURE

"Karrren!" Wallace beckoned me with a holler that carried out of her office, past the doorways that separated us, and into my classroom. I had second period off.

I popped my head in. She sat at her desk, hands holding a sandwich together. "Let me see your writing folders."

It was an impromptu test. Was I doing my job? Had my students been writing, or had I pulled punches similar to a recent twenty-something hire, who whined about a back injury, sat behind her desk, and screened an Eddie Murphy flick with her students?

I walked back to my classroom, mentally cataloguing the work my students had done lately. They'd created personal timelines, family trees, and self-portraits with descriptive adjectives floating around their drawn heads, all in preparation for their autobiographies, which they'd also written. "I'm sixteen years old and there are fourteen people in my house!!" "I was thirteen years old and I seen a boy get killed. But I told the police I didn't see anything." "The events of my life show that I had good and bad times in my life like a normal person."

They'd imagined and illustrated fictional characters and they'd plopped these characters into short stories, for which they'd written plots with rising action and dénouements. They'd improvised alliteration. They'd drunk green tea from Styrofoam cups and studied Basho to inspire their haiku, and then they'd counted the syllables of their three-line poems and posted them all over the room.

> The Beautiful Me
> African-American
> King of my own land.

> Get out of my face
> Your breath smells like raw onions
> Go get a breath mint.

Girls are hating on me
and boys say that I'm a dime
but does it matter.

And despite my tendency to ignore requirements I deemed lame, my students had even responded to some Maryland Writing Test prompts, though I discerned which prompts to give and which to bury. I eliminated, for instance, the prompt that read: "Think of a time in your life when you were chased or when you chased someone or something."

It seemed cruel of Maryland to set up a prompt for which its city kids could think of cops and for which its suburban kids might think of Labradors. Or bunnies. Or maybe I was stereotyping the suburban kids. Maybe they just as often rushed into their teachers' classrooms to report the most recent cop-chase story, which often involved the cop wrongfully accusing the kid in a mix-up of "grab the closest black boy in the Timberlands and hoodie."

I chose other, less asinine prompts, and my kids responded to them, and they filed their essays into their new writing folders, recently mandated by the state. Or the city. Someone up there, sitting on high at the right hand of a bureaucratic Baltimore God.

I returned to Ms. Wallace's office with a random sampling of the legal-sized manila envelopes, each with a students' name and a state-designed spreadsheet glued onto the front.

She set her sandwich down on the aluminum, wiped her hands on a napkin, and fingered the covers. "What is this?" She shook her head. "Ms. Kirn, why haven't you had your students do any writing?"

"They have."

She didn't open the folders to see. "There's nothing listed." She pointed to the spreadsheet and then looked up with a damning expression—eyes wide enough to show the full circles of her irises, head tilted so far back she used the bridge of her nose as an arrow to point at me. She gestured to the folders' white covers, which listed types of writing—*business letter, personal letter, expository essay*—and provided plenty of blanks for titles and dates. Because I hadn't been very good at making my students record each sample of writing they shoved into their folders, a lot of the spaces were blank.

"Your students haven't listed any writing."

"But they've been *doing* writing."

When Wallace opened a folder, a few pages fell out. Their randomness hardly captured the extent of my students' projects. The pages needed the accompanying list to glorify their worth.

"How do you think this looks for your evaluation?"

"Really, we've been doing writing. We've written poems, a narrative prompt, an explanatory prompt, an autobiography, a character sketch, a short story, a business letter . . ." but Wallace interrupted me.

"When I taught, I had my students writing *five* business letters. *Four* explanatory prompts. *Three* character sketches. . . ." She continued listing types of writing, and with each type, her students had always beat mine out in count.

I didn't protest. Administrators, mentors, and education professors often narrated their dazzling accomplishments from years ago, as educators. They tended to remember themselves as extraordinary.

Wallace shut the one folder and handed them all back to me. She told me that folders like these might lead to a poor evaluation, or worse, The Pip.

The Pip: the Performance Improvement Plan. Being *on The Pip* was a dreaded status, uttered gravely between teachers. In addition to threatening one's job, it meant constant scrutiny from administrators, previews and approvals of lesson plans, frequent observations, regular meetings, which at Southwestern took place on some insane, alternate universe where minor t-crossings and i-dottings took precedent over student learning. Lately, a surge of Pips had been dealt like playing cards to whomever got caught in a bad moment. Noelani had entered my room one day during lunch to announce the news.

"Did you hear? Brooke said Jackson scoured the whole Social Studies Department. She put Sypher and Willis on The Pip."

Though I never liked what I'd perceived to be Sypher's temper barely kept at bay—his white face reddening easily throughout the day—word from my students was this: they learned in Sypher's class. They cited actual content: civil rights, a listing of all the states, World War II. And I didn't even need to pry about Mr. Willis's class—my students volunteered it. They loved it, they said, *and* it was tough. They seemed to love it *because* it was tough, which was a double anomaly at Southwestern. They said he taught about black militant revolutionaries and made them write five-page research papers. They often rushed into my room from his, genuinely pumped by some grain of knowledge about white supremacists and black uprisings. Willis's was the *only* class my kids talked about unsolicited, and I was shocked: Why was *he* now on The Pip? No one knew for sure.

I pressed the edges of my unworthy folders against my palm—they aligned neatly in my hands. On my way out of the office, I spotted both the water cooler and the bona fide Xerox machine that the main office had provided for our department. Wallace prohibited teachers from using either—there wasn't enough water for all of us, she said, and we'd break the copier. I silently cursed both.

On this afternoon, I exhibited a sweet naïveté. I hadn't yet learned that while a teacher is grading her students, someone above is grading her, and that the teacher's ability to pass those tests, designed by the higher-ups, is just as crucial for her own survival as her kids' ability to write essays about being chased. Not a soul might care how engaged her students are, how well they've learned to write, how many reading strategies they've acquired, if she can't also jump successfully through parallelogram-shaped hoops. Any teacher probably knows this. Most teachers, if they last, accept this. I was a little late in coming to terms.

Instead, I cursed Wallace. Hoarder of water! Hoarder of ditto machines! Liar of prompt-assigning! This semester, the woman had one class to teach—a creative writing class—and she'd scraped it off her plate and onto Ms. Patterson's.

Not that my department head wasn't busy. Especially with the new principal, she had plenty of paperwork to file, plenty of ways that she had to prove herself and her department accountable to plenty of new rules that I'm sure were unwritten to her, too. And she had to deal with novices like me; I was too busy facilitating my students' creative engagement with "Freytag's triangle" and "poetic tropes" to consult Maryland's standards, which don't actually require students to compose their own short stories or demonstrate proficiency in alliteration, not until eleventh grade. To boot, novices like me didn't fill out folder covers.

I felt like a failure. I sat at my desk, glanced at the clock, and sighed at my remaining thirty minutes. Instead of grading papers or designing lessons, I knew I'd spend my time furious. And desperate to redeem myself.

Indeed, the cover sheets I had ignored listed one or two types of writing that we hadn't completed, and because the cover sheets were designed by people more interested in standardized writing that simulated future tests my students would take, any creative endeavors—those autobiographies and poems and stories—were squeezed onto a single line called "Miscellaneous." But the cover sheets also asked for proof of: Folders for every student (check); responses to those dreaded state-created prompts (check); first drafts, second drafts, final drafts; peer reviews, the use of rubrics (check, check, check, check).

I split the twin sides of one folder open with my fingers and, sure enough, the random writer had included all those requisite stages. I was caught in another classic case of: if it isn't documented officially, it doesn't exist. Nothing in Baltimore existed if it wasn't written in triplicate and filed away, and not much, it seemed was filed away correctly in Baltimore and so it seemed that, aside from the cemetery that lay just behind me and to my left, nothing really existed in Baltimore. Just rows and rows of tombstones. Those were the realest things, other than my students, who'd be arriving for third period in less than half an hour. I gathered the folders again and left my room.

I was about to raise my voice against authority, something I'd rarely done. I'd rehearsed the speech in my mind, and it contained a bulleted list of points to make:

- *Ms. Wallace, I bust my ass. Try my hardest. Plan extensively. And push my kids for ninety minutes every day.*
- *And what do I get in return? No recognition. Just threats that I'll get a bad eval.*
- *And for what? For not making my kids fill out a form? A form that demotes them from critical thinker to cataloguer? A form that exists solely to show someone high up in The State that The State should stay off our backs?*

This would start the speech that would detail exactly how my writing folders exhibited all that the state required, and then drift into a philosophical rant about providing only negative feedback to teachers, how it's discouraging and does nothing for job-satisfaction let alone teacher retention. By the time I actually faced Wallace, the corners of her lips still nesting a few dabs of mayo, my courage waned a little.

"Yes, Ms. Kirn," she asked.

What came out of my mouth was less a rant than a meek complaint: "Every time I come into your room, you only tell me what I'm doing wrong." I mentioned my writing folders, the criteria they met despite their inadequate cover sheets. "You never give me any positive feedback. I find it hard to believe I'm not doing anything right."

I waited.

She made one deep, monosyllabic laugh. "Hah." Her belly retracted and then popped out again. "Ms. Kirn, if I wanted positive feedback, I would've left teaching years ago." She said the two words—positive feedback—as though quotes should go around them, as though she couldn't take them seriously in a city such as ours. In her answer was, I think, the reason for Wallace's cruelness: as a teacher, she too had been raised on a strict diet of negative feedback. The profession, for her, was a lonely and isolating job.

"I never got a paycheck, the whole first semester," she'd once told me. "I kept having to call up my mother. I said, Momma, I don't know why but they still haven't paid me." Meanwhile, at the end of each month, she heard the mysterious intercom announcement, *The eagle has landed*, and nobody thought to inform the young, new Ms. Wallace that the phrase was code for, *Come get your paycheck.* "When I finally went down to the office," she'd told me, "two months of checks waited for me."

Nobody had extended Wallace any courtesy, or such was her view of the Baltimore City Public School Systems, so I suppose Wallace thought she was doing me a favor by breaking me into a system that would get no better with my presence. "Positive feedback? Hah." She turned her swivel chair to grab some papers. "Maybe in *The County*."

Whenever Wallace said The County, she snaked her neck taller, widened her eyes, and over-enunciated her consonants: her pretend bourgeois accent. The Count-tee! It was a magical place, a distant land where pretentious people went to teach and where problems such as ours didn't exist and where people treated each other with touchy-feely goodness but looked down upon the dingy city that was, in actuality, only a few miles away.

"Why not, positive feedback?" My anger surprised me. "How am I supposed to get any better if I never know what I'm doing right?" I paused, wondered if I had the courage, and then I went for the jugular. "I'm not the only one who needs it. Any time any one of us comes into your office, we leave feeling bad. We only hear about things we've done wrong."

She stiffened. I'd pulled a catty tactic—calling on the collective opinion of the group, making Wallace feel unpopular. But it was the truth. I saw teachers pass my door, heading down the hall, presumably into Wallace's office, and when I saw them pass the other way a few minutes later, their shoulders slumped forward. They looked defeated. They sighed. Sometimes they stopped into my room to roll their eyes or shake their head. "I shouldn't even *go* in that room," a veteran once said with her hand on her hip and her finger pointed at Wallace's side of the hall.

"Alright, Ms. Kirn." Wallace nodded. "Next time, I'll tell you what you're doing right." She said the last word, *right*, with a high, round I-sound and a snapped T, and I realized her words were once again over-pronounced. This was her Count-tee accent. But this time, it wasn't used as a joke; it was a wall against me.

I didn't have the time to consciously process what I subconsciously wondered: Why was kindness, in Wallace's eyes, a class issue? Why, in a neighborhood of poverty, was encouragement seen as frivolous? And more importantly, was she right? In Southwestern, where kids advertised the deaths of their young cousins on their silk-screened T-shirts—*RIP, Bubba, 1982–2001*—was positive feedback a luxury?

But I had neither the time nor the energy for philosophy. Instead, I took my moment. "Thank you," I said, and left my spot in front of her desk, along with any forgotten items from my mental list of things to say. On my way out of her office, I spotted the barrel of filtered water. Its forbidden, blue-tinted allure now glimmered like topaz.

• • •

In reality, Wallace was probably trying to save me from the wrath of Dr. Jackson. Mr. Willis and Mr. Sypher ended up on The Pip because Jackson had spent a random, unannounced day ransacking the social studies department. Brooke informed us that Jackson had "ripped Sypher and Willis new assholes." Maybe Ms. Wallace knew that, at any moment, Dr. Jackson could walk into my classroom, point out an error like incomplete writing folders, and toss me onto The Pip.

The Pip was not, by its nature, a bad thing. Ostensibly, if you got put on The Pip in Baltimore, your students weren't learning, you couldn't manage your class, and you didn't plan your instruction effectively. The Pip was an intervention strategy for incompetent teachers, teachers like Ms. Back Injury who parked it at her desk and hardly taught.

While the title sounded optimistic, The Performance Improvement Plan—sounded as though the administration was hopeful that performance could indeed be improved—nobody seemed to regard The Pip in this altruistic light. Instead, it was seen as the administration's decision to fail its teacher at teaching, and to make improvement nearly impossible because, as that teacher reached his hand out again and again in small and large efforts to better his performance, the administration used the stipulations of The Pip to slap his wrists over the more minor failures that all of us teachers experienced, which, had said teacher not been "On The Pip," would have snuck by without any other scrutiny but the teacher's.

In other words, at a school such as ours—a school that was by its very nature *failing*—all of us, newbie and veteran alike, experienced plenty of failures, and we knew that they could have been cast by some outsider as warrant for putting us on The Pip, which would have made our jobs all the more difficult.

It seemed especially ludicrous to me, for instance, that a teacher on The Pip was required to submit lesson plans a full week in advance and follow them to a T. If excellent teaching required constantly assessing students' progress, then an effective teacher adjusted her instruction to meet the needs and progress of her kids. In other words, on Monday, what you think you'll teach for Friday's lesson will change by the time you reach Friday because Thursday or Wednesday or even Monday will go differently than expected—you couldn't possibly know for sure how the moody minds of your students would absorb the lessons. Why write a full-blown, step-by-step lesson plan so far in advance that, by the time you reach the day, its carefully designed and multi-modal activities are irrelevant? And why make teachers who need "performance improvement" labor over and then commit to irrelevant instructional decisions that they're then required to impose on their kids?

This was just one reason why The Pip seemed to be a bureaucratic trap more than a positive intervention. Ironically, neither Mr. Johnson of the sexual innuendos nor Ms. Back Injury of the Eddie Murphy cinema were put on The Pip. Willis was. Sypher was. Hardworking teachers swallowed hard at the facts and then looked around their rooms, wondering what state-mandated poster they'd forgotten to tape to the cinder blocks, speculating on how Jackson might "get" them.

Shortly after the social studies hunt-down, Jackson announced that she and the assistant principals would formally review every single teacher in the building. This began the school's Pip Culture, during which everyone feared becoming the next target, the next scapegoat, the next ear to press down onto the chopping block.

• • •

No wonder: the same was happening in the city at large.

In the winter of 2002, the *Baltimore Sun* ran a roughly 1,900 word exposé on Northern High School. With about 2,000 students (a few hundred more than Southwestern), Northern was the third-largest of Baltimore's nine "zone high schools"—although the CEO of Baltimore schools would have wanted me to call them *neighborhood schools. Neighborhood schools* sounded better: communal, friendly, like a building on Sesame Street. *Zone high schools* evoked a certain image of violence, decay, and apathy, an image fairly captured in *The Sun*'s article.

The headline read, "Students, Teachers Call Northern out of Control; Violence Escalates at City School with New Administration; 'Ugly, ugly place to be.'"

The article described dire conditions, including students carrying knives, fights breaking out in the cafeteria, teachers locking classroom doors to keep intruders out, a seventy-seven percent attendance rate, the smell of marijuana wafting up the stairwells. The list went on. The story was shocking, outrageous, an uproar to most citizens.

But Baltimore's high school teachers had a different reaction. "Did you read the Northern story?" a Northwestern high school teacher asked me. "It sounds just like my school."

And it sounded just like Southwestern. "Students swear at and threaten teachers, roam the halls during class, light fires in trash cans and lockers, gamble in classrooms and stairwells, throw food and smoke marijuana in the cafeteria, break down doors, crawl in and out of windows, vandalize classrooms, drink alcohol and buy and sell drugs, those interviewed said." The descriptors could have been used for any "neighborhood" school. At Southwestern, empty bottles of Smirnoff Ice sometimes waited on the steps. And yes, we sometimes caught the kids shaking dice in the hallways and tossing them against the wall, and this was also the way students passed time in some classes where teachers didn't teach or when teachers didn't show. And our students shook their heads when we asked them about the metal detectors that supposedly ensured a weapon-free learning environment. "That thing don't work, Ms. Kirn." They'd seen knives. They'd said they'd seen a gun. Of course they wouldn't tell who carried it.

All across the city, zone high school teachers could now read about their lives in print. Despite our kids' regional patriotism, Northern was Dunbar was Northwestern was Walbrook was Southwestern. There were slight differences between the schools—while knife-possession seemed the crime of choice for Northern, Southwestern had record-high incidents of arson. Some of us tried to use the variations to rank our schools. Which was the worst to work in? Walbrook's kids wore uniforms, which meant students at least complied with one major school rule. Northwestern's classes were packed, thirty to a room, which meant at least their attendance rate was a reasonable ninety percent instead of Northern's seventy-seven or Southwestern's sixty. But the Northern article, followed by our ubiquitous declarations that *It sounds just like my school*, confirmed that our schools were, for the most part, all equally bad.

And now our lives were captured in newsprint for the rest of Baltimore to read. I got strangely, vaguely excited. Citizens of Baltimore would finally see the messy truth. Residents of The County would sympathize with the disaster that was their fellow Marylanders' educations. Something would happen! People would respond! Baltimore City Schools would change.

But the story didn't become the representative tale that I'd hoped. I hadn't paid attention to the blame that the article cast, insinuated in the title and only a few other lines: "Teachers say the problem began when a new administrative team more accustomed to middle schools was assigned to Northern. Several teachers said [school principal] Donaldson—the fourth in five years—has not been a visible presence in a school that desperately needs one."

It's a small paragraph in the exposé, and other interviewees, namely parents, cite the entire school system as responsible. Still, the reporters implied an easier target for the system to go after—the principal—and Carmen Russo fired Donaldson, a woman that Russo herself had once described as "no-nonsense" with a "very good track record." Now, this principal was "afraid of the students," said one parent.

I gulped. The *Sun* had worked hard to get their story. Russo had barred reporters from entering the school for months, a tactic Mayor O'Malley knew nothing about until reporters told him. "It doesn't promote open and transparent government, does it?" he replied. Once reporters got inside, they noted that "Getting people to talk about conditions at North-ern on the record is difficult. Teachers are worried about their jobs. Parents and their children fear retaliation." To speak one's mind was to snitch, and snitching in Baltimore—whether on the streets or in the halls of insti-tutions—had consequences. During my first year, the teachers' union at Southwestern held a meeting, and the few teachers in attendance com-plained about the state of our school; they arrived the next morning to find transfer forms in their mailboxes. In Baltimore, veiled or blatant threats pressured people to keep silent about violence, catastrophe, and failure. Outsiders weren't trusted. In a decision that probably damned her, Donaldson herself declined to be interviewed for the article, which only confirmed speculation that she was an elusive, disengaged leader.

Had reporters trekked up Font Hill, they would have met the same resistance they'd found at Northern. And had any courageous folks talked, whether teacher or student, they would have risked being branded with that word, *snitch*, forever. In other words, the Northern article was an impressive feat. It succeeded in penetrating a closely guarded catastrophe; it shone a huge spotlight on the ugliness of a "neighborhood high school"; it finally captured an urban reality for which many had laid their necks out. And the only result? A simplistic solution in which one principal was replaced with another.

In my mind, I saw a set of hands wiping themselves clean. Job done. Problem solved. The world could nod and get on with life. I gulped because, with such response, I never saw Southwestern improving.

People wouldn't necessarily learn the hardest truth: there was nothing unordinary about the outrageousness of Northern.

When inner-city teachers describe their jobs, listeners sometimes want superlatives. *It was the worst-performing school in Chicago*, they want the teacher to say. I once read an essay about my former student, Jerome Smith, to a crowd in Columbus, Ohio, and before I began, the emcee introduced my piece with the superlatives—*the worst school, the worst kids in Baltimore*.

I cringed. That single word, *worst*, suddenly turned the enigmas of my students into entertaining horror stories.

Former director of Teach For America-Baltimore, Peter Kannam, once wrote about this phenomenon in a newsletter to us TFA corps members. He described a holiday dinner with his family, where, after he survived his first few months of teaching, his relatives wanted to hear "horror stories." They wanted to learn about those crazy kids of the inner city. Peter admit-ted that he sometimes complied. I have too. I've told about how many cop cars sirened up our hill in that first week of school, about my door being set on fire, about Brandon Ward's threats. But the real horror stories, Peter said, were not the ones that our listeners usually wanted. The most horrific stories that I can think of were ones like Andre Tufts, whom I met in my final summer at Southwestern. He strutted into a two-hour class one full hour late and handed me the keys to his Lexus—equipped with a remote control for doors, locks, and lights—in exchange for a pencil, which he used to write misspelled, dyslexic, choppy sentences in print as large as a third grader's. *Write about a time when you were in a difficult situation*, his assignment asked (a Maryland state prompt), and he started, "Onse I was in a dificlt stuashin." In four barely coherent sentences, he described the first time he got locked up. The horror, to me, was in Andre's writing— that he lived the dangerous life of an adult in Baltimore, and wrote like a child. That, statistically speaking, he'd probably die this way: young, hard, barely literate. That none of us had ever figured out a way to show Andre he could do more than sling on the corner.

I know the tactic of superlatives heightens the stakes of teachers' stories. But it also makes movies of real lives, and I think it disavows the listeners: *this is unusual*, the superlative implies. *This is a freak institution. This is cinematic.* And when it's over, we can stand up as we would in a movie theater, or we can fold the story up as we would a newspaper, and get on with our lives.

No *Sun* reporter exposed the innards of any other "neighborhood" high school. No photographers knocked down Southwestern's chain-linked, school doors. But they could have. And so, while Northern and its principal became the victims of overexposure, and while the *Sun* readers shook their heads at what they thought was an anomaly semi-solved, high schools internally panicked, which might have explained the sudden threats of Pips and the rush of formal reviews that sprouted upon us teachers.

"You're supposed to lie." Omar Ali said to Noelani and me, as we all stood in the parking lot during a fire drill. Or a fire alarm. I forget which. "How is your year?" Omar simulated the question and then simulated the optimal response: "Oh, it's great! I love it! Never have I had such brilliant, motivated students. I really feel like I get through to them!"

Our laughter fed Omar's monologue.

"And the administration here is *sooo* supportive. I receive *constant* constructive criticism." Omar laughed at his emphasis of the word constant.

"Constructive!" Noelani repeated.

Omar was a broad, energetic guy with dreadlocks that grazed his shoulders and a passion for spoken-word poetry that he spread to his kids through a student organization he founded, called Rhythm Movement. He wore baggie, dark jeans and sweaters to school. He had a casual style of dress and teaching, and none of this gelled with administrators. I thought Wallace was tough on me, but her criticism paled in comparison to Omar's constant "constructive criticism," which seemed to include more frequent check-ups, more intense scrutiny over the minor wordings of his lesson plans, and yes, more frequent Pip threats.

But after a year and a half at Southwestern, Omar had his own coping mechanisms. "Oh, yes," Omar continued to feign optimism. "Constructive is the operative word. Seriously," he turned to me. "You have to lie to these people. You're never supposed to tell the truth."

Since my defiant stance against Wallace, I had been considering truth-telling to administrators, reviewers, and anyone higher on the totem-pole of Baltimore City's Schools. I suppose I wanted to write my own version of the *Sun*'s exposé. I wanted to call out our errors, to name all that was wrong. In particular, I wanted to say that our students—mine included—were barely passing. Though my lessons were more engaging in my second year, though I had chosen texts that my students could relate to, and though I figured out how to get them involved in the messy business of their own learning processes, that didn't mean that I, in any semester, had erased the huge gap in a student's reading and writing levels. None of us TFA corps members could boast the kinds of turn-arounds we were hired to achieve. Amy and Ellen described kids who still scratched their heads at basic multiplication. Noelani's and my students still struggled to write paragraphs. Open my gradebook, and you'd see columns of 60s and 65s, interrupted only by the unusual 85 or 90 that was achieved by that quiet, lonely student like Renee Woods, who should have transferred into a "city-wide" school, a.k.a. a far-more-selective institution than a "zone school." Otherwise, even my relatively mediocre expectations, which had lowered slowly as the weeks and months wore on, were bars set so high my students just looked up at them and shrugged.

Why not just tell the world? Admit the inadequacies. Dear Baltimore, Dear World, despite my hard work, despite my night and Saturday afternoon classes at Johns Hopkins, despite my monthly professional development with Teach For America, despite applying all the newest research on *learning modalities* and *performance-based assessments* and *ways of making learning meaningful*, my kids were not much better prepared to graduate high school than had they never entered my room.

But this suggestion of truth-telling provoked Omar's emphatic protest. "No," he'd said. I heard it in my mind regularly after this fire-drill day. "You're supposed to lie." I got the feeling that Omar, in his straight-up, get-real, causally-clothed style, had already tried "the truth" with someone. "They don't want to know how your year really is," Omar added. "They'll just think less of you."

• • •

I felt a little, cold stone descend in my esophagus when I learned who would perform my formal review: Mr. Rawls. Unsmiling, impersonal, no-nonsense Mr. Rawls. The only administrator that the kids seemed to fear. I'd never heard the man speak. I'd only heard him grunt, or yell, which he rarely had to do because his very presence struck our kids with uncharacteristic trepidation. Mr. Rawls would assess my performance as a teacher.

My anxiety mounted. As the date neared, I envisioned the failed scenarios. Would he stumble upon some minor error I'd never noticed in my lesson plans? Would he scorn me for my students' low grades? Would his tight, unsmiling face render me unable to explain that I kept my standards high (a semi-truth) and that in so doing, grades aside, I still served my kids well? Would Mr. Rawls toss me onto The Pip?

On the day of my formal review, lesson plan binder tucked underneath the crook of one arm, I walked into Mr. Rawls's office and sat down opposite from him.

Without looking up, he said, "Ms. Kirn." I waited, my enormous binder in my lap, while he shuffled through carbon-smelling forms.

His bald head was shiny. His lips were thin and terse. To me, Mr. Rawls exuded the kind of torment I imagine a prison guard must feel—the sense that one's job makes none involved happy, but that one's job must be upheld regardless because of some unknown and unknowable good that exists beyond the gray interior of one's prisony world. Mr. Rawls possessed a resignation to his suffering, indicative in his stern, unfriendly mouth and his drooping eyelids. His face seemed to say, *I've been through this before*, and *this* meant absolutely anything you could toss his way.

He found a paper and slid it across the table: my formal review, every category and column already marked. Beside several statements, a large *S* had been written.

Having never spoken to me, having probably never known my name, Mr. Rawls had declared me *Satisfactory*. Only one category had an *E* beside it, and before I could figure out why he'd marked me *Excellent*, he gestured to a record book.

"You have very good attendance." He ran a leathery finger along lists of dates. I focused on those three days I'd been marked out, which reminded me of those belabored mornings when I sat on my bed coughing, phone in hand, and felt guilty that I was too ill to make it through the day. But Mr. Rawls was pleased with my attendance. "You come to every faculty meeting," he added.

The comment puzzled me. I had never thought of those monthly, hour-long sessions in the "Media Center" as optional. I nodded.

"So I gave you an *Excellent* rating for Professional Responsibility." He pointed to the form. As a result of my stellar attendance record alone, I had been deemed *professionally responsible*. All I'd had to do was show up.

"Thank you," I said.

But when I looked more closely at the categories, I saw that I'd received an *S* for "instruction" and "management," both of which were probably justified though neither of which Rawls had directly assessed himself. I'd also gotten an "S" for "planning and preparation," another oddity because, despite all the Pip threats and despite Wallace's sporadic check-ups on things like writing portfolios, nobody had ever even peeped at my lesson plans this year. Nobody knew a thing about how I taught my kids. I could have been teaching the cinematography of horror films, or the nutritional content of cheese puffs for all Mr. Rawls knew, and he'd just branded me *Satisfactory*.

"Now all we need to do is sign." Mr. Rawls offered me a pen. That was it? No checking my students' grades? No discussion of my teaching strategies? Of my goals for my students? I realized my much-anticipated formal review was just another bureaucratic hoop that bogged the administration down, indicative in Rawls' drooping eyelids.

"Do you want to see my lesson plans?" I asked, and he looked up. "Here." I handed him my fat three-ring binder that contained every daily and long-term plan, every handout I'd ever given, every activity my students did, every goal, everything about how and what I taught my kids. "Nobody's ever seen my lesson plan book."

His arm dropped a few inches when he took the weight of the book into his hand. "This is huge." He opened the book at random.

Why did I do this? Sure, I was ogling for another *Excellent* somewhere on my report. But I also wanted to give my formal review some integrity. In order for Mr. Rawls to decide whether I'd planned, and how well, he should have at least seen some evidence.

But when I handed Mr. Rawls that binder, the mood of our meeting changed. He was no longer my superior, plugging through some mandatory paperwork. He flipped through my binder with intrigue. "You're teaching *Romeo and Juliet*, huh?" he said. "Do they read the whole thing?"

"They do."

"That's good." He flipped another page. "I always thought *Macbeth* was Shakespeare's best."

"They like the love story and the gang fights, though."

He nodded. He flipped the pages again, and paused at my long-term plan, a two-page document that outlined every major goal I had for the semester. "And you spend three weeks on *Black Boy*?"

Before I could confirm, Mr. Rawls started on a mini-monologue. "I never understood why people emphasized black literature in the city. As a kid, I didn't want to read another story about my own life." His eyelids no longer drooped; they lifted. The topic energized him. "Why would I want to read about another black boy? Why would I want to read about my own life?" he asked, and when I smiled, he pressed his lips together so that the edges lifted just slightly. "You know? I want to learn about someone else's life when I read. I want to go to a different world. Why are we always having kids read what they already know?"

We were sitting in a cinderblock office on the southwest side of a city that I think Mr. Rawls might have spent his whole life living in.

He listed his favorite stories, ones that took him out to sea or deep into a jungle or on some aristocratic adventure. And I was entranced. I was giddy. It took me a few beats to understand that Mr. Rawls was challenging my choice, but even when I did, my giddiness grew: someone was taking me and my teaching choices to bat. Someone cared enough to engage me in a real discussion, not about forms and the correct way to fill them out, but about literature, about reading, about what and how to teach our kids. It was the first philosophical conversation I'd had with a Southwestern administrator.

"I used to teach literature, you know," he said.

"No," I said. "I didn't know that."

"Yeah, used to be an English teacher. Before I did *this*." He waved his hands over the forms, and added, "Chasing kids down the halls all day, writing them up."

I imagined Mr. Rawls's usual day. While my kids laughed at awkward Shakespearean syntax, he wrote incidents of violence on official documents that, by their very existence, would only raise the school's negative statistics, and outsiders' negative opinions. His choices in syntax didn't matter.

"Well," he closed my binder. "A copy of that will go into your official file," he said, nodding to my formal evaluation. Business as usual. I signed the form.

But I marveled about it for weeks after. For a few moments in Southwestern, the unlikely duo of me and scary Mr. Rawls had been pedagogical philosophers. Literary colleagues. We'd cared deeply about how best to teach students. We couldn't afford to do so for long; what felt like a meaningful conversation was only a two-minute digression in the seven-minute interaction of my formal review. Still, to this day, I remember Mr. Rawls's pontification. It defines him in my mind, and offers a possible glimpse into other administrators. Maybe, somewhere beneath the Pip threats and the anal-retentive remarks about writing portfolios, the passions of real educators were buried. Even for Dr. Jackson and Ms. Wallace. And maybe each of those wary administrators longed to be taken, as Mr. Rawls had said, to "a different world," one where they felt those passions had a place and a meaning and a reason.

Enormous binder in hand, I left Mr. Rawls and his paperwork behind.

• • •

During my first year, two pop-rap songs played repeatedly across American airwaves, Baltimore's included. The first was Shaggy's, "It Wasn't Me." Kids sang along to the innocent-sounding, high-pitched voice of Ricardo "RikRok" Ducent, who gets caught cheating on his girlfriend and confesses his infidelity to his friend, reggae artist Shaggy. Shaggy's advice is to deny the affair at all costs. But RikRok confesses all the places that his girlfriend found him—doing it on a counter, doing it on a sofa, doing it on camera. It doesn't matter. After each undeniable confession, a group of men intrude with the recommended reply: "It wasn't me."

For months, whenever I caught students at some mini-crime—throwing paper, drawing on a desk, cutting class—they repeated Shaggy's mantra. "It wasn't me," they said and smiled.

The smile was an acknowledgment of the irony; they knew they'd been caught. They knew that insisting on their innocence wouldn't change their guilt, a knowledge that was evidenced when I doled out their punishment and they accepted it.

But the school district didn't seem to know. *Don't acknowledge any failures, especially your own. If we don't tell the world how flawed our schools are, then maybe our schools won't be flawed.* The threats of Pips only led teachers, even good, hard-working teachers, to feel that they had to cover up even more the failures they lived with, which were all of our failures. Like thick make-up over a break-out, the covering only made the condition worse, as no one would or could look honestly at the causes of, and solutions for, a dismal school.

Meanwhile, another song overplayed, a far better hit by Andre 3000 and Big Boi, of OutKast. Half-rant, half-apology, "Ms. Jackson" is supposedly addressed to the grandmother of Andre 3000's kid. While the chorus apologizes again and again to Ms. Jackson, the other lyrics are a father's fume, and an insistence that, despite his break-up with Ms. Jackson's daughter, he'll still be responsible for his son. He'll be there for the first day of school, for graduation, for all the milestones. The song holds the fragments of a broken love, owns them, and apologizes for pain regardless of who's to blame. The song, in other words, is the polar opposite of Shaggy's "It Wasn't Me."

When I think of my time in Southwestern, it's not by accident or sheer Billboard preference that these two songs play as musical backdrops for my memories. In Baltimore, blame and responsibility pulled on each other like a game of tug of war. It was hard to acknowledge responsibility without receiving disproportionate blame. Shrugging off both, however, was easy. And it probably wasn't melody alone that had Noelani and me preferring OutKast.

When the opening notes played on our drive home from school, we turned up the volume on the car stereo. We sang blaringly and badly along, apologizing again and again. We were sorry, Ms. Jackson. And for what? I'm not entirely sure. Probably for our inability to fix what was broken in Baltimore. We were sorry. We were for real. We sang on our way from the rough, trash-ridden west side where our kids lived, to the more upscale, central neighborhoods where we resided, and as the city's row homes and idle stoop-sitters passed by, we apologized, we apologized a trillion times, with our windows rolled all the way up, with no one able to hear.

CHAPTER 14

ELISABETH SHUE LOVES US

Because it was a weekday night, we had sore feet from standing all day and sore throats from speaking (slash shouting) all day, but by God, we were going anyway, because tickets that cost forty dollars for the general public had been given to us for free. Because we Taught for America. Because we served the nation's underprivileged schools, underprivileged kids. Because Davis Guggenheim thought we were worthy of some reward. It was spring, nearing the end of our commitment, and in my two years of teaching I hadn't been given anything but the laminated posters from my special education teacher. So Amy, Ellen, and I were going.

The event was made fancier by its title: The Something-Something Film-Screening and *Gala*. I'd never been to anything called a *Gala*, a fact I announced to Amy and Ellen, who sat in the front seats of Amy's car.

"I've never been to a *gah*-la."

"I think it's pronounced *gay*-la," Ellen said.

But a *gay*-la did not evoke for me what a *gah*-la did. I imagined ball gowns. Not on me, per say, as I was wearing my standard tan poly-blend teacher slacks, the ones I'd bought at the beginning of this TFA road, the ones that had pilled week after week in the wash. By the end of the second year, the knit could pass for pajama fabric. But I envisioned ball gowns on *some*one at an event called a *gah*-la, especially at a place called The Charles Theater. The TFA Program Director had said The Charles Theater was the only place of its kind in Baltimore: a hundred-year-old building that played old Hitchcock movies and sold fancy coffees with steamed milk, which were advertised on a café-style chalkboard above a gourmet concession stand. This would be no United Artist or AMC theater, with artificial buttery flavoring. This would be an old-fashioned venue of style and charm, a building whose very existence justified the *Charm* in our affectionately coined Charm City.

"I heard Elisabeth Shue's gonna be there," Ellen said.

Elisabeth Shue? Of *Leaving Las Vegas*? And of the very first *Karate Kid* movie? Sandy-haired and otherwise fairly nondescript Shue: I'd never been especially interested in her until now. As we drove south in the dark, down St. Paul, over North Avenue, passed more vacant houses with windows covered by plywood, passed people sitting on stoops and women standing in knee-high boots and ass-bearing skirts, I thought about Elisabeth Shue. In a ball gown. At our *gah*-la. I now imagined, not just ball gowns, but red carpeting and gilded columns.

North Avenue always marked the nadir of shady in downtown Baltimore. "North Av," as we referred to it, wasn't just a street but the name educators used for the school system's central pulse. *North Av* made decisions about enrollment. *North Av* pulled plugs on whole schools. *North Av* did this and *North Av* did that, and we grunt-working teachers talked about it like it was an omnipotent dysfunctional computer, the Hal of our *2001: A Space Odyssey*, the broken authority over our labor. We called it *North Av* because the administrative building for all of Baltimore schools had sat for many years on the actual avenue that cut east to west across the center of the city, just north of downtown. But the administration moved farther north this year. Now *North Av* no longer resided on North Avenue. It had been pushed toward Towson, toward the beltway and the edges of this "shrinking" city as though—along with industry and middle-class homeowners—even the bureaucratic brain behind the educational system was trying to find a way out of town.

We crossed over North Avenue, to the gala, to the anomalously hip Charles Theater, which was surrounded by dingy B-more blocks too unsafe for us to walk alone. The theater did not have velvet rope after all, but we proudly showed our free, forty-dollar-value tickets and, once inside, contemplated the latte-touting chalkboard menu.

The lobby was urban-chic: concrete floors, high ceilings, silver and gray metal as décor. The aesthetic had a kind of rhetoric to it. It said: city is cool; urban is now. It said: live in the city. I saw mostly white-haired, middle-aged white couples. They looked like they'd driven in from the county, like they didn't live seven blocks north of North Av, as I did, literally one house away from where the graffiti became ubiquitous on the plywood-covered windows of row homes. Here, the women wore pashmina stoles and warm-toned make-up. I looked around for Elisabeth Shue. No sign of her.

"*Why* will Elisabeth Shue be here?" It suddenly dawned on me that Elisabeth Shue's presence made no sense. We were at the screening of a movie about five first-year teachers. Three of the five were TFA-ers. We would be watching approximately an hour and a half of footage about lives pretty much like ours, except in sunny Los Angeles. This was the very reason that Noelani and Brooke and many other TFA teachers decided not to come. *Why would I watch a movie about my life?* Noelani had asked me.

Always the bargain-hunter, I'd said, *Because someone paid forty dollars for it*, but she wasn't in the mood. She'd rather catch a TV show and an early bedtime.

As the doors between the lobby and the theater opened, Ellen said that Elisabeth Shue was married to Davis Guggenheim. We filed in with the crowd and chose our seats, which felt to me like a luxurious reward for two tiring years. I let my body fall into the plush, springy, forty-dollar velvet fullness, let the curves of the cushion catch me as the lights went dim and on came *The First Year*, a documentary about five newbie teachers trying, like me, their damndest to make a difference. And often failing.

But in the film, they don't totally fail. Otherwise, what kind of teaching movie would that be? Ms. Genevieve DeBose, a twenty-three-year-old kid out of college who doesn't even know how to get the electric turned on in her new house, admits that her sixth graders aren't engaged in school. The camera shows her turning the classroom lights on and off, on and off while she pleads with her kids: stay focused, stop talking, stop fighting. It's been a good day, she tells them. Don't screw it up.

But the film doesn't just show her problem—an unruly, uninterested class. It offers her triumph. Like a good plot, it has a zenith. Her low point is the foil to her inevitable high one. Ms. DeBose writes a grant for her kids, and receives it. She and her class will study the textbook-outlined "elements of culture" by photographing images of their own lives. Forty disposable cameras arrive, and the documentary captures her excitement as she opens the cardboard box, fiddles with the plastic-wrapped cameras, then distributes them to her kids.

In the days to come, they photograph uncles playing instruments in a basement, dinners their aunties and grandmothers cooked. The photos, along with the writing they produce to accompany their art, are all posted in a fancy room somewhere outside of school, and the display is unveiled like a gallery exhibit. The girls arrive in skirts and black shiny flats and the boys arrive in sweater vests and pressed khakis, and they admire their projects with parents by their sides. In other words, the class has gone from disengaged to passionately immersed in school. Hooray for Ms. DeBose!

And Mr. Nate Monley, at twenty-five, is instantly charismatic: a blond-haired, blue-eyed, fluently Spanish-speaking, guitar-playing guy who commands the attention of his fifth grade kids. He starts the year with a troubled student named Juan. Juan writes on Monley's shelves, has to spend quiet time in a corner away from the other kids, laughs off a serious presentation about gang shootings, and seems impervious to adult inter-vention. Juan even draws a picture of a monkey on a toilet with the head-ing, *Mr. Monley*. But by the end of the year, Juan and Monley are fishing together, eating burgers together at a greasy spoon, having heart-to-hearts, and Monley will definitely be back for a second, a third, a fourth year of teaching. . . .

Mr. Maurice Rabb says he'll jump through any hoops to get his kids to learn, and does. Kindergartener Tyquan, who's missing his front teeth and has gold-plated bicuspids, is in serious need of speech therapy, says *no man, no man,* and when nobody can understand him, points to a picture of a snowman. "*Snow*man!" an adult says in an *a-hah* voice. He's legally entitled to a speech therapist but the only one that serves the school seems to be on permanent sick leave, and despite the bureaucratic hoops that Mr. Rabb tries to leap through—the special meetings with school administrators, the phone calls to this person or that—Tyquan never gets a tutor. So Mr. Rabb decides to tutor Tyquan himself, three days a week, after school. To make sure Tyquan succeeds, Mr. Rabb performs the job of two.

The small victories are captured in scene after scene—Tyquan counting all the fingers on one hand and then saying "pive," and Mr. Rabb saying "yes!" and high-fiving him. Right answer, Tyquan! Mr. Monley, casting his fishing line into the river aside Juan and Juan's brothers, weaving out of English, into Spanish, into English again with the suavity of someone who's lived with his bilingual students and their families all his life. Ms. DeBose, singing gospel and clapping in a church with one of her once-problem children and his whole family. In the epilogue—narrated by the recognizable voice of Elisabeth Shue, a voice that's equal parts innocent, sultry, and serious—we learn that all the teachers are still teaching. Still Teaching for America.

Why didn't I write a grant for my students? Why didn't I sing gospel at their churches on Sundays? Did they *go* to churches? Why didn't I know? Was I too selfish to become an after-school therapist for someone? My eight-hour teaching days and two-hour night classes and weekends of homework and grading surely left another inch of time, somewhere, somehow, during which I might have done more, might have redeemed some poor kid's proverbial pronunciation of *snowman.*

Plenty of instrumental music plays throughout the film: the worried, lone violin at a time of trial; the quiet, synthesized rhythms in a time of achievement. Guggenheim's hope, at least as he words it in an article, is that the film "will change the way people view education and see it as a human issue."

But this film wrecked me. I saw all that I did not do. I did not go to church with my kids, did not go fishing with their families, did not call photo-developing places on my off-day to determine the most economical way to use my grant-money, which I did not acquire because I did not ever write a grant. A draft of a grant sat unsent on my hard drive. After seeing the film, I even felt strangely guilty that I did not fluently execute a second language in my classroom, despite the fact that all but two of my students—refugees from Cuba—were native English speakers. This guilt about language was metaphorical, I think. Listening to Monsley's rapid, enthused Spanish made me want another tongue with which to reach my students, one that I could have studied in a textbook long before I stepped foot in Baltimore, one that would have brought us instantly together. *Hola, me llamo Senorita Kirn.*

What would Guggenheim have done with David Turner? Would the filmmaker have captured a victory in our occasionally cordial back-and-forth banter, and would cameramen have focused on a shot of my grade book, which showed David's passing score of 65 percent? Guggenheim probably could have turned my Timmy Rogers tale into triumph—Timmy throws fit in class, busts open closet door, makes full turnaround, attends class regularly, develops rapport with teacher, "passes" English I. But I would have wanted a caveat, an addendum, a parenthetical "excuse-me, but." *Excuse me, but* Timmy didn't always attend my class; he skipped plenty of days, and skipped other classes too. *Excuse me, but* Timmy barely "passed," and barely "passing" at Southwestern would not bring Timmy any nearer to his suburban, middle-class, grade-level-performing counterparts. And *excuse me, but* I don't believe Timmy ever went on to college, which meant that Timmy was not a walking embodiment of the TFA mission, printed in discreet font across my TFA T-shirt and blasted around the circumference of my TFA mug: *one day, all children in this nation will have the opportunity to attain an excellent education.*

Maybe Guggenheim's film-making eye would have spotted the successes that I, too distracted by all the failure, couldn't see. But even my biggest successes seemed to devolve into failures. Takira Webb, my brilliant tenth-grader who'd gotten kicked out of a top city school because she couldn't get herself out of bed in the morning. She was absolutely college-bound. The year that I taught her, she came to school nearly every day, and we sat atop the student-desks together, reading and analyzing revision possibilities for her far above-par essay. But the next year, Amy, Takira's math teacher, had to dial Takira's house before school each morning just to get her butt out of bed, and eventually, even the daily calls didn't work. Takira stopped coming. College-bound, and she was on the way to tossing her ticket.

I never saw in myself what I saw in Mr. Rabb or Ms. DeBose or Mr. Monley. In the film, triumphs outweighed struggles. Triumphs actually *resulted* from struggles. Each teacher's true joy at connecting with his or her kids was the ending note of the film, the highlight, the pinnacle, the thing toward which all struggles pointed. My true joy at connecting with my students was only one emotion in a broad spectrum of difficult days. In the movie, teaching appeared beautiful, worthy, and righteous. In my life, teaching was gritty, draining, and felt sometimes all for naught. Noelani had been wrong; the film was nothing like our lives.

Earlier in the semester the program director for Teach For America had sat down with me and asked, how did I plan on bridging the achievement gap? What was my strategy to locate my students in whatever nook or cranny of the standards that they'd gotten lost in and raise them to the proud platform of the national average? And unlike the year before, I didn't gulp and confess doubt about my capabilities. Instead, I talked goals. I talked benchmarks. I planned on having my students write analytical essays comparing two film versions of Shakespeare's play, and that was my goal, and my benchmarks were comparison activities of the films, and graphic organizers for each paragraph of the essays, and due dates for rough drafts, and peer review days, and final due dates, and in the end, I would collect these essays and grade them. Jeremy nodded and said this sounded genuinely impressive—"a big, hairy, bodacious goal"—and he wished me luck and told me if ever I needed anything, *anything*, feel free to call, because Teach For America people were insistent on dropping personal boundaries. Jeremy meant it—any of his TFA teachers could call him any time, on a Saturday evening if we needed. Jeremy would go on to develop and head a nationally ranked charter school, one that served low-income students. Jeremy was serious about the cause. And so was I. But when he left, I sighed. In the end, only about half of my students would even turn in that essay, and the other half would turn in nothing, and would not "pass," and yes, some of the essays I received would be decently wrought and organized, and the writers of them would be better for it, but I doubted that my efforts were doing much to chip away at a national crisis.

The day that Jeremy visited, I went to Amy's room. She was the only teacher around, lingering in her classroom and organizing primary-colored blocks and trapezoids and other unknown contraptions that she used for geometry instruction.

"Jeremy came."

"Oh yeah."

"Yeah." She kept on stacking and organizing. "He wanted to know how I was going to bridge the achievement gap."

I didn't have to say anything else. Amy looked up from a set of books she was boxing up into a new, high-gloss compartment. Amy had sharp, clear blue eyes and I looked into them and waited for some kind of solace.

The other day, when I'd asked her how teaching was going, how "bridging the achievement gap" was going, her response was, "I don't know about you, Ms. Kirn, but here in room 3516, we don't really have an achievement gap. We're just marching on with the rest of the nation, doing our math on target."

On this day, she delivered her comfort with equal sarcasm: "You know," she started, "I'm awfully comfortable in the achievement gap. My students and I, we find the gap quite roomy." She threw her arms above her head, reached her hands toward the ceiling, and wiggled her shoulders. "Plenty of space to stretch, relax." I laughed, and she smiled, and we—the two teachers who'd stayed in school an extra hour and a half, who'd stayed long after others had left—we eventually turned in the towel, too.

But these teachers in the film, *these* teachers were saving the nation. Though the scenes didn't actually show that student achievement had dramatically improved as a result of their teachers' toil, the editing had me convinced that the kids soared, all of them: Juan and Tyquan and Ms. DeBose's entire class of fifth grade photographers. As I watched, I forgot that the documentary was a crafted work, that it was the edited and probably simplified version of several messy lives, that it needed tension and resolution and that it featured a soundtrack to elicit feelings of *hooray*. My teaching arc felt like a little roller-coaster operating so far below sea level that any rise upward was already in the zone of failure. In other words, my little triumphs didn't count. Davis Guggenheim and Teach For America and American viewers wanted big, rosy-ended accomplishments. I wanted the same. I might not have known yet that the world wouldn't always redeem itself. That sometimes we'd find ourselves at the end of a story with little more than broken pieces in our palms. Or rather, at twenty-three, I probably did know this, but I didn't want to believe it. So despite the fact that the film's endnote was a glorification of the profession, the message I got from the film was different: if I lacked a bona fide success story, I didn't belong in Baltimore.

When the lights came on, Davis Guggenheim walked across a stage beneath the screen and sat in a chair. Three unnamed adults followed, along with a blonde woman who I suddenly realized was Elisabeth Shue. But I was no longer star-struck. And not because she wasn't beautiful. She was. She was also far shorter than I ever realized, and had faintly cut muscles in her lean arms and strong, solid, back-curving posture that made her look regal, but still, what did Elisabeth Shue know? What did Guggenheim know? The forty-dollar gift of the *gah*-la was not a gift after all, but a mirror for my feelings of failure.

Among the three other adults on stage were the Maryland Teacher of the Year and the Superintendent of Maryland's schools. While audience members asked questions of the panel, I yawned and looked at my watch. It was nearing nine and my bedtime, and tomorrow I had to wake to the reality of a world that most of the audience would leave behind once they lifted from their Charles Theater seats. Still, they had questions. *How are the problems in the film's LA schools similar to the ones here in Baltimore? What is your hope in creating this film?* Though I can't recall exact answers from the spokespeople on stage, in an interview, Elisabeth Shue once said, "It's my hope that everyone who sees the film considers becoming a teacher." The film was half-recruitment for a job we already had. I looked at Ellen and Amy, who looked tolerant, but Ellen went to bed even earlier than I did; if this Q and A dragged on, we'd squeeze out of our aisle-side seats.

A black man in the audience who looked to be in his thirties raised his hand. He asked, nay, demanded to know what Maryland planned to do about one of its staggering statistics. "I've got dyslexia, okay, and I want to know." His voice wasn't quite as friendly as the one that inquired about Mr. Guggenheim's hopes for his film. "What are we gonna do about the fact that seventy percent of all inmates in this state have learning disabilities? Seventy percent!" he emphasized, and I leaned forward on the edge of my seat. His voice was urgent; he sounded like he knew a little something about the world beyond the film.

The question was directed at the Superintendent of schools. What would Maryland do? What would it do, I thought, about the third of Southwestern's kids who've been diagnosed with some enigmatic obstacle or series of obstacles that stood between them and their statistically improbable diplomas? Baltimore's "special needs" kids were often the least engaged, lowest performing students, and I'd seen my fair share of paper-pushing in an effort to comply with some rule that allowed a school to dot its *I*s and cross its *T*s and yet let a child fail and/or dropout, regardless. How would Maryland help?

Guggenheim had lovely hair. It was a little long everywhere, especially on top. It was full and thick and shiny and brown and seemed soft between his fingers and just long enough that he did justifiably need to wipe it aside or back from his face, but it was not so long that it looked scruffy. The length said, *I can defy cultural conventions with taste and class. I can defy cultural conventions in a way that creates new conventions.* He belonged at a gallery opening. He pushed it from his face and turned his eyes to the Superintendent.

She started by complaining about the state's nonexistent funds for students with learning disabilities. It was the system, she said. "A child needs to fail before he or she is considered eligible for special needs services," she said with exacerbation, and her hands went up to feel the invisible rain pouring from the ceiling of the Charles Theater. "Which means that a child is already struggling before he or she is allowed the extra help."

That's so frustrating, I thought. *How frustrating for her. For us. For our kids.* I sighed along with the Superintendent and thought that her defeatist attitude was the comfortable end of the conflict until, smack in the middle of another defeated explanation of the system and its woes, the Maryland Teacher of the Year interrupted Maryland's head of education with a righteous, angry tone.

"The state of Maryland needs to care about its children with learning disabilities *before* they get to prison!"

The audience applauded. I sat up and clapped and, as the applause grew louder, even made the conscious, awkward effort to "wooo!" I *woo*ed for the Maryland Teacher of the Year. I'd been shaken from my "the system is impossible" coma.

Then the Maryland Teacher of the Year added, "*Before* they get to high school!"

And that's when, perched there at the edge of my plush seat, I paused mid-clap.

Before they get to high school. A line that implies that struggling kids are beyond hope once they reach their pubescent ninth grade. And the line *before they get to prison* created a parallelism that I cringed at: Baltimore's high schools had once again been equated to its commonest, most cliché metaphor. Prisons? High schools? All the same here in Charm City?

Though I was used to the comparison and could shirk it off, I was most upset by the insinuation that once kids got to high school, the course of their lives had been charted, their destinies had been drawn, and the charade I performed at the front of rows of kids or in between clustered groups of desks was altogether earnest and pointless. The sentence cut at my tired efforts. The insinuation raged against everything TFA had taught me: I was supposed to have high expectations, to believe anything was possible, to aim high and watch my students follow suit. But then why *didn't* TFA ever cite major grade-level advancements from its high school teachers? We only ever heard about Ms. First-Grade Teacher of Baton Rouge or Mr. Third-Grade Teacher of Houston who each started the autumnal first-days with thirty kids one to two grade-levels behind, and ended in the warm, blooming spring with students completely on point, on target, on the central dot of the national average, as they waved them off to the next grade. Which meant that the so-called forgotten kids in the shacks of Baton Rouge or the projects of Houston were now performing alongside remembered kids in any white, middle-class county across the country. And that was the whole point, *is* the whole point, of Teach For America. But I'd never heard a story like this about any high school teachers. Nobody had claimed that they'd taken their tenth graders and risen them three or four grade-levels in their short semester, maybe because there are limits to what a teacher can achieve in a given semester. Maybe because by the time students get to high school, too many habits are learned, too many paths are laid down, too many behaviors are carved.

Did I honestly believe that? The idealist in me, a pom-pom waving crusader of just causes, a prominent part of myself before I started TFA, would have said no. Absolutely not. There are no limits to humanity. But I mourned that I now had a newly born realist lurking inside, a jaded woman who felt simultaneously angry that each story didn't end in redemption, and tired of believing that it could. *Yes,* she thought. *Some things were probably impossible.*

Before they get to high school. I thought of the many things I wished had happened before my kids got to Southwestern. *Before they get to high school,* I thought, *kids should learn to spell Wednesday.* One afternoon, while my students were working, I graded carbon-copied question guide after carbon-copied question guide. Ten questions total, and one was simple—*On what day is Paris and Juliet's wedding now?* Nearly anyone who paid any attention to act four scene two that day could get the answer right. Papa Capulet wants to push the wedding forward because he's brash and Mama Capulet thinks the family should hold back because she knows her daughter is not at all into Paris, and to keep my students on point as they read this all-too-subtle but still plot-specifically crucial Shakespearean tension, I asked them tedious questions on those carbon-copied reading guides, including *On what day is Paris and Juliet's wedding now?* The answer is written plain as day and spelled correctly in the words of the characters: *Wednesday.*

But reading guide after reading guide, nobody spelled it right.

Wensday.

Wenedsay.

Wesday.

Wesnday.

I read what seemed like an infinite array of creative but worrying spellings. Nobody, nobody knew how to spell *Wednesday* but for Renee, the quiet girl with lovely pencils and eraser-sets and handwriting far neater than mine, nearly font-worthy in its cursive consistency.

At Southwestern, the number of errors on any batch of student papers was so high they often eluded my B-plus-type personality, but seeing the same day of the week incorrectly written again and again and again, and hardly ever the same way twice, was disconcerting. *By God,* I thought, *these kids are fifteen, sixteen. Don't they learn the days of the week in elementary school?*

I called on a student who sat nearest to my desk. "Can you spell Wednesday for me?"

Without a question, he did. "W-E-S-N-D-A-Y."

"Thank you," I said.

Before they get to high school, I thought, as I tuned out the Guggenheims' discussion, *they should know how to spell all the days of the week.*

Or what about the time that I witnessed what Amy and Ellen strove to conquer every day? Even while they taught subjects like algebra and geometry and pre-calculus, they often had to combat students' incompetence with basic math. Prior to reading Shakespeare, my kids and I spent a class period learning about "The Elizabethan Age." I hadn't anticipated the confusion over the phrase, and my kids spent a full thirty minutes under the misconception that we were discussing the literal age of this new woman, Queen Elizabeth.

"But how old *is* she?" everyone kept asking, and I finally got why.

"Well, let's figure it out." *Ellen and Amy would be proud*, I thought. A little math practice in the middle of English class. "She was born in 1533. She died in 1603." I wrote the biggest number over the smallest and drew a line underneath. "How old was she when she died?"

The class argued a full minute. Someone called out thirty. Someone called out sixty. These became the most likely options, and they argued about which was right. Was it thirty? Or sixty? Everyone chose a side. I watched, my eyebrows crinkling closer and closer together as that long minute of mathematical debate passed.

From the front row I heard someone reluctantly murmur, "She was seventy." It was a murmur both confident in its correctness and discouraged by its necessity.

"Yes!" I shouted. "She was seventy!"

The voice came from Renee, who looked as defeated as I felt. There was no victory over a mere one student's subtraction of 1533 from 1603, and it seemed Renee and I were the only people to know that.

At the Charles Theater, the Q and A ran its natural span, though it never got any more heated. Everyone had agreed that the state of Maryland needed to do more to help its learning disabled, and everyone had agreed that the film was inspiring. And when the number of seat-shifters and coughers greatly outnumbered the number of hands that popped up in eager quest of some world-changing answer, Davis Guggenheim thanked the audience, and the audience clapped, and Amy and Ellen and I stood up to go.

As we made our way into the river of strangers shuffling out to the lobby, Amy's roommate found us and smiled. "Did you see Elisabeth Shue?"

Amy's roommate, who was also a TFA teacher, had snagged a seat right up front. She wore a big smile.

Amy nodded. We all saw Ms. Shue.

"Wasn't she beautiful!" said Amy's roommate. "She was so beautiful!"

The open-mouthed smile didn't stop, and it was clear that Amy's room-mate was star-struck. I thought about how lovely it was that Amy's room-mate could focus on the beauty of Elisabeth Shue and not on whatever lessons any of us had to teach tomorrow. She seemed genuinely uplifted.

"Yep," said Amy half-heartedly.

Ellen nodded, and said flatly, "She was beautiful." Then Ellen looked down at the crowded pathway between the seats, careful not to step on any heels or toes.

I didn't say anything, didn't even ask myself why Elisabeth Shue's beauty, which seemed quiet and simple from so many rows back—under-stated and classic, innocent and all-American—all of a sudden hurt in a place I couldn't quite name. Maybe because this beauty was unreachable, with Shue high up on stage and the audience in obedient rows like parish-ioners in pews. It was unreachable like the other side of that achievement gap my students and I were meant to bridge. I always visualized the gap as a southwest-American canyon of red clay and cracks, where my stu-dents stood on one side, and the rest of the nation's children and teachers stood on the other. Shue's beauty was yet another thing in this world that I thought couldn't be reached. Couldn't be met. Could only be admired from a distance.

CHAPTER 15

ONE HUNDRED AND FORTY

The grass surrounding the half-charred tree in the school's front yard had turned from straw-yellow to rich green. The kids in the hallway—or whoever remained—no longer wore hoodie sweatshirts over their T-shirts. By June, the building was warm. It was also kind of sleepy. Southwestern succumbed to heat like a beast that submits to some hypnotic charmer and rolls over. This was no longer early spring. Early spring usually brought with it the amped-up hormones of teenage girls who shortened their skirts and teenage boys who surveyed the girls with extra devotion, *tsk-tsk*ed the ones they liked. With early spring also came quick tempers, ready reflexes, the need, it seemed, for kids to throw fast punches or jump each other. In April and May plenty of fights had erupted. But by June, the building was quiet. About half of the enrolled kids had been officially seduced by sun and streets. Whoever still came up the long hill was in it to finish it. The ones who'd remained were often quiet. They'd waited out the chaos; they'd survived a semester worth of Southwestern mayhem and still came, day after day, all the way to June. That phrase, *all the way to June*. It felt like *all the way to China*.

I, too, had made it, however exhausted. My shoes went from hard-soled and supportive to floppy and toe-exposing, and I still couldn't pick up my feet. When I approached my kids' desks, my backless slides shuffled across the dusty linoleum floor. I hung over my remaining students, shoulders curling forward, spine uninterested in straight posture, and heard their inquiries through a tunnel of fatigue. At twenty-three, I felt ancient.

So it was with a weary body that, during the last week of school, I donned a polyester zip-up robe and a mortar-board cap. Having never taught seniors—having only taught kids at least three years and several growth-spurts away from possible diplomas—Southwestern's graduation for me was an afterthought. A way to spend a Saturday afternoon. An obligatory pomp and a circumstance for students I didn't know but would applaud nonetheless. I lined up with the rest of the faculty, adorned in an outfit I wore at my own college graduation only two years before, and

217

processed into the rarely used auditorium. An audio recording of violins played, half of them keeping us in step, the other half wandering up and down the sentimental melody of every American graduation.

"We look good," someone said of our uniformity.

We did. In our caps and gowns, we looked regal. We looked like what teachers had often thought we weren't (which they confessed in mutters when no administrator was in sight): an institution of learning. The graduates—one hundred and forty of them—paraded onto the stage, their tassels swinging with their struts and swaying in front of their broad smiles. The women-graduates wore royal purple, the men, bright gold. One hundred and forty southwest Baltimore teenagers stood before the audience, looking suddenly very grown. They sat down in unison, their smiles uncontainable. They glowed like beacons in shimmering polyester.

The audience was far from reticent. The families shouted and cheered. That's when I began to grasp the magnitude of what I was about to witness. This was not just any graduation. In my own adolescent world, a high school diploma had been a given; the rolled-up paper to mark, in a sense, the beginning of one's choices, the end of living out the script that someone else had planned for you. Everyone went to school and everyone graduated. The audience in my own hometown was polite, offered steady, simple applause. One after the other, names were called like numbers at a burger joint. The graduates seemed to retrieve their diplomas obligatorily.

Here, the diploma was a different feat altogether. Ms. Brown's formal, overly articulate voice proved perfect for the occasion. As she called out the full names of students, the students did not walk across the stage to retrieve their diplomas; they did not march or strut or saunter. They danced.

"Abraham Otis Jenkins," Brown called. No one knew who she meant. Up jumped a gangly kid with shoulder-length cornrows and a wide, mischievous, gold-plated grin that the staff had sort-of grown to like. "Mouth!" voices from the audience called out. We usually saw him pressed up against the glass windows of a class he didn't belong in, or lurking around the corner of yet another hallway during class. "Mouth!" Noelani said in instant recognition, and turned to me with a smile. Who'd known his name was Abraham?

Who'd also known he was graduating? Last I'd heard, he wasn't. Word was, a little massaging of numbers allowed him to pass his classes by the gold-plated skin of his teeth. Family members whooped and hollered. Voices kept calling out, *Mouth!*, and Mouth shimmied to the podium, paused, shimmied a bit closer, and paused again like a football player extending an end-zone ritual. When he got to his diploma, he busted a move before rigid Ms. Brown and grabbed his high school degree. Then, after years of driving every Southwestern assistant principal mad with his hall-walking, his suspensions, his wide, flashy smile always popping up in the very place he wasn't meant to be, Mouth *hugged* Ms. Brown. Abraham Otis Jenkins grabbed Ms. Brown by the shoulders, pulled her against his gawky gold gown, jumped up and down, and released.

For each graduate, the crowd didn't just cheer. It exploded. It was a Mount Vesuvius of pride. It produced an outpouring of raw, loud, uninhibited elation that manifested in top-of-the-lungs hollering and top-of-the-head shrieking. Full-sentence shout-outs emitted from grown men and hyperventilating women. Family members didn't just clap their hands; they lifted arms in the air, waved them to a range of personal rhythms, jumped up and down to makeshift tempos of their cacophonic outbursts. The whole typically drab, windowless, rarely used auditorium now burst into bright gold and purple jubilation, bouquets of carnations waving about, oval helium-filled balloons lifting, not to the dingy distant ceiling, but to some unseen but easily imaginable blue and promising sky.

Brown continued reading names, and the graduates shimmied and/or slid and/or jiggied and/or jumped their ways to that podium. Each graduate's personal procession was long and glorious until each arrived at that precious thing, that golden ticket, that glowing white rolled-up document that said *I accomplished. I achieved. I'm victorious.* It was the best ceremony I'd ever seen. The proudest I'd ever felt for near strangers.

The bigness of their achievement was reinforced by the valedictorian's speech. These students on the stage, she told the audience, were the one hundred and forty survivors of an entering class of nine hundred.

Nine-hundred. The number dampened the moment. Upon hearing it, I could feel the collective gasp in the audience. Nine-hundred. Maybe we needed the sudden inhalation to make space for the emptiness. Subtract one hundred and forty from nine hundred; you get seven hundred and sixty. Seven hundred and sixty students gone elsewhere—maybe to other schools, but more likely, to no school at all. Absent. Vanished. Failed.

They felt like ghosts in the auditorium, suddenly invoked by the valedictorian as the ones who hadn't "survived." They'd passed onto another dimension. They lingered. They haunted. The principal winced on stage.

The remaining one hundred and forty—theirs was a feat I now began to understand. Just stay in school, I'd always thought. The cliché poster that was somewhere plastered on any American public school wall had an easy mantra. With my ninth graders, I sometimes recited it. Like a Nike Just-Do-It ad, *Stay in School* had a simple ring to it. Keep coming to class. Do your work. Just *stay in school.* When they didn't, I wondered on my weaker days why they couldn't follow the uncomplicated instructions? It had been easy in suburbia, I'd thought.

But that was just it: *It* had *been easy in suburbia*. In the mornings, the long, yellow buses stopped at clean, convenient neighborhood corners, picked us backpack-wearing kids up, dropped us off at school on time. In Baltimore, students competed with the public to catch lines of an unreliable, often late bus system. They needed tickets, which their schools sometimes erratically distributed, and which they couldn't supplement with their own income. And the buses only scratched the surface. In suburbia, I'd never had a single friend quit and enter night-school because, as Derek Hayes had once said, his Mom needed him to stay home and take care of his siblings. While my high school's "parent-teacher meetings" were packed with nine-to-five working guardians, I'd only ever seen one students' parent at Southwestern's infamously empty parent-teacher night. When I'd once told one student that maybe if he had such a difficult time with Mr. Willis, his mom could arrange a parent-teacher conference, he gave me a look like I'd just said the shape of the world was flat. He cocked his head and squinted. "Ms. Kirn, my mom doesn't have time for things like *that*."

Our worlds, I'd always known, were different. But I'd still thought the answer for these kids—*my* kids—was easy: stay in school. Above all else. Follow the mantra on the cliché educational poster. Just, stay in school. Get up each morning, grab your bag, catch the bus, go to class. How hard can that be? You have fewer advocates? So what? More household responsibilities? Doesn't matter. A lifetime of traumas and no counselor to talk to? An empty fridge and a parent you haven't seen in two days? Keep going to school. As for those temptations on the corner, the ones to either get quick cash if you want to sell, or quick escape if you want to buy? Keep walking. No matter how easy it would be to take cheap offers for a bag of groceries. No matter how badly you need release from your neighborhood landscape, from a home where maybe your mom's new man comes into your room unwanted at nights, from your past that inflicted wounds on you so regularly you'd started believing you deserved it: *school*, my students. School is your ticket.

But why should you believe me? When the school you're supposed to "stay in" is crumbling and always, every faithful year, at the brink of a state takeover, which means Maryland itself thinks your school is failing you. When some of your teachers have a plan to teach you each day, but others pass the time making lewd comments, or still others, with twenty-some working years' worth of accrued sick leave, have taken a permanent paid hiatus, and the city has no money to hire someone else. Why would *staying in school*—so you could sit in that abandoned class and watch Martin Lawrence films with the substitute—be your answer? Why not stay home, help out your grandma, help out the bare cupboards with a street-based sales job? Or why not have a kid, bring something soft and beautiful into this world, love him fiercely, vow to make him regal, the new prince of Baltimore city. So much more sensible to do these than hike up that very long hill every day, the one beside those 34,000 tombstones, for an education you half believe will take you nowhere.

Despite all persuasions to the contrary, these one hundred and forty jubilant teenagers found a way to their diplomas. They completed the tour de force I now saw as closer to a miracle. Every ounce of their euphoria meant a flipside to their journeys. Every smile and squeal and dance-move was the proportionate inverse to their pain, their labor, their countless obstacles. They were *this incredibly happy*, I thought, because it had been *that incredibly hard*.

Lord Have Mercy! They were giants on that stage. Triumphs. They were—all of them, even Mouth with his barely passing scores—brighter beacons than I'd ever known.

• • •

But Baltimore had made me a glass-is-half-empty woman. Graduation was victory, and I still harped on sad math. Though I'd left a hot black-top parking lot of squealing, whooping graduates with bunches of helium balloons in hands, I felt the ghosts of all those dropouts when I crashed on my living room couch. Also, God bless the kid, but I wondered what Mouth had really learned from his well-worked *D*s.

If my two years at Southwestern High School had been captured on film, by Davis Guggenheim or some other director, maybe he or she would have ended with the graduation scene. It strikes a high note of success, and it's uplifting. Students do make it, they do survive The Terrordome. Takira Webb would, in two more years, become one of them. She'd graduate and head to community college. The results of my hard work would not be for naught, could result in high school diplomas, at least for some. For thirty-five percent of the kids I'd ever seen.

A similar graduation scene concludes *Lean on Me*, that classic inner-city tale of Joe Clark's resurrected Eastside High. While the credits roll, Morgan Freeman hands each graduate a diploma like a ribbon-tied baton, and the students, sun-soaked on an outside stage, nod their heads and subsequently their tassels at Freeman's presumably wise but muted words. A cover of the Bill Withers classic, "Lean on Me," gets the last say.

Forget that Joe Clark tosses out a significant portion of the troubled school—kids known for smoking crack or dealing drugs or starting fights or walking halls. Kids like Mouth. Never mind that the real-life Clark admits to commandeering a school of superior discipline, but not superior instruction. That the real-life statistics of Eastside High indicate little to no academic progress. "Basic skills," shouts Morgan Freeman in the film. I know the lines too well—I can say them along with Freeman as he scolds the faculty for their shameful work: "That means our kids can *barely read*!" Apparently, Eastside High's kids could barely read with or without Clark, who himself said, upon resigning after seven years as principal, that his biggest accomplishment at Eastside was proving to the world that "black and Hispanic students in the inner city can behave. Educating them is another story."

Educating them is another story. A funny sentence, considering that "educating them" became *the* story in *Lean on Me*. The message of the movie's end-note fit with the desires of many viewers of teacher-films and possibly readers of teacher-books, but most certainly with the expectations I had of myself at the end of my two long years. And the message was this:

The students are healed.

The wretched school is transformed.

Though it began gray and graffiti-riddled, the world ended in springtime, and sunny.

Even in the roughest corners of this odd planet, success outweighs failure.

And the narrative destiny of us all is, regardless of obstacles, Happiness.

Who doesn't want redemption, transformation, the bluest cloudless sky?

• • •

The fresh, recently graduated, brand-spanking new Teach For America corps arrived in Baltimore. They sat at round tables in The Radisson Hotel's "White Oak Room," a windowless conference space. Some were Asian and some black, some brown and most white, and many looked a little stunned, like they'd unexpectedly landed in this town without an identity, their student-existences stripped down to suitcases. They'd *just* graduated college, as in last week or, in some cases, yesterday. Their clothes revealed the awkwardness of their new, unknown roles. The clothes seemed to wear *them*: men in crisp white button-ups and silk striped ties, women in knee-length skirts and heels or blouses and slacks. Some looked wide-eyed and ready, faces bright and smiling, heads nodding at every utterance. Perhaps, like me, they'd felt that little euphoric lift in the solar plexus when, back in January, they'd perused the TFA recruitment brochures. They'd seen the pictures: young white teacher smiling at the front of a classroom, pointing to a kid whose hand stretched toward the ceiling; young black teacher leaning over a table of students, each one peering into a microscope. The images contrasted the nearby statistics: "By the time they are nine, children in low-income areas are already three to four grade levels behind their peers in higher income areas." Be the change the nation needs, the brochure said to them. Make a difference. Have an Impact. Matter.

They didn't know each other, and most didn't know the city. They didn't know their new jobs, and they certainly didn't know themselves in those jobs. But they were here to teach America, change America, and tomorrow they'd interview for a job they did not know how to do.

"Wow," said Noelani. "Is this what we looked like two years ago?"

"No," I told her. "We were never this young."

She laughed, but the fib felt true, and while I looked at what seemed like the new teachers' smoothest, unblemished, shiny faces, I added, "*Never.*"

I had no ribbon-tied baton to pass these not-yet-teachers, no bona fide certificate of accomplishment other than my survival at Southwestern, and still I was passing it. And what was "it"? The broken bureaucracy, yes, the dangerous work environment, yes, but mostly, the achievement gap. The students I "passed" were still grade levels behind. *Be the change the nation needs*, the brochure had said, and I had not been.

Noelani and I were here anyway. Tomorrow Baltimore was holding a huge teacher-recruitment fair, and this new TFA corps, along with floods of other teachers-for-hire, were preparing for impromptu interviews with Charm City's principals in need. Noelani and I had volunteered to prepare the interviewees for the jobs we'd decided not to keep. The two of us were now numbers in another statistic; we were little stories in the abstract phrases of *teacher turnover* and *teacher shortage*. We were leaving for all the reasons that studies had shown—"unsafe and unstable work environment," "lack of parental involvement," "lack of support by administration"—well-analyzed reasons in Johns Hopkins research. Due to a pervasive *teacher shortage*, year after year the city had no choice but to hire completely inexperienced teachers. Even Dr. Jackson, who'd supposedly said she wanted no new TFA people, was sending representatives—administrators like Ms. Brown and Ms. Wallace—to recruit new faculty. These well-dressed, half-scared, half-eager college grads were crucial in filling the holes, were very much needed.

Two years. That's all they were asked to serve. To their twenty-two-year-old selves, it might have sounded like a huge chunk of their lives. It did to me when I'd stood where they were now, at the start of that long, two-year tunnel. So I suppose I didn't have to feel guilty now. I'd completed my commitment. I'd done what TFA had asked of me. I'd serve[d] *in an under-privileged school*. I'd taught approximately two hundred Baltimorean ninth graders who, in some cases, could now boast about reading an entire

Shakespearean play, could maybe write an essay with greater focus, could probably write a paragraph with greater clarity. These were reasons to celebrate.

And TFA agreed; it had thrown us newly inducted alumni a banquet at a fancy art gallery. We'd drunk cabernet and munched on finger-foods between the white walls and modern art. After cocktail hour, we settled into seated rows and, like Southwestern's graduates, our names were called. As we each walked to our diploma-sized certificates that honored our service, the audience of ourselves hooted and cheered. We shook hands. We smiled for cameras.

I allowed this celebratory love to wash over me. I accepted it because of the long, loud, potentially volcanic days of teaching, because of the weekends planning and grading, because of the countless calls to my students' homes, and *despite* the fact that I felt, after all the toil, that I had not been enough. My students had not been catapulted to their current grade level. They still struggled to pronounce words in our literature textbook that some education expert had deemed grade appropriate. I had not brought *the change the country needed*. And now I was tired, I was burned out, I was leaving.

But I clung to Southwestern that summer like a survivor on some half-wrecked ship, a ship that still needed to transport kids to an improbable shore. During an oppressive Baltimore heat-wave that coincided with or maybe caused Southwestern's broken air-conditioning, I taught summer school. In my old room that felt like it could bake pizzas, I taught kids who'd officially failed, sometimes by my own hand.

Summer school is, by operation, a school of failure, a school for the almost but not quite left behind. The ghosts of my own Southwestern past revisited me. Trey Knight, of second year, first semester, first period. Despite several one-on-one discussions and parent-teacher conferences, he failed my class. He used to arrive early in the day with a fat wad of green in his pocket that he'd eagerly display, and he kept himself so high he couldn't remember yesterday. Yesterday? He wasn't in school yesterday, he insisted. Yes he was, I told him. Didn't he remember the in-class debate about teenage love? Blank-faced, he stared at me, then turned away to tease a girl. Like a bad rerun, here again sat light-skinned Trey Knight, half baby-fat and half-grown-man-bulk, still showcasing pupils dilated to the size of dimes, still believing he was the cleverest person in the world to talk about his "best friend, Mary J."

And here again arrived Nikkya Arnold, of second year, second semester, third period. Actually, when she was meant to attend that class-period, she almost never showed. But, on days that she graced me with her presence, I was her immediate enemy. She scowled at my hellos, scanned me up and down, and sat in a corner to talk up a storm. At my warnings or my checks by her name or my promise to call home, she rolled her eyes or shouted out invectives. I couldn't remember what I'd ever said to Nikkya, but I'd remembered how her responses felt—like a wall, with an instant, loud imperative that said *I will not let you in*. I couldn't make her *do* anything, she'd tell me. Now, Nikkya was coming to summer school. Remember me? she said on the first day, smiled, and sat down.

And now appeared Michael Casey, of second year, second semester, fourth period. Michael Casey of the mostly male fourth period, of the class of racist tension, of the very last group I'd ever taught. He had also not been a faithful attendee of school, but when he had come, he spent all those minutes with his cheeky face buried into my rectangular-shaped *To Teach is to Touch a Life Forever* pillow. Around the words were classic school images: an apple, crayons, pencils and a ruler. It was the kind of Hallmark souvenir that students usually gave their teachers, but no student had given me the pillow. Perhaps if one had, I would have loved that pillow. Instead, I'd received it from a colleague; how did she know I'd touched any lives? As Michael slept on the words, the token of teacher-accomplishment became a prop for teacher-failure. Michael wasn't high like Trey or raging like Nikkya. He was vacant. Completely disengaged. He'd checked out of school. Though I tried to teach him, I did not touch his life, let alone forever. Some days he came, and he tried his hardest to sleep on that pillow, and other days he didn't come, and I, occupied with the feud between David Turner and Bobby Hudson, made the effort to call home a few times, but mostly I let Michael Casey go.

"Why you fail me, Ms. Kirn?" This was Michael's first question in summer school.

"Um, because you did nothing in my class?" I waited to see how he digested the truth laid to him as inquiry.

He furrowed his brow and stuck his lips out. "I did too." I'd forgotten how puffed out Michael's cheeks were. They made him look kid-like and innocent.

I shook my head. "You did *not*. You sat right at that desk," I pointed to one near the back, "and curled up on my little teacher pillow."

He furrowed his brow again. "Nuh-uh."

I nodded. "Yuh-huh."

Michael sighed and took a seat in the middle of the room.

• • •

I dismantled classroom 3536 slowly that summer. I boxed up my poetry handouts in one hundred degree heat. I gradually peeled the laminated posters off the sweating, cinder-block walls. The Southwestern Code of Conduct. The Core Learning Goals. The Special Education Goals. The Attendance Improvement Plan. The After-School Coach Class Hours. Signs of a school well-meaning were gradually all unstuck, and with each, I felt the weight of disappointment. I was dismantling the props of a heavy task that I did not feel I completed.

This was not how my two years were meant to end. I still craved the *Lean on Me* moment, the huge redemption, the bona fide success. If I lacked the obvious victory, then hadn't I failed? Michael wasn't the only kid to ask why I'd failed him. Several former students popped their heads into my room, demanding to know the same. "Why you fail me? Now I gotta go to summer school." I offered the classic teacher response: *I didn't fail you. You failed yourself.* The kids usually scowled and disappeared from the doorway. But what if they were right? What if I *had* failed them? Couldn't I have done better, taught a more interesting selection of stories, met with parents or grandparents one more time, or given a more relevant writing assignment? Sure my students wrote poems and short stories and letters to friends and autobiographies of their lives, but maybe I'd neglected some magical written assignment that instantly hooked every kid into loving literacy and language.

Or what if I'd been someone else? My hamster's wheel of doubt kept endlessly spinning. What if I'd been, not a suburban Philly poet but a twenty-something girl off Gilmore Street, from just around the way, who'd somehow made her way in the world and returned to west Baltimore to teach. I would have been able to motivate them then, I thought. I wouldn't have failed as many kids.

Still, with each sign I removed from the classroom walls, I also felt the levity of relief. I'd no longer demand magic or miracles from myself. How does one *complete* the task I undertook, anyway? How does this long journey end, if not by just saying farewell? This problem would no longer be mine, I'd thought, and kept dismantling the classroom.

And still, I taught. Trey and Michael and Nikkya sat in their little desks with the others, looking like they'd melt in a pool on the floor.

"None of the other classes be doing work, Ms. Kahn," Michael said. His cheeks looked especially puffed out in the heat. "This *sum*mer school!"

"Yeah, Ms. Karen. People don't *do* work in summer school." Nikkya said it kindly, like I needed schooling myself. They would come, she told me, and I would give out the passing grades. They would show their faces, and I would show them the door to tenth-grade English. This was how summer school at Southwestern went.

But we read. We wrote. They sometimes stared outside the open windows that looked down Font Hill, or put their hands outside the windows to feel the stagnant hot air, or told me how they could be at home right now or at so-and-so's house, who had air-conditioning. They described how amazing their summers would be without me, without this, without summer school.

"Should have thought of that during the school year," I said.

The temptation of elsewhere was too great for Trey Knight, and he didn't finish. But Michael and Nikkya stayed.

"Why didn't I just do my work?" Michael asked one day, his neck craned to lift his face from a half-written page on his desk. It was the first time he'd admitted that he belonged in summer school, that it hadn't been some huge injustice or administrative mistake. Because he snagged it from my desk each day, my little *To Teach is to Touch a Life Forever* pillow sat beside his work. His head, though, resisted the urge to lie upon it.

"I don't know, Michael. Why didn't you?" Michael never answered.

Nikkya was now an entirely different Nikkya. She smiled when she entered the room. She said "Good morning, Ms. Karen," and then narrated in enthusiastic detail her evenings with her grandma. Who was this girl? Or more importantly, where had she been in the fall semester?

Day after smoldering day, Michael and Nikkya arrived ready to make good in five weeks what was meant to be taught in twenty. And for the most part they did, except when Michael felt the pull of the summer streets and left his classroom seat vacant on a few instances. I called immediately, repeatedly, and left messages on a machine.

"Why you gotta call my house?" Michael asked first thing the next morning.

"Where were you yesterday?" I asked back.

He didn't answer.

"Do you want to fail again?"

"No, Ms. Kahn."

"Because you *can* fail again."

He dropped his head, his fleshy cheeks facing the floor.

Inside me, though, was the opposite voice. *Because you can't fail again, Michael. If you fail again, then I fail again, which is why I have to call your house immediately when you miss even one day of summer school.*

Michael strode to his desk, but not before grabbing that pillow off my own. *To Teach is to Touch a Life Forever.*

"Why do you want that? You know you can't sleep on it."

He set it on his desk and brought out his notebook. "I like it." He reached across the desk and patted the pillow like a pet.

The lame teacher-gift that had made me feel like a poser now had a purpose. The pillow was Michael's academic muse. And with it by his side, Michael completed his work.

In fact, Michael completed summer school and went on to tenth-grade English. Our last day together was another one-hundred degree scorcher in August. Unlike the usual days, though, when Michael would bolt out the scorched building as soon as possible, he idled. I wish I could narrate exactly the exchange between us, but I don't remember what we talked about. I only really remember that, instead of the typical urge to flee the building as soon as possible, Michael lingered around my desk, his white T-shirt hanging below his knees like any other Baltimore boy, his black sweat pants bunched up around his boots. While we talked, he picked up the pillow, threw it in the air, caught it, and hugged it to his chest. It was a discordant, charming image: city kid nearly cuddling a page-sized pillow. Around us, the walls were bare. So were the closets and the drawers in my desk. Only a few boxes remained in the room, remained of my two-year life here at Southwestern. A few boxes and Michael.

"Can I keep it, Ms. Kahn?" Michael held up the pillow.

That was how a Hallmark gift, usually bestowed by student to teacher, was given from teacher to student. I said yes, and Michael's joker grin spread across his face and lifted his round, fat cheeks. Though we talked some more, what I best remember is our farewell. There were no hugs or promises to write. Just one single gesture that stays in my mind. On his way out of the classroom, Michael thought to pause and turn around. Michael stood in the door's frame a moment, marking it in my memory.

A lot had come through that door: the fire, lit from a napkin that was shoved into the door's vents and then stomped out by Dennis Moore; that six-foot-something man with his bottle of wine, stumbling to the front of the room with his cronies, all lit as bulbs; the principal; my department head; The State with their clipboards and clicking ballpoint pens; and roughly two-hundred Baltimorean ninth graders. Letisha Clark, Jimmy Nizbin, Takira Webb, Jerome Smith, Brandon Ward, Yolanda Perry, David Turner . . . I couldn't possibly know how many lives I'd influenced, how many little successes went unseen as my students passed in and out of my room. "I have to believe," said Ms. Simmons, a fellow TFA teacher, as we drove home from a parent-teacher night where once again none of our kids' parents showed. "I have to believe that if they're in my classroom, I'm reaching them somehow."

I liked her optimism, but I was skeptical—I still wanted proof. I thought of Davon Green, a.k.a. Lor Busta, who bounced into my room one morning before school and said, "Ms. Kirn, I'll never forget what you told me last year." Ellen was sitting beside me. I looked at her, eyebrows raised, a little smile creeping across my face: here it was, the rarest of teacher-rewards, where a student actually confesses what he or she has learned.

Then he revealed the kernel of wisdom I bestowed: "Any number divisible by three," Davon said, "is a lucky number!"

Ellen, the math teacher, choked on a laugh.

"Thanks, Davon," I said flatly. I thought he would praise the virtues of some meaningful lesson on shaping paragraphs or reading stories or even living life. "If I were your math teacher over here, I might be very proud of myself."

But none of us could know the small ways we affected our kids. Such was the lot of the teacher. Eventually I would cradle the last of the cardboard boxes in my arms, haul them through the doorway, and turn around to flick the light of room 3536. *Southwestern is a better place because you are here*, said the walls at one point. I had become something in this room: a teacher, yes, but something else. Perhaps as often as I had taught in my classroom, I'd also failed. And all I'd felt I'd really done was survived, that same word praised at graduation, that same idea I'd hated to hear from Ms. Brown—*let's weather the storm*—or from my students—*Am I passing?* We were meant to do more than survive. Weren't we? The wavering optimism gave way to what Baltimore had now made me: a realist, a person who, for better or worse, now fully believed without a doubt that while Hollywood shaped perfect tales of triumph, the world's stories sometimes remained flawed, broken, and we all still had to live them.

But right now stood puffy-cheeked Michael Casey, holding my teacher-pillow in his hand. Right now, Michael Casey couldn't quite let himself leave as fast as he'd done all the days before. He was a symbol, to me, for all the little successes that would forever go unknown. Would Michael make it to eleventh grade? To twelfth? To graduation? I didn't know. I only knew that, because of me and because of himself, he made it to tenth. "Bye, Ms. Kahn," he said, and then lifted the pillow into the air, its cliché slogan slanted upward toward the ceiling. "Thanks," he said and smiled.

EPILOGUE

Today, I have one photo on my desk from the final Teach For America banquet: Noelani, Amy, Ellen, Brooke, and I are standing in front of a patchwork quilt of cherry-red circles and emerald green squares. Our arms are wrapped loosely around one another. The flash of the camera reflects against our foreheads, causing them to shine. We're smiling broadly and, due to the Baltimore humidity, we're literally glowing.

None of us drive up Font Hill anymore. In fact, nobody does. In 2006, the state finally attempted what it had threatened: a full take-over of Southwestern High School. But under the state's control, the school still didn't improve. Maryland's high schools now had to demonstrate their students' competency in high-stakes pre-graduation exams, and the percentage of Southwestern students who passed those exams was in the single digits. In other words, about ninety-five percent of Southwestern's students were deemed too ill-prepared to receive diplomas. Southwestern High School, seen not only as a perpetual failure but also a shrinking community, was shut down.

A week before the official closing day, alumni from the school's thirty-six years descended on Font Hill for a grand reunion. Students from across the decades came to reminisce, to flip through old yearbooks, to swap stories about former teachers. But when they arrived, they found the inside of their alma mater pitch black and nearly abandoned. The school-year wasn't over yet, so what had happened? The power had failed earlier that day, and students and staff, unable to work in the dark, had been sent home, which meant even on its last hoorah, the building that was Southwestern High couldn't hold up. The party resumed in the parking lot.

I keep the photo of my four fellow TFA alumni and me on my desk partly because it marks a moment of accomplishment. We'd finished. We'd completed the two-year feat that, at its beginning, Tom Sypher and other Southwestern teachers had bet we wouldn't finish. *You'll never survive The Terrordome.* I am prouder of my time in Baltimore than of any university degree. And maybe I keep the photo of those four other weathered, young, tired and shiny teachers on my desk, beside other snapshots of my husband, my closest friends, and my late stepfather, for the very reasons those Southwestern graduates had celebrated so outrageously: because it had been *that* hard.

But that's only partly the reason. I haven't lived in Baltimore since my stint at Southwestern, yet in some ways I feel I'll never leave it. I became, in the best possible sense, haunted by what I saw there. Baltimore, with its vacant row houses and abandoned lots, is the landscape of an unbeautiful home I forever feel both alien in and a little sick for. Its brokenness is partially always mine to puzzle over. Its students eternally feel like my responsibility. And by "its students," I don't just mean Baltimore's. I mean any student in this nation who gets robbed of a decent education, who flounders in an impossibly flawed school. Baltimore: pronounced Ballmore or Bald-more. Either way, there is *more* in it for me, more to it.

And there was more to it for Ellen and Amy, Brooke and Noelani as well. All of us eventually moved away, but our experiences at Southwestern led us to related work and shaped how we viewed the world. Noelani worked in an education nonprofit for a few years and then became assistant principal of a bilingual charter school in D.C. She now manages curriculum and instruction at a Pre-K charter school in D.C. She believes that her work in TFA led her to program leadership in early education, where she can help kids get the right foundations to succeed in school. At Southwestern, Brooke realized that she wanted to become a legal advocate for disenfranchised voices, so she went to law school and became a public defender. She now says she uses her degree to fight for the same kinds of communities in which she taught. Amy worked at an experimental magnet school in Baltimore, then delivered professional development to math teachers across the country, and has now moved back to her hometown of Pittsburgh, where she designs and delivers professional development for twenty-five school districts in Pennsylvania, in addition to offering nationwide consulting. Ellen taught at Southwestern another year, then wrote innovative math curriculum for the city and tested it out in her classroom. Eventually she headed to Harvard, where she's currently finishing her Ph.D. in education, studying how our current standardized tests influence, often negatively, the instruction that students receive.

As for me, I'm still in the classroom, though I've drifted into higher education. I currently teach at an open-enrollment community-based college, which vows affordable higher education to anyone who's willing to attend. I've also taught developmental reading and writing to underprepared freshmen in California, often non-native speakers, first-generation college students, and kids who attended high schools very much like Southwestern. In many cases, they'd made it into college on sports scholarships or because the UC system had promised to accept the top students at any California school, even the most failing ones. When these students described their former high schools, I gave a knowing nod. The English teacher played movies instead of explaining grammar; the principal allowed total chaos in the halls. As college students, they couldn't construct a coherent paragraph, which some of my colleagues complained about. I tried to remind those teachers that our students' under-preparedness wasn't entirely their faults. At their schools, they were the *A* students. When I sat one-on-one with them, we acknowledged their difficult pasts, and then we set to hard work. At the semester's end, they often remarked that they learned more in four months than they had in four years.

My experience in west Baltimore is the reason I'm still, despite all the struggles, a fierce advocate of TFA's mission: that all students should have the opportunity to attain an excellent education. Baltimore is the reason I vote, above all else, on matters of education: on increasing funding for schools (or, more often, on *not decreasing* funding), on increasing scholarships for low-income kids. It's the reason I loved teaching in California, a state that declared, in 1960, that every one of its residents should have access to a free, excellent college education. So it—Baltimore—is also the reason I marched with thousands of UC Berkeley students and faculty when the university said it would raise fees another 45 percent, all but erasing the state's original mission and thereby rewriting the diversity of its student body.

"Whose university? Our university," thousands cried. The September sun shone down on 5,000 students and faculty, and I snapped a photo of the masses holding placards. Within the camera frame I spotted, to my surprise, a Teach For America recruitment banner hanging over a railing: "Solving the nation's greatest injustice," it said.

On the last day of my two years at Southwestern, I would have read such a banner with a skeptical eye. Really? "Solving the nation's greatest injustice"? I didn't feel I'd reached such a high standard by motivating Michael and Nikkya through summer school. My two years didn't bridge the great achievement gap. On that last day, I turned the light out and I shut the classroom door, and it rattled in its frame one more time. I never returned to room 3536. But I now see the irony in what became Michael's pillow. *To Teach is to Touch a Life forever*, it read, and I'd thought the life I was meant to touch was a student's. Teaching touched mine, not because I walked away with Hallmark lessons on life and love and personal transformation, but because I witnessed just how steep were the odds against my students. My two years didn't solve the nation's greatest injustice; they helped me see exactly how *great* the *injustice* is. And the experience empowered me to use whatever gifts I have to continue fighting for students who, based primarily on their community's income, have far less than a fair educational shake in this world. This, I believe, is the often overlooked power of TFA—it turns thousands of promising young people annually into witnesses of an American crisis.

There are plenty of fair criticisms of the program. Skeptics say that TFA teachers—completely inexperienced and vowing only two years—can't possibly bridge the achievement gap in their classrooms. Some teachers do demonstrate remarkable gains in student learning, advancing their kids two and three grade levels in one year, and TFA touts these stories on its websites and in recruitment literature. But TFA's own statistics don't prove that this is a sweeping trend. A 2004 study by Mathematica Policy Research found that students of corps members achieved only slight gains in math and none in reading. In fact, TFA doesn't yet have proof that its corps members, on the whole, achieve the significant gains that it intends for them. The huge success stories *are* possible, it seems, but they're rarer than TFA would like.

Most corps members seem to have an experience somewhere in between devastation and victory, one more akin to mine—messy, heartbreaking, with achievements peppered here and there among daily struggles and a lot of jaw-dropping moments. Of course, there are others who exit more jaded than when they entered. One of my roommates felt abandoned in a school without any other corps members and quit after her first year. She still curses TFA to this day. Another roommate hated her elementary gig the entire two years. When I talked recently to my third roommate, who'd always seemed the happiest of the three, she said she's ambivalent about the program. "I still think a lot of people use it as a rung on their career ladder," she said. She thinks it might do more harm than good to create an engine of primarily white teachers who leave every two or three years.

Some administrators agree with her. When an administrator at Southwestern asked Mr. Barnes, the social studies head, if he wanted any more TFA teachers to replace the five of us once we left, Mr. Barnes just shook his head stoically. Brooke, who was sitting right next to him, gasped. "How can you *say* that!?" She'd served as Mr. Barnes' right-hand-woman, and she was genuinely hurt. But all he said in reply was, "Many will come. Few will stay." Mr. Barnes was tired of the turnaround.

I understand all the criticisms. But I'd still venture to say that all five of us—Brooke, Ellen, Noelani, Amy, and I—were decent teachers to our students, something they were in danger of lacking had we not shown for our interviews on that first day with Ms. Brown. No one wanted the jobs we were filling. And, while people often measure TFA's success on whether or not its corps members achieve the mission in two years, an equally crucial, possibly more powerful result of TFA has been the movement of advocates it's generated once the teachers become alumni. There are now nearly 24,000 alumni, and because they encountered the nation's educational crisis firsthand, they inevitably carry their eye-opening experiences into their chosen fields. These, remember, were the high-achieving college seniors who may never have entered teaching were it not for TFA. These were listless graduates like me, or the graduates headed for law or medical school before their idealism somehow derailed them. TFA estimates that only one in ten would have pursued teaching without the organization. Today, over 4,000 still remain in the classroom, and two-thirds are still working in education. Those no longer teaching are principals, policy advocates, founders of charter schools (such as Mike Feinberg and Dave Levin, who began the nationally recognized KIPP schools), and high profile administrators (like former Chancellor of D.C. Public Schools, Michelle Rhee). Even my ambivalent roommate, who works for an ecological research and teaching nonprofit organization and still visits Baltimore City schools to this day, admits that she would never be in education if it weren't for Teach For America. "I love teaching," she told me, seeming genuinely surprised by the fact. And while not all alums remain in education, even those who exit the field take their experience into the most unexpected places, like business, biology, or technology. We're on school boards. We volunteer. We donate. We advocate. If we aren't serving low-income schools directly, we're carrying with us this indelible experience that informs our lives, our career choices, our voting decisions. Even politicians are noticing the potential impact of TFA alum: Rahm Emanuel, San Francisco Mayor Gavin Newsom, and Howard Dean have all urged TFA alumni to run for public office. As Brooke once said, "My experience with Teach For America changed my life. The experience is a lens through which you see everything in life."

Ultimately, we know firsthand that the odds are brutally stacked against the nation's low-income kids, and many of us still use whatever gifts we have to see that their American Dream is just a little more reachable than it was before. There's that old argument that we should all just "pull ourselves up by our boot-straps." It was implied in a quote from the lieutenant governor of South Carolina, Andre Bauer, who likened poor kids in need of free lunches to "stray animals" begging for food. But if your school accepts a culture of failure, if your reading teacher calls out sick for a year, if you don't have enough money to eat lunch, and if at age fifteen you still can't spell "Wednesday," do you really have those proverbial boots to pull up?

Most of middle-class America doesn't get a full, honest view of the schools we've entered and served. They get glimpses, maybe, usually in the same ways that I did before I arrived in west Baltimore—through mainstream media, through triumphant teacher-films, and inspirational teacher-books. These stories follow a predictable narrative arc. Michelle Pfeiffer enters urban school, meets troubled kids, shows a karate move or two, eventually helps troubled kids succeed. Morgan Freeman enters anarchic Eastside High, where students toss a toilet out of a window, sexually harass the assistant principal, and bash a teacher's head into the ground until it's bloodied. By the end, the school is a thriving, smooth-running ship of academic achievement. In *Stand and Deliver*, Edward James Olmos (playing real-life Jaime Escalante) enters another failing school, takes on a class of unmotivated basic math students, and trans-forms them into calculus masters. I could go on listing the stories. Since 1980, there have been nineteen inspirational teacher-films, and most begin in devastation and conclude in full redemption. Among the most popular "ghetto-teacher movies" (*Stand and Deliver, Lean on Me, Dangerous Minds, Freedom Writers*), all four are supposedly "true stories." All promise total turnarounds. All cast a single teacher or administrator as the film's hero. In the end, the message about school-reform is always this: one person, a Joe Clark, can change any one of the downtrodden, violent, drug-infested schools in a year. Nay, in nine months, in the time it takes for a single human to form. It's simple, really, the fixing of the inner-city education dilemma. It takes a messiah.

But these films say more about us and what we would like from our world than they do about the real plight of low-performing, low-income schools. In real life, Jaime Escalante didn't singlehandedly transform in two years a dozen students from basic math to calculus. It took him nearly ten years to build the calculus program that eventually made him famous, and no student jumped immediately from basic math to calculus. Escalante and the colleagues who collaborated with him had to redesign Garfield High School's math department and even work with neighboring middle schools to improve the curriculum of their future high school students. In other words, the program's success required not just the savior-tactics of one but the hard work and support of many. And the progress took five times as long as Hollywood's version.

In 2002, Jerry Jesness, author of "*Stand and Deliver* Revisited," argued that "The Hollywood fiction had at least one negative side effect. By show-ing students moving from fractions to calculus in a single year, it gave the false impression that students can neglect their studies for several years and then be redeemed by a few months of hard work." In my opinion, though, the film and others like it perpetuate even more damaging myths. The classic redemptive teacher-narrative implies that reform can and should occur in a year or two, that teachers can do it alone, and that the only missing key to our many failing schools and their underperforming students is this "touch of a master," as Jennings calls it. Which means that anyone who falls short of this success feels like a failure.

We're often too eager to craft or hear the same full-proof story of redemptive victory. We tend to want, as the TFA alum shared back at the Opening Ceremonies of Institute, the simple conflict, rising action, climax, and dénouement of the perfect teacher-tales. But real life is invariably messier. The answers to the nation's educational inequity are more complex than TFA's simple "have high expectations," a fact I quickly learned at Southwestern.

Before working in west Baltimore, I was both wary of the Rocky-esque crescendo of teacher-films and simultaneously captivated by their inspirational messages. After my time in west Baltimore, though, I began to see the oversimplified stories as damaging to education reform. They let viewers believe that the solution to the nation's failing schools is easy. They teach us that what those schools need are saviors. They place the onus for a student's success heavily on a single teacher. And once the credits roll on such films, after the black and Latino kids smile with diplomas in their hands, the viewers believe the story is complete; they may lift their bodies from the theater chairs, let the seat cushions flip up and fold toward the seatbacks, leave the darkness of cinema and squint at the blinding daylight. Some savior-teacher is out there, fixing things with his or her unorthodox methods and high expectations and what-not. The viewers can go home to their lives. They can forget about it all.

But I think most Teach For America alumni cannot forget. As Brooke once said of her TFA experience, "I live it every day. I miss my students and their families. I agonize over where they are today." I believe many are, like me, haunted to some degree. We know most American children born into poverty are still only fifty percent likely to graduate high school. If they do, they'll still perform, on average, at a ninth-grade level. And we know that in a country which lists, among its rights, the pursuit of happiness, we know our low-income schools simply aren't good enough. Those of us who are honest with ourselves know there is no magic bullet to kill the monster of educational inequity, or else someone would have annihilated it long ago. No one person can solve the crisis. No Joe Clark, no Michelle Pfeiffer, no single smiling, young, new TFA corps member. It will take collaborative multitudes.

By seeing this flawed school and its students in entirety, by intimately knowing the many challenges our under-resourced schools and their teachers face, my hope, dear reader, is that you too will now have the experience that thousands of TFA corps members possess, and you too will see how the traditional definitions of American success are far less accessible to Southwestern's and the nation's low-income kids. As Richard Rothstein, author of *Class and Schools: Using Social, Economic and Educational Reform to*

Close the Black-White Achievement Gap, once said

> People who are not teachers, who aren't in daily contact with children from disadvantaged communities, can easily believe that the only reason kids don't go to college and don't have middle-class outcomes is because they are lazy or their teachers aren't any good. Teachers know better, and because teachers have such a unique insight into these problems, they have a responsibility as citizens to educate the rest of the country about them.

Maybe, just maybe, something in this book will lead you, dear reader, to become an advocate too, in whatever small or large way you can: through voting, through career choices, through volunteerism, even through conversations with neighbors.

To this day, I still dream about Baltimore. I dream of teaching teenagers in enormous T-shirts. I dream of losing lesson plans in stacks of poetry worksheets. I dream of trying to hold thirty-something kids' attentions. Not all the time, but about once a season I dream of the place that not only showed me the grittiest this world can offer, but still, despite the odds, challenges me to seek even the smallest redemptive endings amidst the most broken of places.

ABOUT THE AUTHOR

PHOTO BY JUSTIN LANIER

Heather Kirn Lanier is Visiting Assistant Professor of English at Miami University in Hamilton, Ohio. She is the author of *The Story You Tell Yourself*.